The Campus History Series

MONTANA STATE UNIVERSITY, BOZEMAN

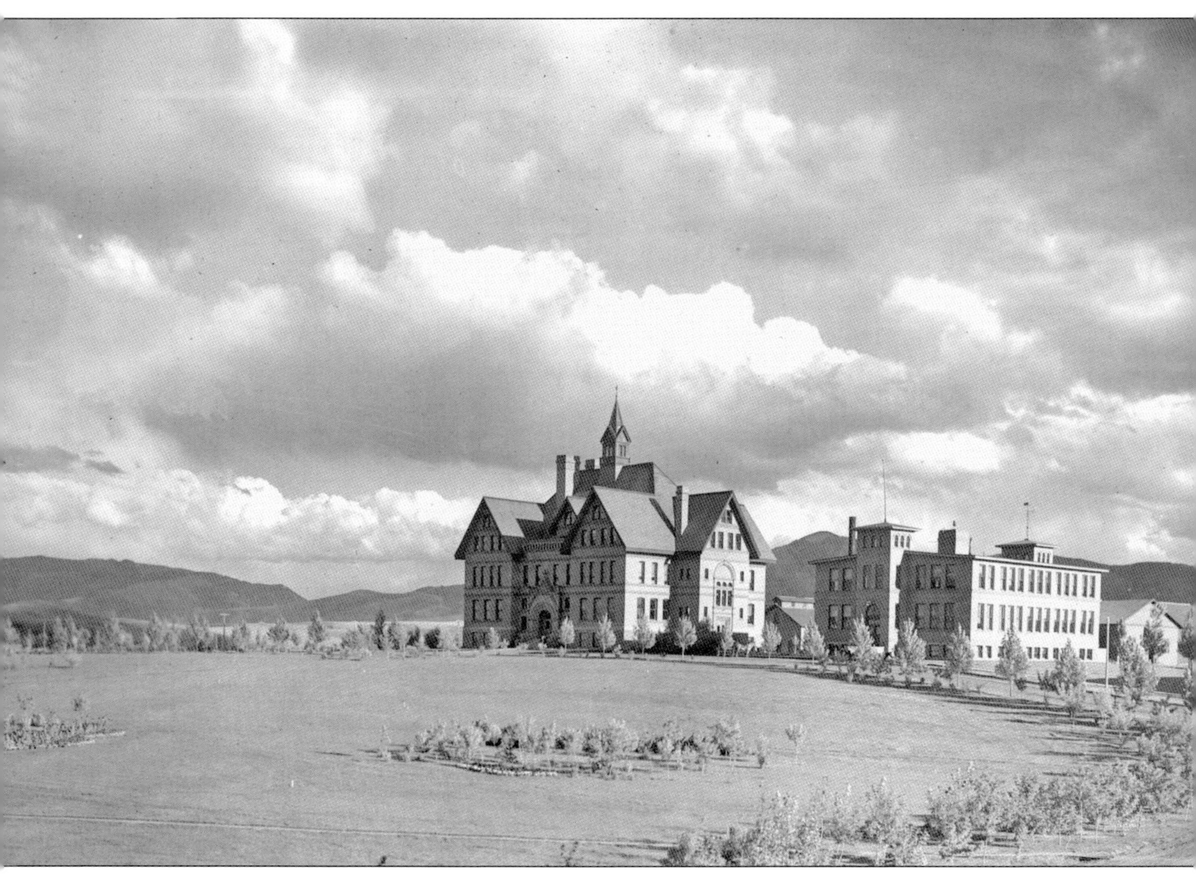

This early image presents a striking view looking up a hill to Montana Hall and the Chemistry Building in 1912. The image portrays the promise of the future in rich agricultural pursuits, leading engineering departments, and a strong foundation that enable the institution to function as an integral part of the community in which it resides. (Montana State University Library, Merrill G. Burlingame Special Collections.)

On the Front Cover: Hard at work sketching out plans, these students are learning to conceive, plan, and design a wide variety of machinery and systems on their drafting tables on the top floor of Montana Hall in 1906. Included in the image are mechanical engineering students Donald Butter and Stanley Yergey. (Montana State University Library, Merrill G. Burlingame Special Collections.)

Cover Background: The mountains provide a scenic backdrop that enhances the beauty of Montana State University. Seen here is a campus view in 1909 taken from the southwest looking northeast toward the Bridger Mountains. The Experiment Station buildings are in the foreground, with Linfield Hall beyond. (Montana State University Library, Merrill G. Burlingame Special Collections.)

The Campus History Series

MONTANA STATE UNIVERSITY, BOZEMAN

JAMES J. THULL AND HEATHER C. HULTMAN

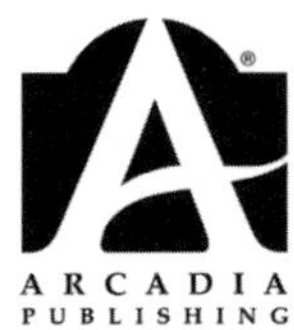

ISBN 978-1-4671-2825-4

Published by Arcadia Publishing
Charleston, South Carolina

Printed in the United States of America

Library of Congress Control Number: 2017951698

For all general information, please contact Arcadia Publishing:
Telephone 843-853-2070
Fax 843-853-0044
E-mail sales@arcadiapublishing.com
For customer service and orders:
Toll-Free 1-888-313-2665

Visit us on the Internet at www.arcadiapublishing.com

This book is dedicated to Kim Allen Scott, university archivist at MSU, Bozeman, who has been our mentor and constant source of support and guidance.

Contents

ACKNOWLEDGMENTS

Unless otherwise noted, all images appear courtesy of Montana State University Library, Merrill G. Burlingame Special Collections.

Introduction

Montana State University, Bozeman, was founded in 1893 as the Agricultural College of the State of Montana with an initial class of eight students. Within a few years of being founded, it began to be known as the Montana College of Agriculture and Mechanic Arts, and in 1913, the name was officially changed. By act of the Montana legislative assembly in 1965, the school officially became Montana State University (MSU). While the university has changed names, its dedication to educating students and serving the citizens of Montana has been constant for the last 125 years.

MSU offers baccalaureate, master's, and doctoral degrees in more than 225 academic programs. It is the state's land-grant university and the largest university in the state of Montana. In the fall of 2016, MSU had 14,400 undergraduates and 2,040 graduate students, a total enrollment of 16,440. The student body was 55 percent male, 62 percent were Montana residents, and four percent were international students who represented more than 72 nations.

Land-grant colleges were established under the Morrill Act to help fund, establish, and sustain institutions of higher education across the United States. Research and development of agriculture was a prime motivation for the act—this has been part of MSU's focus and traditions since the founding of the school.

The first building on campus was the Agricultural Experiment Station Building, in 1894. It is still in use but is now called Taylor Hall in honor of J.C. Taylor, an influential and dedicated county extension agent who served the citizens of Montana. The university's College of Agriculture currently oversees the Montana Agriculture Experiment Stations and is home to six departments, including Agricultural Education, Plant Sciences and Plant Pathology, Animal and Range Sciences, and Land Resources and Environmental Sciences.

The university continued to grow and build in the early years, and much of that early infrastructure is still utilized today. Montana Hall, which until 1914 was called Main Hall, began construction in 1896 and was completed in 1898. Originally housing the library, classrooms, and administrative offices, the building is currently dedicated solely to administrative services. Much of the original architecture both inside and outside the building remains; some items are still in use, including the tables from the original library, which now live in the MSU Library's Merrill G. Burlingame Special Collections Reading Room.

The library has served the research needs of its faculty, students, and staff since the creation of MSU. Renne Library was named for Dr. Roland Renne, who served as the fifth president of the university from 1943 to 1964. The library is located at the center of campus, just west of the Strand Union Building and south of Montana Hall. It collects materials to support all areas of the curriculum, is open to the public, and serves as a hub of student activity as the second most used building on campus.

Engineering was another of the early focuses and areas of excellence for MSU. The original engineering building, Roberts Hall, was completed in 1923 and named for the civil engineer William Milnor Roberts. It housed the departments of Civil, Electrical, and Architectural Engineering. Today MSU is in the process of building the Norm Asbjornson Hall, which will serve as the new home of the College of Engineering and include an innovative laboratory and modern classrooms. In keeping with the college's history of innovation and developing solutions for the problems of today and tomorrow, it is home to some forward-thinking institutions like the Center for Biofilm Engineering, the Montana Wind Applications Center, and Western Transportation Institute. The college is also home to the departments of Electrical and Computing Engineering, Civil Engineering, Chemical and Biological Engineering, Computer Science, and Mechanical and Industrial Engineering.

The growth of MSU has been continual over its 125-year history. In addition to engineering and agriculture, the university offers degrees through the Colleges of Business; Arts and Architecture; Education, Heath, and Human Development; Letters and Science; Nursing; and Honors. It is also the home of Gallatin College, the Museum of the Rockies, and numerous other departments and programs.

Many of the chapters in this book focus on and celebrate the special events, traditions, cultures, and lifestyles of MSU, its students, faculty, staff, and the greater Bozeman and Montanan communities. Bozeman sits in the heart of the Rocky Mountains and is surrounded by five mountain ranges: Bridger, Tobacco Root, Big Belt, Gallatin, and Madison. In nearly every direction, snowcapped peaks rise above the city. The Yellowstone, Gallatin, and Madison Rivers are all a short distance from campus. Also near campus are high mountain lakes, hundreds of miles of hiking trails, national forests, and Yellowstone National Park.

The students, faculty, and staff of MSU have long taken advantage of the multitude of outdoor activities just outside their doors. Montana has some of the best trout fishing in the world. Not coincidentally, MSU has an active fly fishing club and the world's largest collection of trout and salmonid materials housed in the library's special collections. Hunting, hiking, rafting, ice climbing, skiing, and spending time outdoors exploring the Big Sky Country are not only favorite pastimes but also a reason why many students pick MSU.

"Go Cats Go!" is a phrase that can be heard at nearly every sporting event on campus. MSU sports teams include men's skiing, cross-country, tennis, track and field, basketball, and of course, football. They also include women's tennis, cross-country, golf, basketball, skiing, volleyball, and track and field. The Cat-Griz football game with the University of Montana–Missoula, known as the "Brawl of the Wild," has become one of Montana's most celebrated sporting traditions. Rodeo is another long and celebrated campus event. MSU hosted the College National Finals Rodeo for nearly three decades; its student teams claimed eight national team titles, 32 individual national championships, and a multitude of Big Sky Region crowns.

The American Indian Council's MSU Pow Wow is one of the most important, celebrated, and anticipated annual events on campus. Officially turning 43 in 2018, the event is one of the largest pow wows in Montana and has always been free of charge and open to all.

The long history of student life, academics, expansion, and the larger history of the Bozeman community is reflected in the images within this book. The authors hope you enjoy viewing them while reflecting on the past as you learn a little more about Montana State University, Bozeman.

One

Montana State University from 1893 to 1943

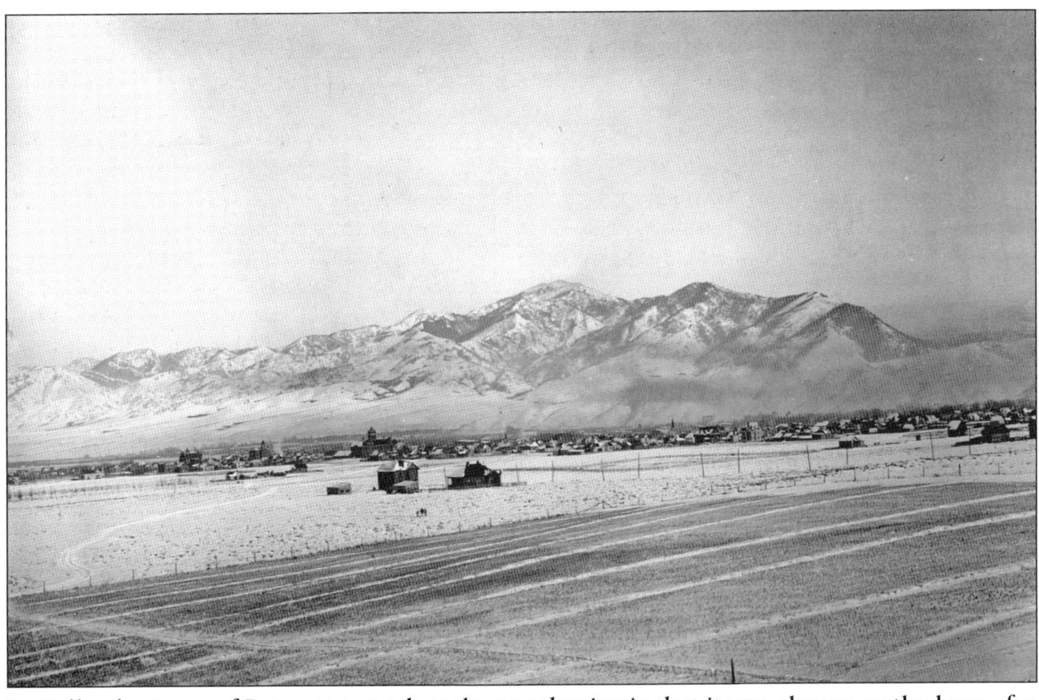

Initially, the town of Bozeman was less than enthusiastic that it was chosen as the home for the Montana College of Agriculture and Mechanical Arts (later Montana State College, now Montana State University) at a time when funds were tight and an economic depression was worsening. Local pride in the institution eventually developed as it successfully provided students with the knowledge and skills to enrich the community and country.

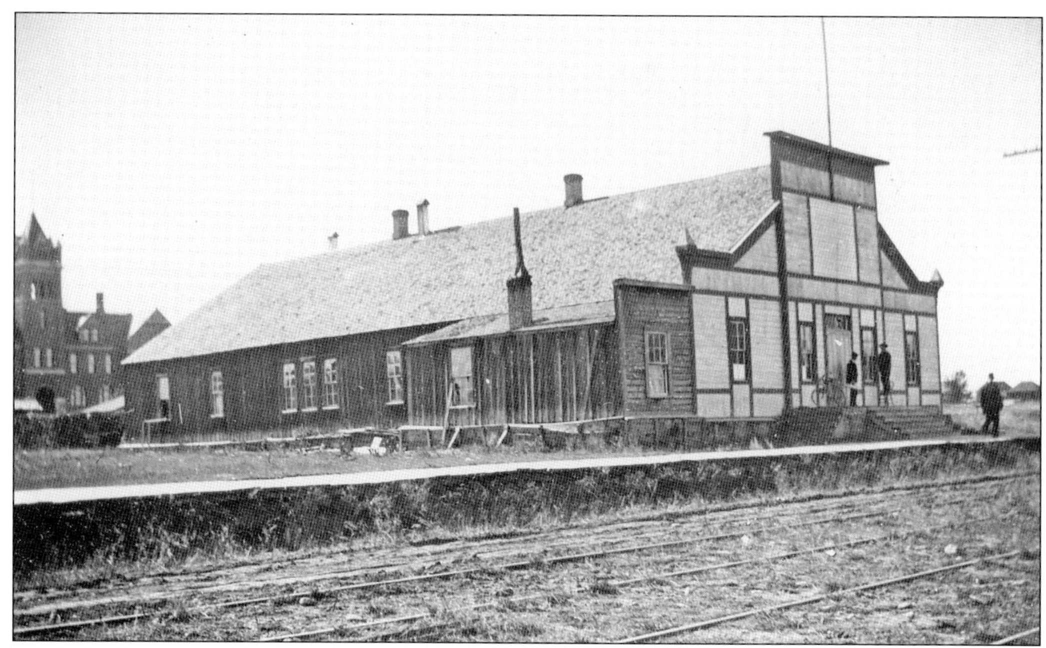

Originally a roller-skating rink and later a Presbyterian academy, the Old Academy Building was home to the university's first classes in 1893. Luther Foster, S.M. Emery, Walter Cooper, and Homer G. Phelps served as instructors to the first class of eight students, which consisted of five men and three women.

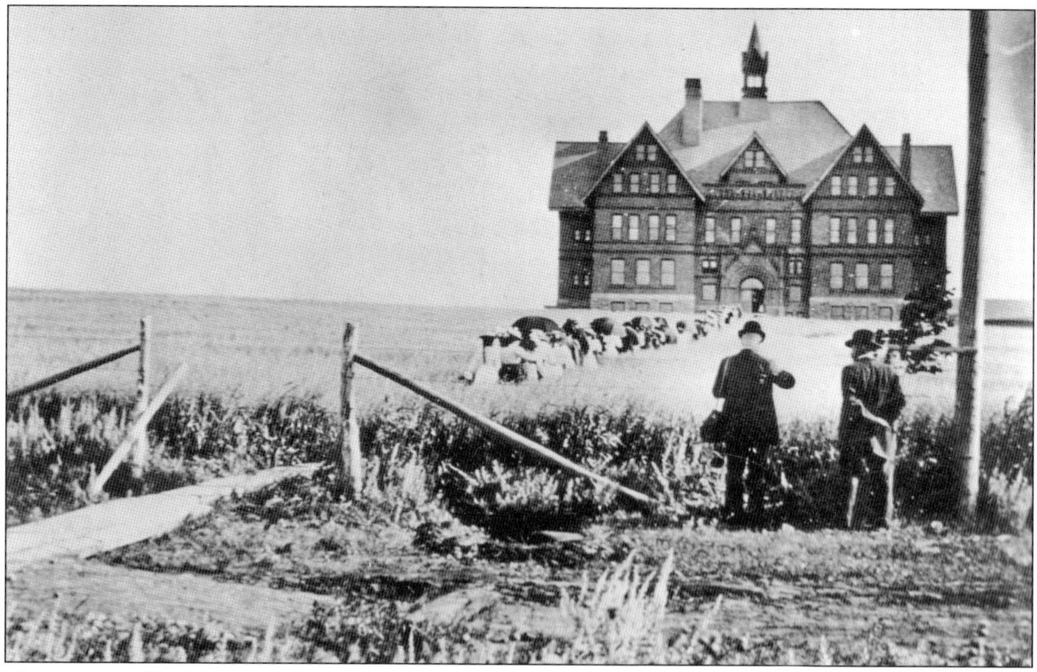

The Main Hall at Montana State University had its cornerstone laid on October 21, 1896, and was completed in 1898. It was renamed Montana Hall in 1914. Montana Hall is the second oldest structure on campus. The visitors seen here are delegates at a state Epworth League convention. (Photograph by Charles D. Crouch.)

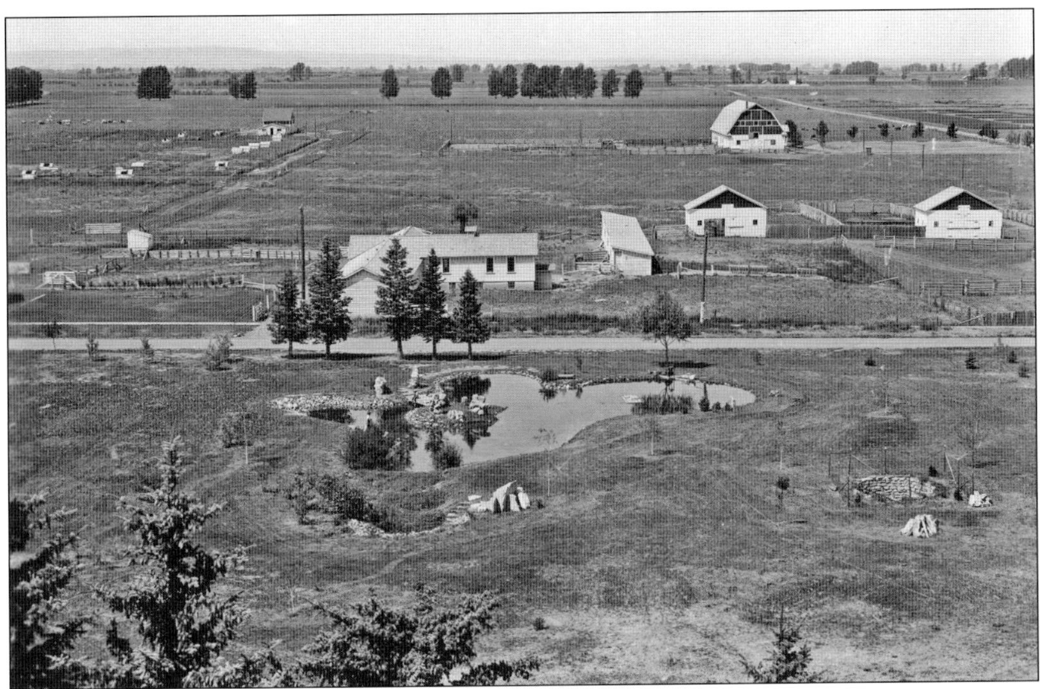

The Frog Pond, seen here in 1935, was located on campus near the poultry office, US Bureau of Entomology building, and veterinary laboratory. The pond served as the scene of the annual tug-of-war between the men of the sophomore and freshman classes. The Fangs, MSU's chapter of the Intercollegiate Knights, also used it as a dunking ground for initiates who didn't observe fraternity traditions.

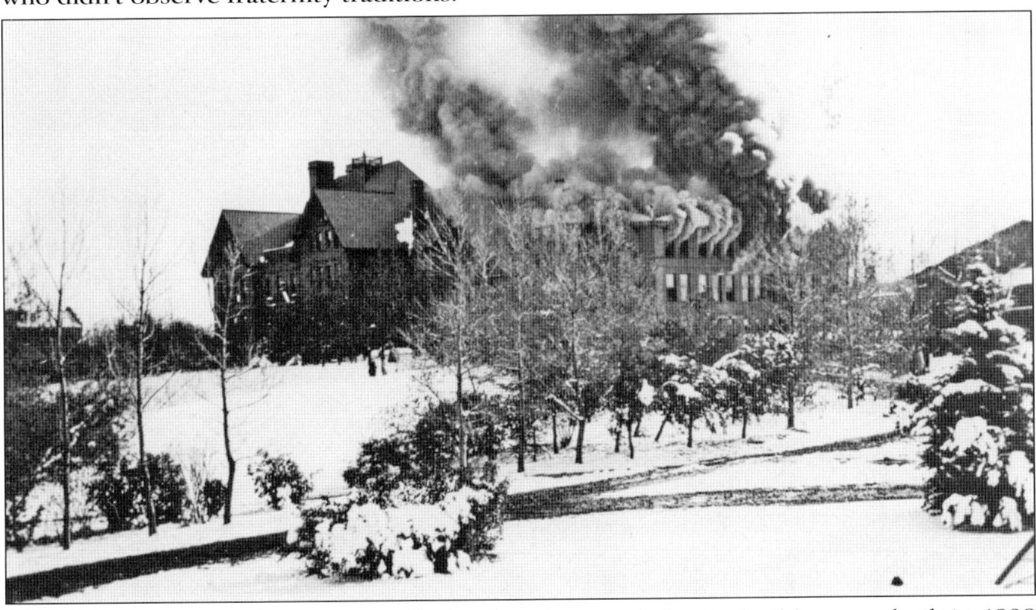

Located to the west of Montana Hall, the chemistry and physics building was built in 1898 and provided the first home to the sciences on campus. In October 1916, a lab explosion started a fire that sent smoke billowing from the windows, leaving a snowy spectacle of a destroyed building on campus grounds.

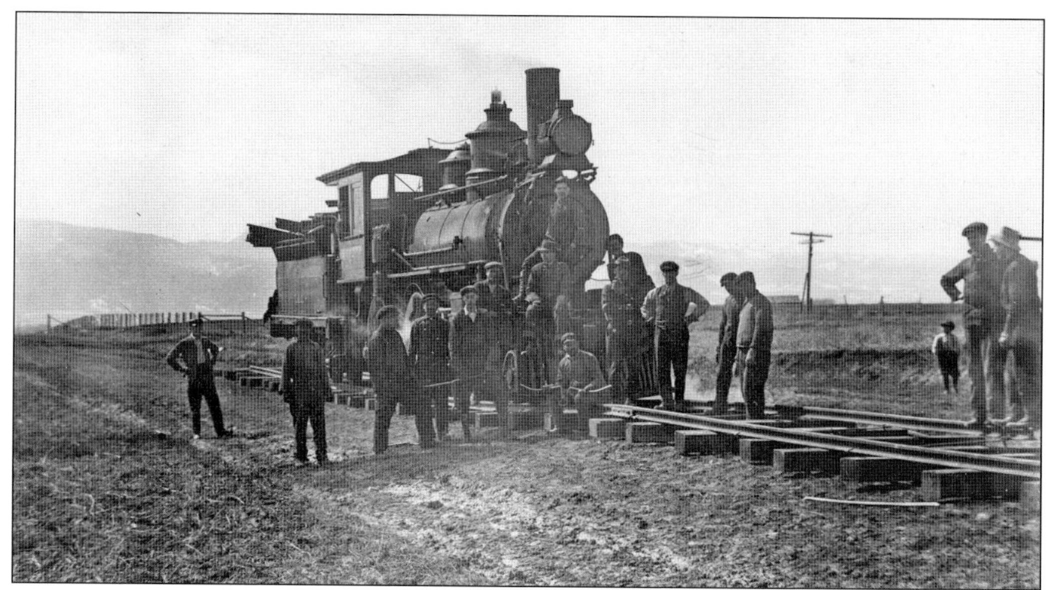

These men are standing with the locomotive engine kept at the edge of campus in 1917. The Northern Pacific Railroad kept an engine on campus to bring coal for the heating plant. The male students often used the engine as a smoke house, since smoking was prohibited on campus.

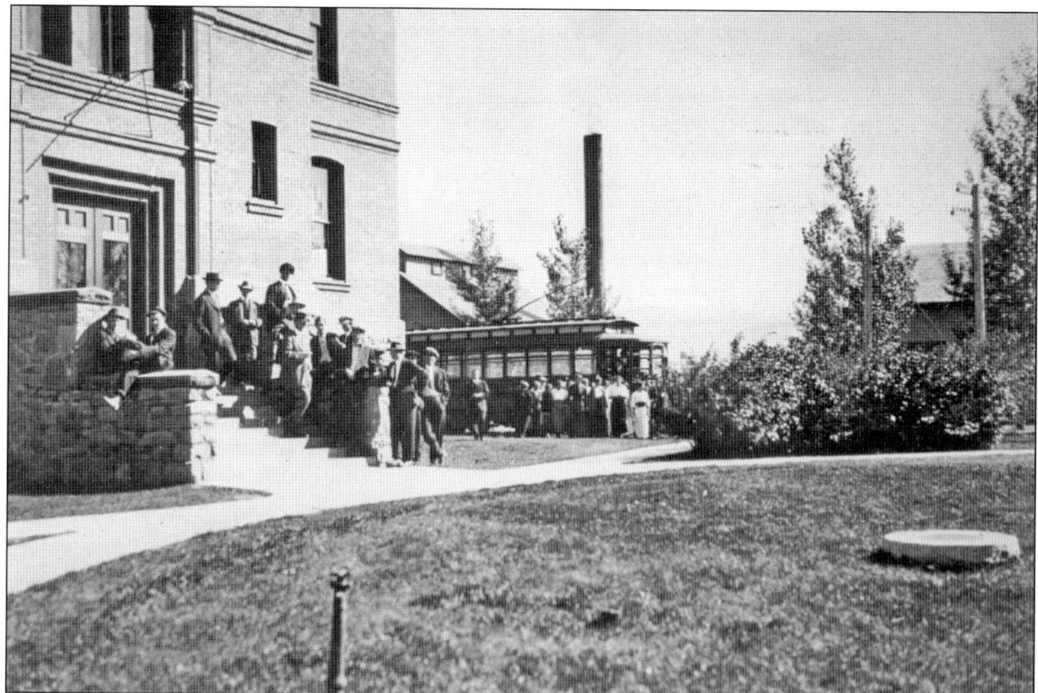

Early transportation to the university took many forms. Seen here in 1914 is a group of students waiting to board the streetcar. Near the electrical engineering laboratory and heating plant, the streetcar once ran from the corner of Montana Hall to the Northern Pacific Railroad station in Bozeman.

A man climbs the flagpole on campus to retrieve a pennant. Described as a battle royal, a pennant would be tacked high on the flagpole, then the male students would rush the pole to climb the mast and secure the pennant.

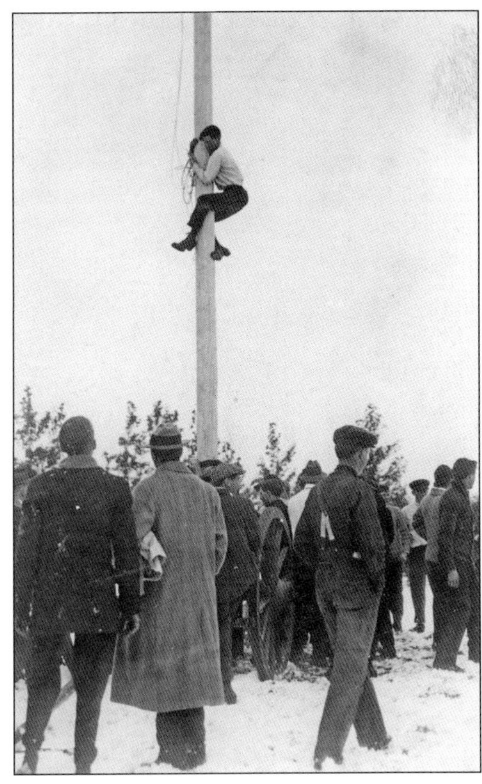

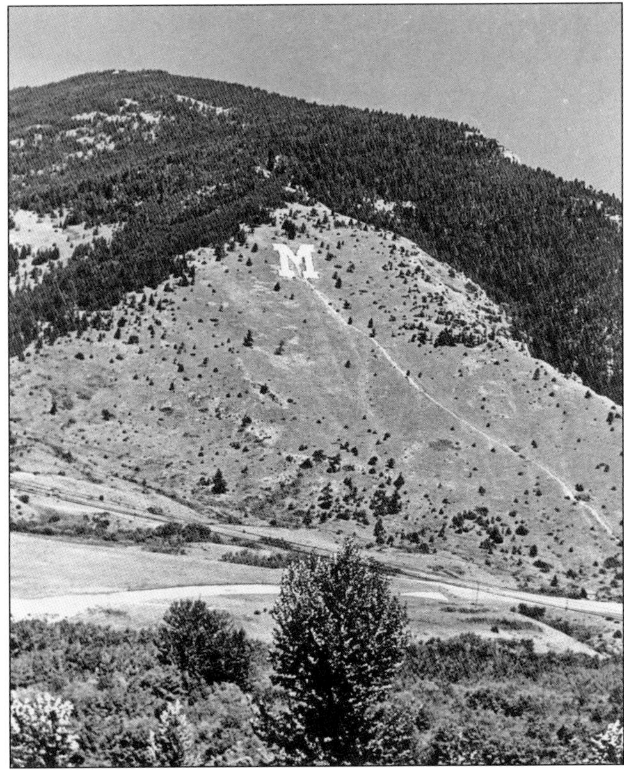

Mount Baldy of the Bridger Mountains northeast of Bozeman plays host to Montana State University's *M*. Work to establish the landmark began with a US Forest Service permit in 1916; engineering students marked out the lines, it was filled in and whitewashed by the class of 1918, and completed in the spring of 1918. The *M*'s legacy as an enduring monument serves as an inspiration to students past and present.

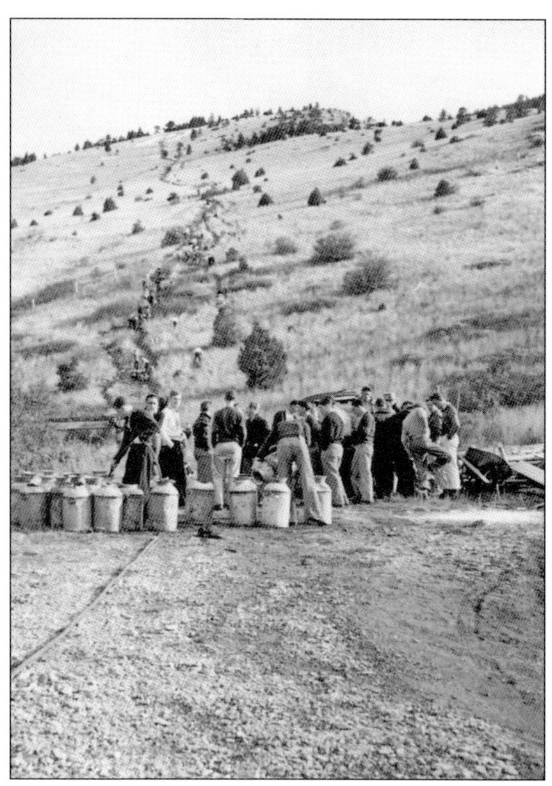

Student pride and participation provide the keys to the upkeep of Mount Baldy's *M*, and 735 freshmen were expected to respond to the call in 1939. Seen here is a group of students gathered around milk cans preparing whitewash to carry up the hill, which other students are ascending in background. (Photograph by D.J. Pletsch.)

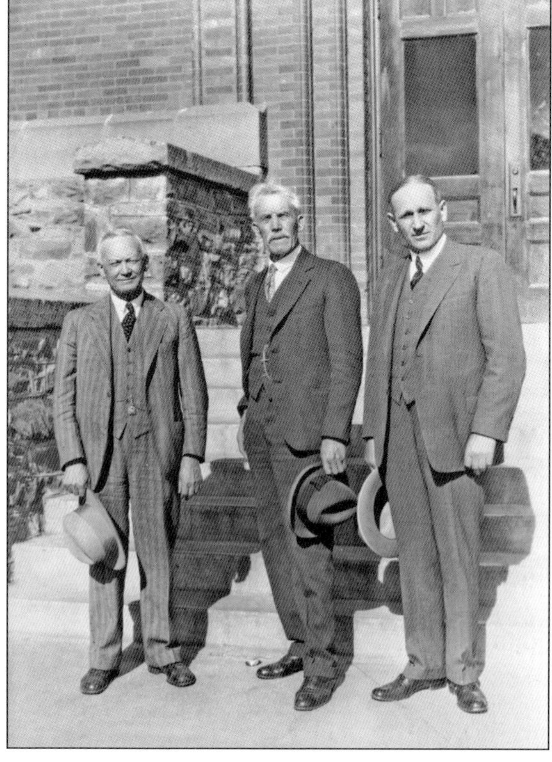

Early Montana State University presidents (from left to right) James M. Hamilton, Rev. James Reid, and Alfred Atkinson stand outside Montana Hall around 1940. Reverend Reid served as the second president from 1894 to 1904. Hamilton led MSU as its third president from 1904 to 1919. As MSU's fourth president, Atkinson's tenure was from 1919 to 1937.

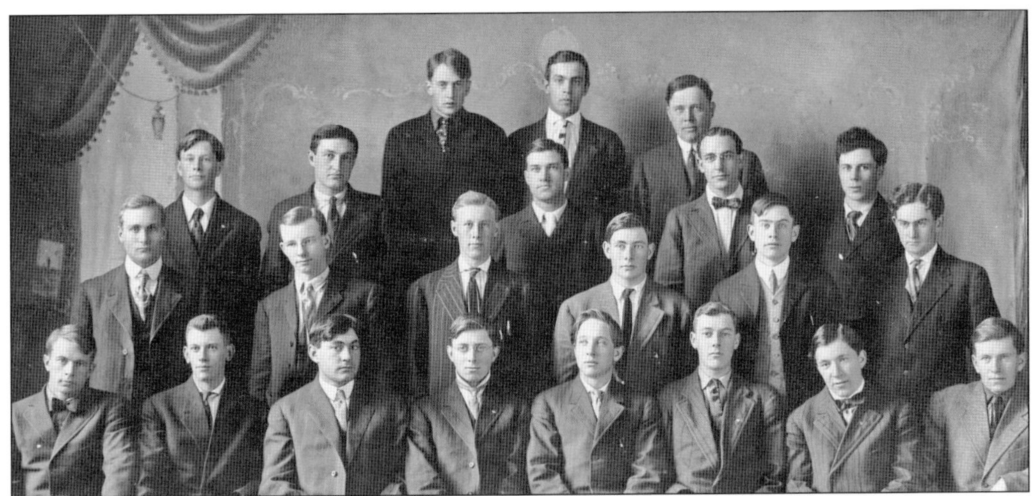

Known as the "Electric Club," founding members of the Electrical Engineering Club organized the local branch of the American Institute of Electrical Engineers on May 7, 1907. The club's purpose was to keep in touch with the latest developments in electricity. Floyd Lorentz served as the first chairman, and the first address was on the design and installation of high-tension transmission lines.

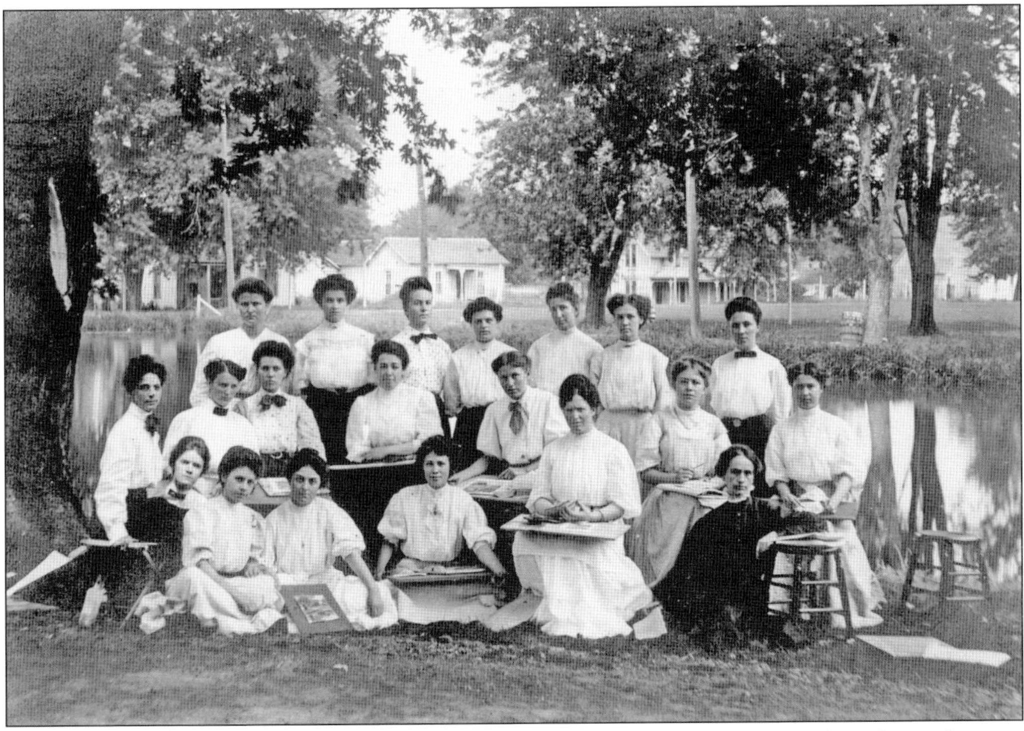

The Hamiltonia Literary Society promoted oratory and debate among the female students at Montana State University in 1908. Established in 1904, the society encouraged members to speak intelligently on a wide range of themes ranging from current events to books, history, music, and art. From left to right in the first row are Anna Krueger Fridley, Belle Osborne, Louis Hartman, Gladys King, Annie Breneman, Ruby King, and Sara Chaffee.

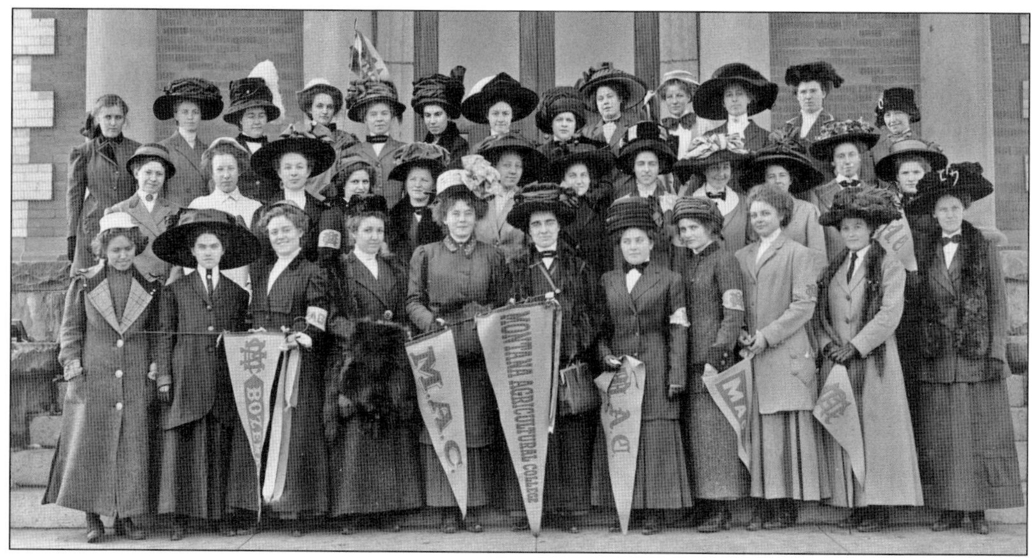

The Boosterines, a group of women students organized in January 1910, are seen here holding spirit pennants on the steps of a campus building. From left to right in the top row are Elsie Gerber, Inez Dusenberry, Olive Clark, Vie Vaileau, Irene Carr, Inez Moore, Blanche Metheny, Frances Read Moxley, unidentified, Mildred Eckles, Natalie Sacket, Alberta Borthwick, and Alma Bancroft. Bess Robertson and Nan Morgan are in the second row from the top.

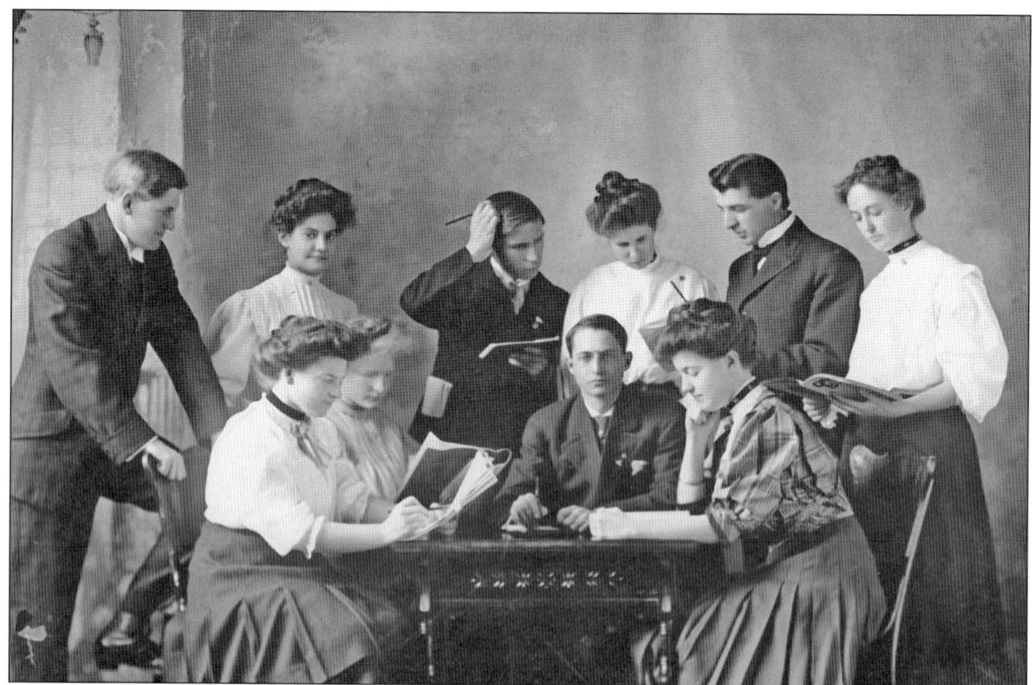

Montana State University's student paper, the *Exponent*, was first published in 1895; according to the staff in 1907, the *Exponent* as a representation of the student body reflected its successes and failures. The 1907 *Exponent* staff members seen here include Lisle Henderson (seated second from right), Frieda M. Bull (standing second from left), and Amy M. Cooke (standing third from right). (Photograph by Schlechten.)

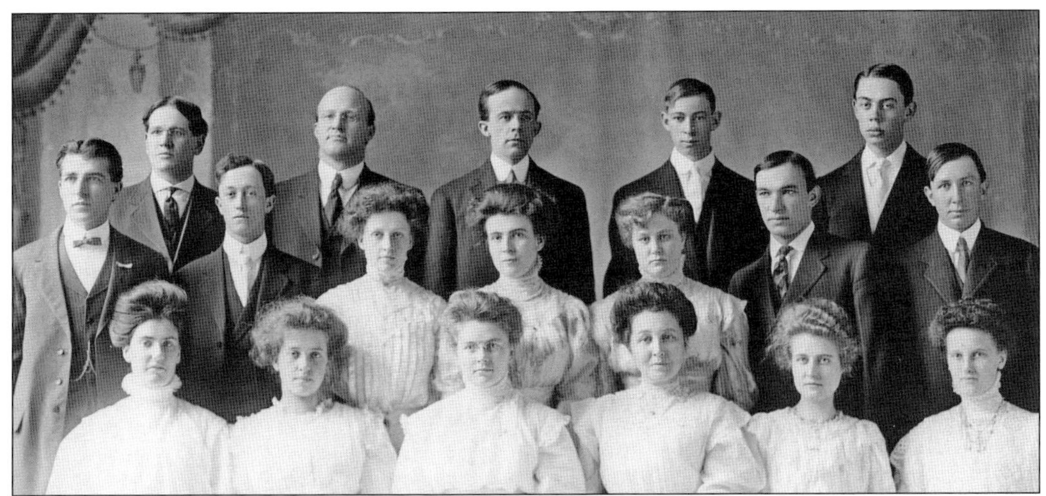

These 18 men and women comprised the Chorister Club in 1905. The club was organized in January 1905 and performed its first concert in April 1905. The group was the first organized choral club at Montana State University; its conductor was F. Arthur Oliver.

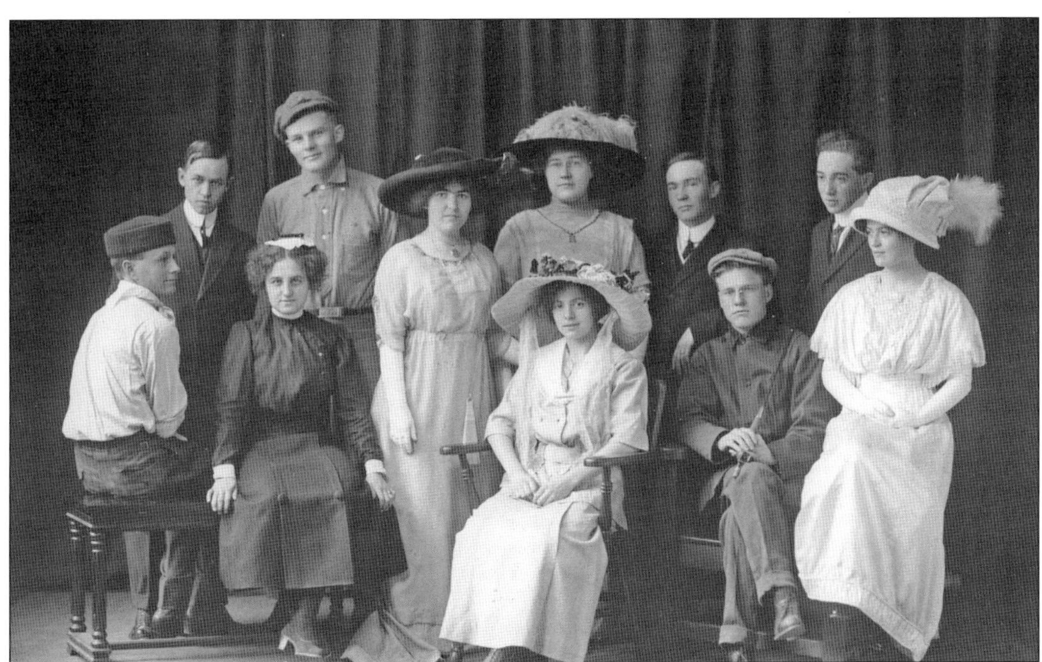

The cast of the Jack-'o-Lanterns, Montana State University's dramatic club, performed *The Professor's Malady* in Bozeman Opera House on December 6, 1912. From left to right are (first row, seated) Joseph Truman, Georgia Cullum, Mae Myers, Kyle Jones, and Rhonda Dawes; (second row, standing) George Roosevelt, John Edward Hodgskiss, Myrtle Alderson, Olive Clark, Alonzo Burket, and Kenyon Talcott.

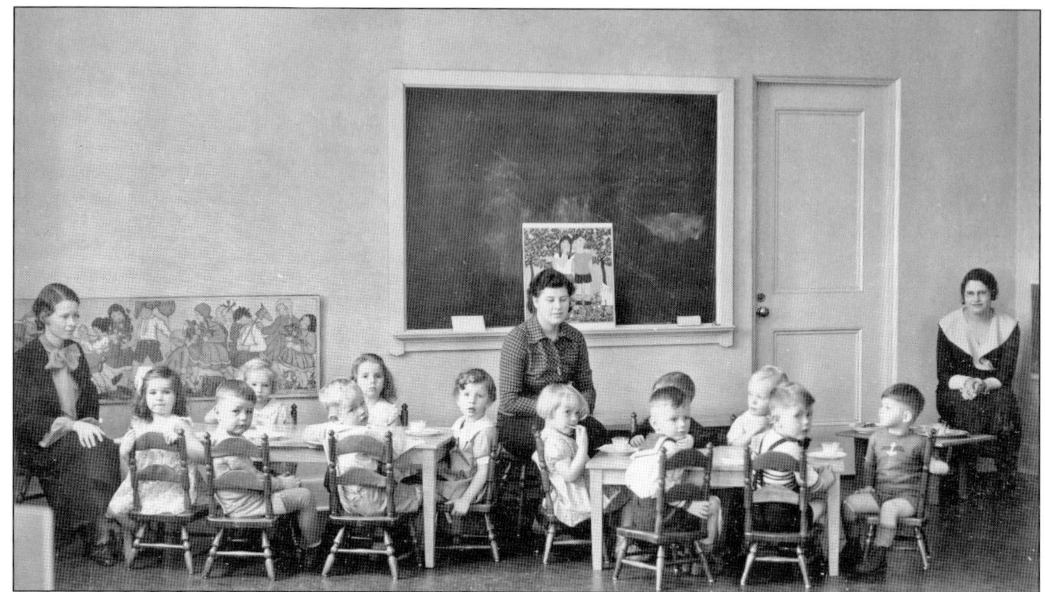

Educational opportunities can come in little packages—home economics students were able to observe the children of faculty and townspeople through appointments in Gladys Branegan's first nursery school in 1934. Among these children are Greta Gay, Wesley True, Joe Bowman, Judy Johnson, John Cannon, Paul Hansen, and Roy Graham.

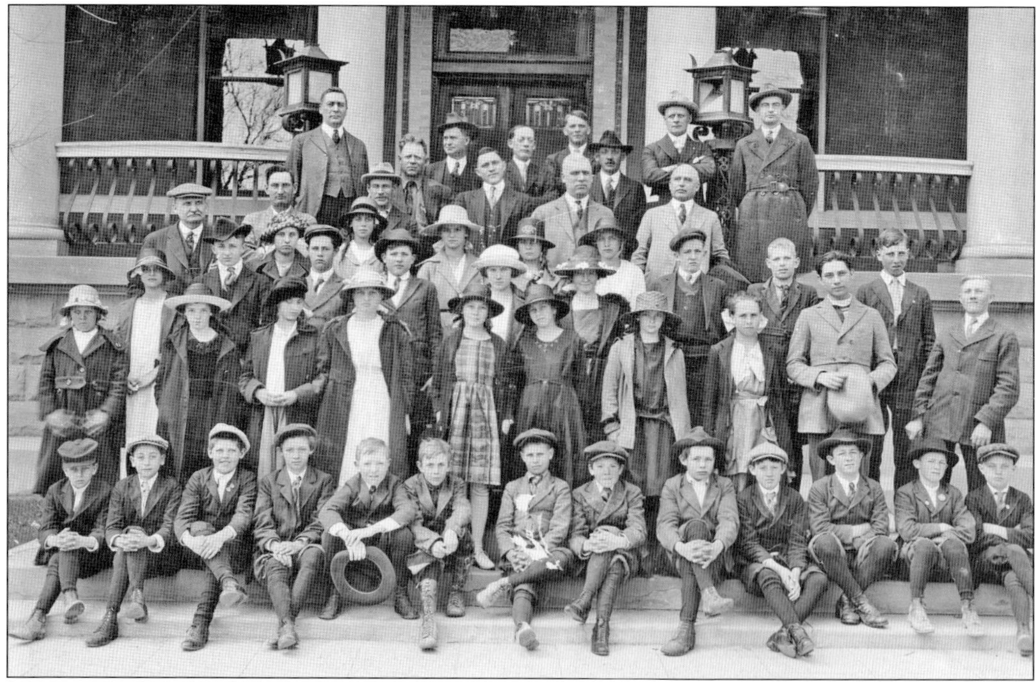

Montana State University's 4-H program provides youth with a variety of activities associated with real-life situations. A successor for earlier boys' and girls' clubs that included corn, pig, calf, canning, sewing, and garden clubs, Montana's 4-H Clubs were included in the extension program under the Smith-Lever Act of 1914. Seen here is a group of men, women, girls, and boys from the 4-H Congress in 1910.

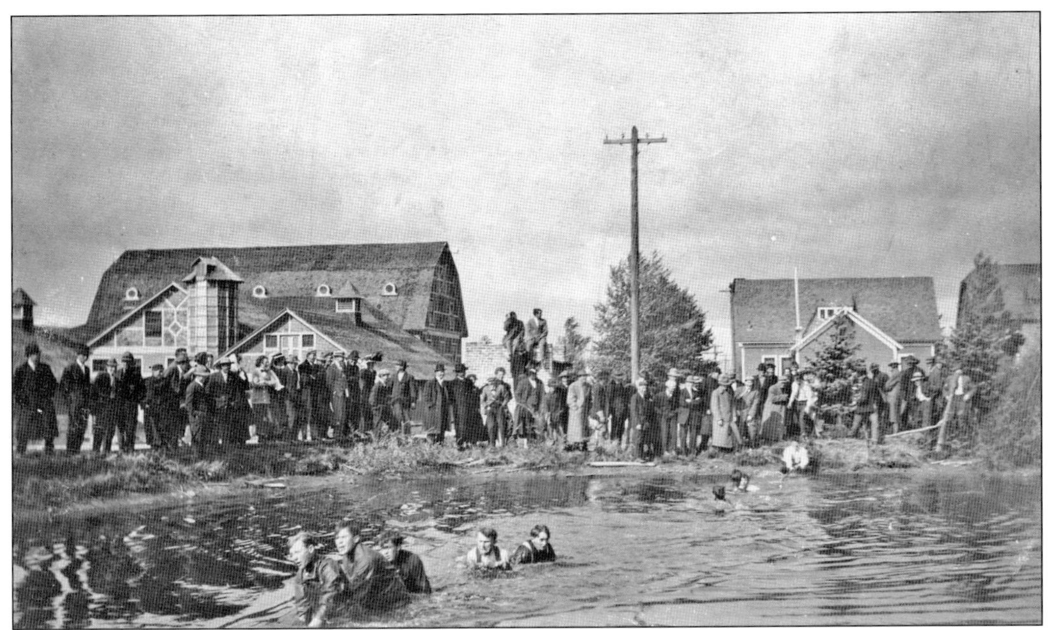

Rivalry between the students at Montana State University can create a sense of competition that can end in a dunking. Here, the young men on campus in 1913 participate in the annual tug-of-war. The tradition originated in 1907 between the freshmen and sophomores and became an annual event with a formal challenge in 1910.

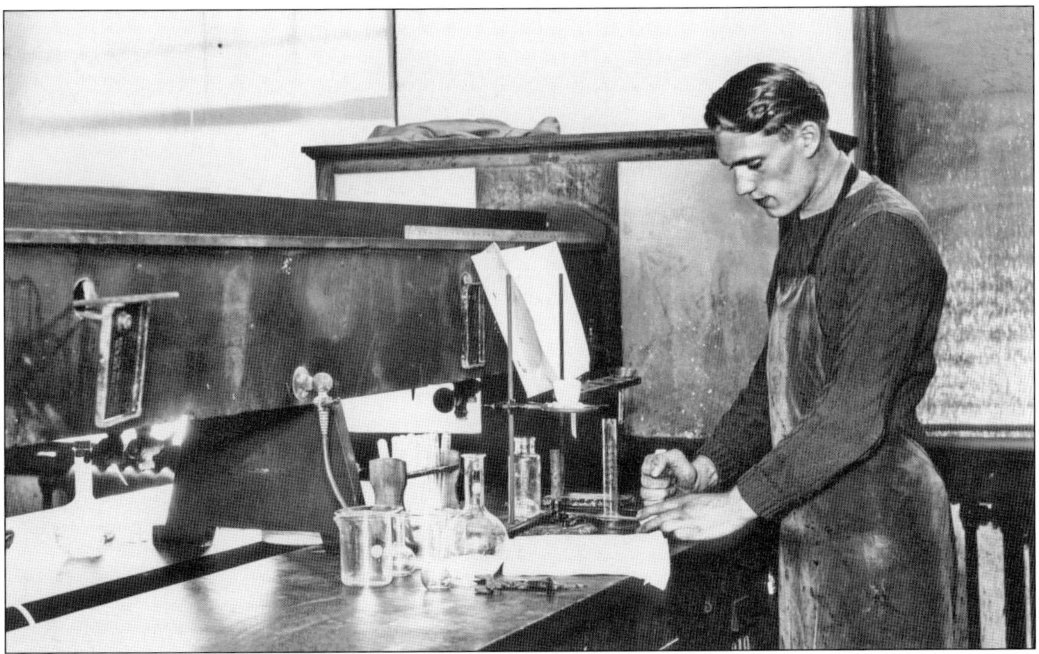

Chemistry courses provided by Montana State University applied to multiple disciplines in the 1920s; chemistry had applications in agriculture, home economics, and engineering. Training offered by chemistry courses opened doors to positions in government jobs, experiment stations, municipal food laboratories, water purification works, and manufacturing industries. Here, a student is working on an experiment in a chemistry laboratory in the 1920s.

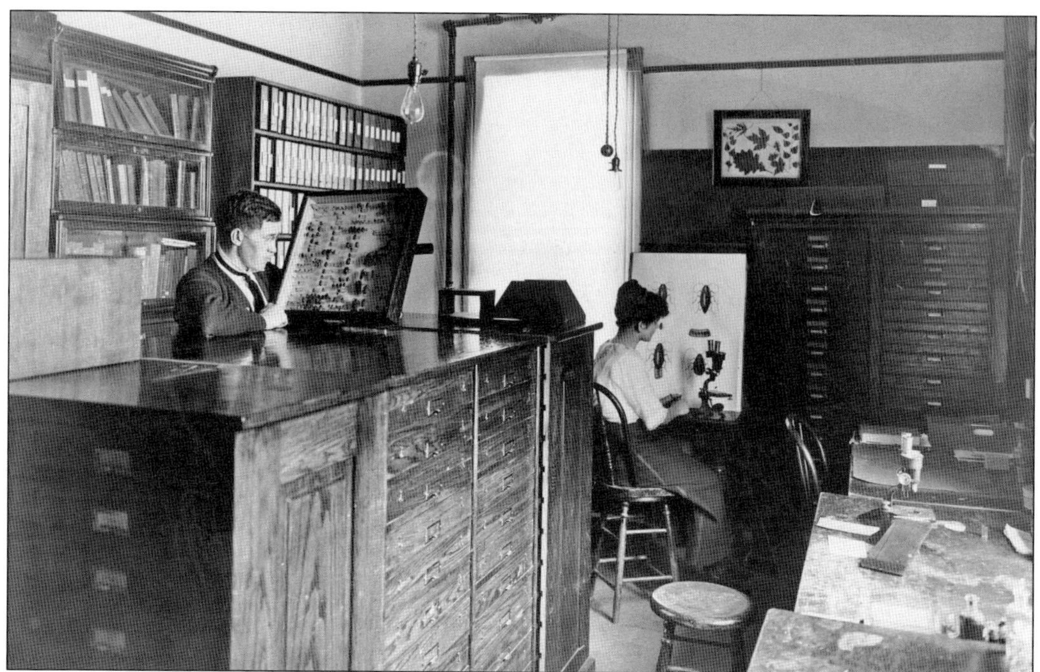

Two students work in the biology lab with zoological specimens in the 1900s. The biology department at the time was comprised of four laboratories devoted to botany and zoology. The laboratories were equipped with up-to-date texts on recent discoveries as well as an extensive selection of botanical and zoological specimens.

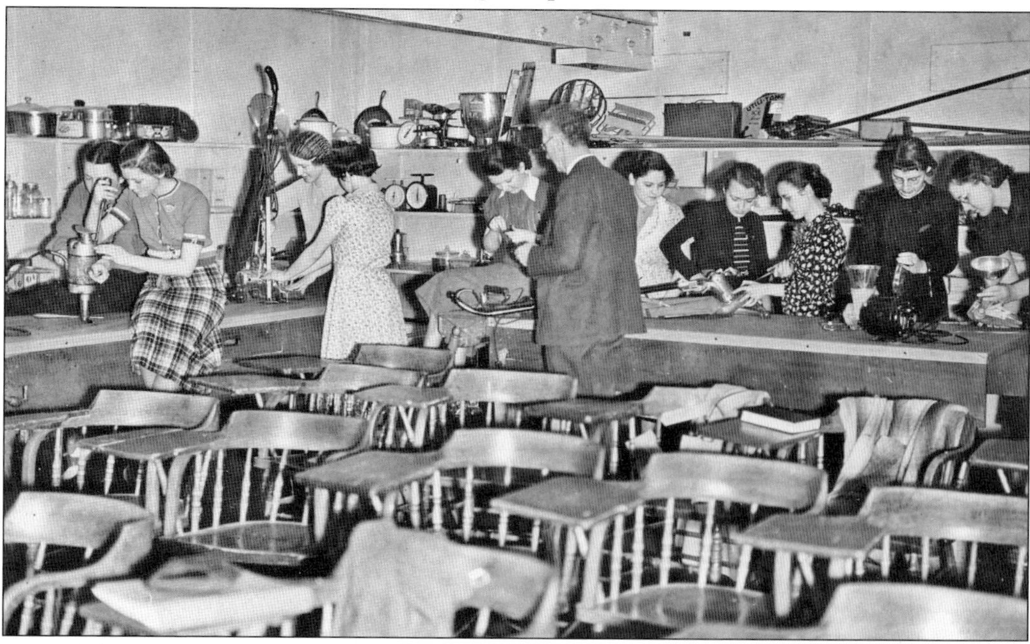

Several female students are pictured in a household mechanics class working with their instructor, Harry Cockrum, in 1942–1943. Household mechanics courses provided students with the knowledge to select and use electrical appliances as well as home water systems. Additionally, the courses taught the principles of home plumbing and heating.

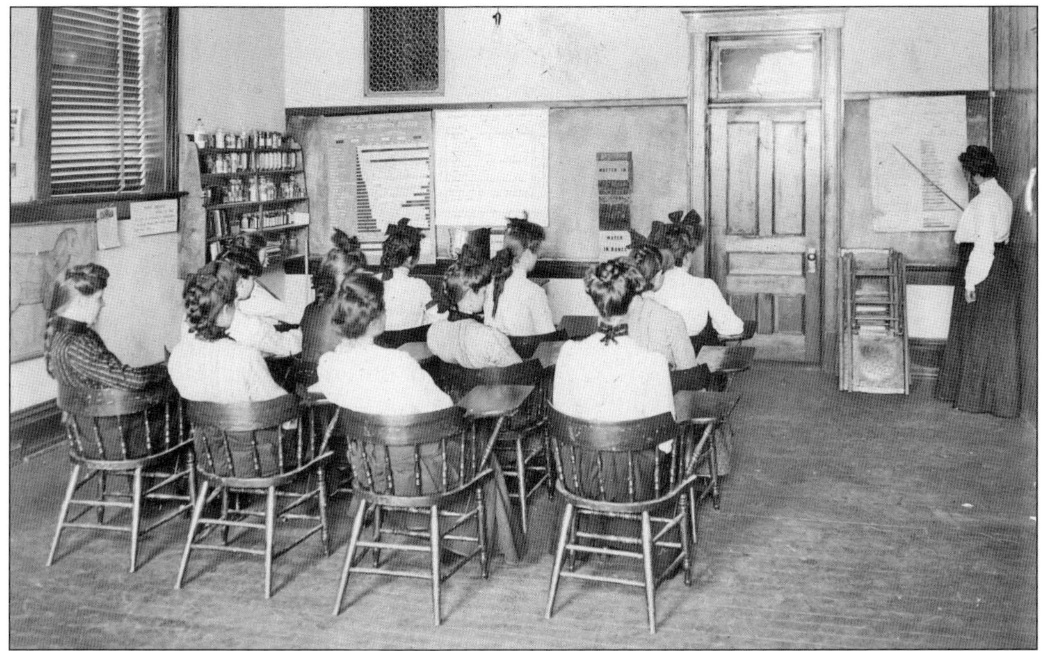

Food chemistry courses offered by the university instructed students in the composition of different foods and their functions, preservation, and adulteration. The female students seen here in the 1910s listen to their instructor discuss food nutrients and their uses in the body as well as the average composition of common foods.

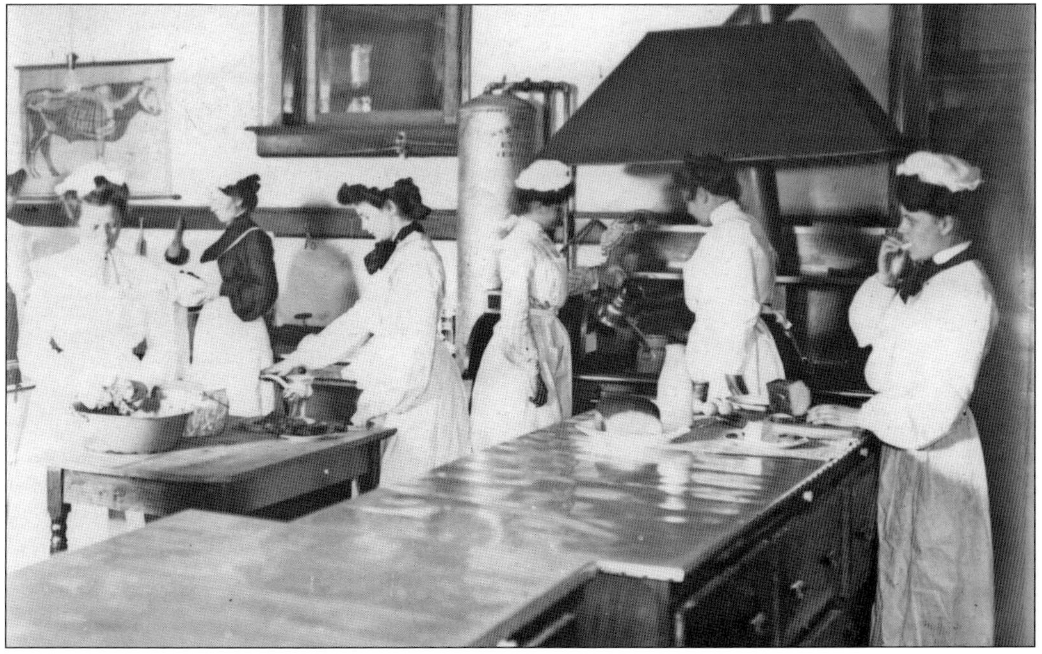

MSU students work on their cooking skills in a domestic science course in 1905. The Department of Domestic Science's program was designed to provide women a liberal education with a scientific basis aimed at allowing them the opportunity to correlate chemistry and biology with household work.

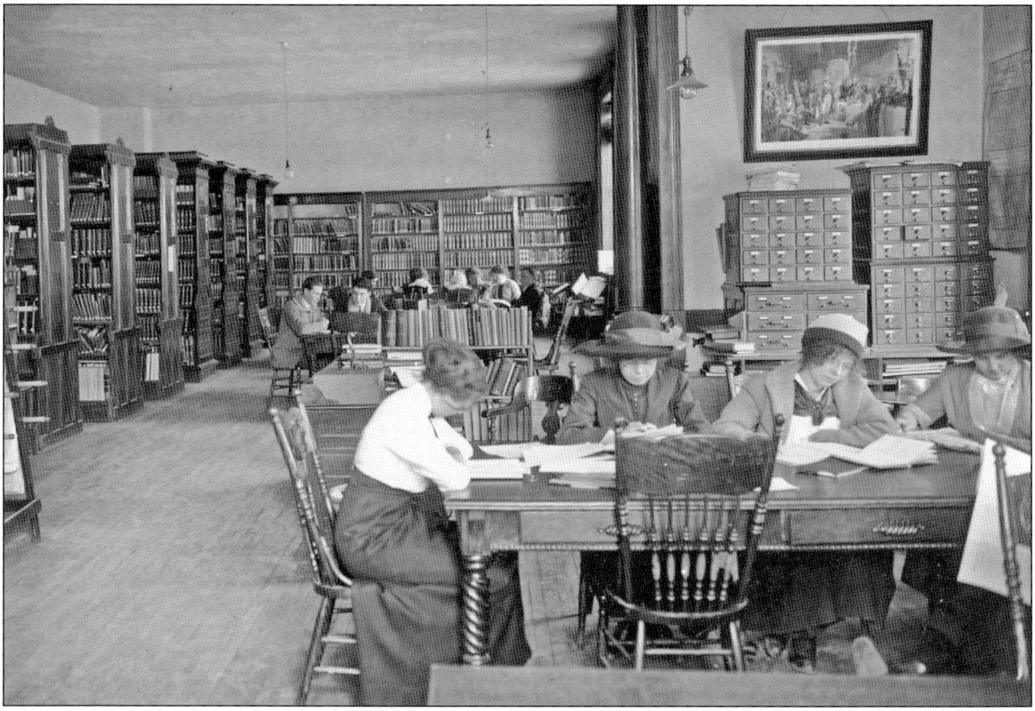

MSU Library was originally housed in Montana Hall, then known as "Old Main." In this 1904 image, students can be seen studying. In 1949, the library moved to its current location, which was dedicated as the Renne Library in October 1978. The tables seen here can still be found today in the library's Special Collections Reading Room.

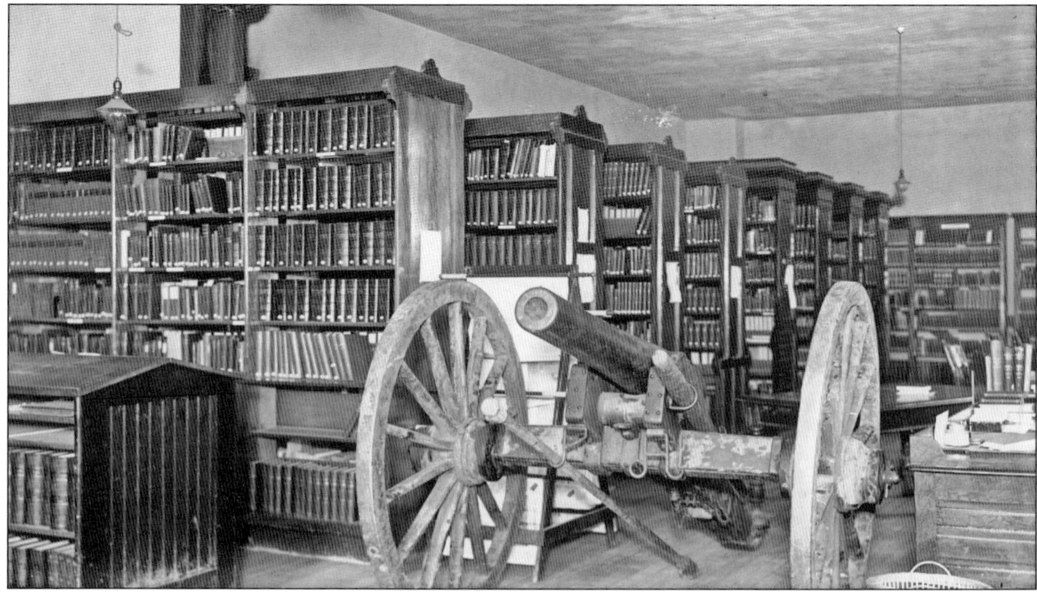

Practical jokes come in packages large and small; on March 25, 1910, a 1,300-plus-pound cannon from Fort Ellis found its way to the second floor of the library at Montana Hall, to the surprise and consternation of the librarian. The cannon was later mounted next to the flagpole as a permanent fixture on campus.

Two

Montana State University from 1944 to Present

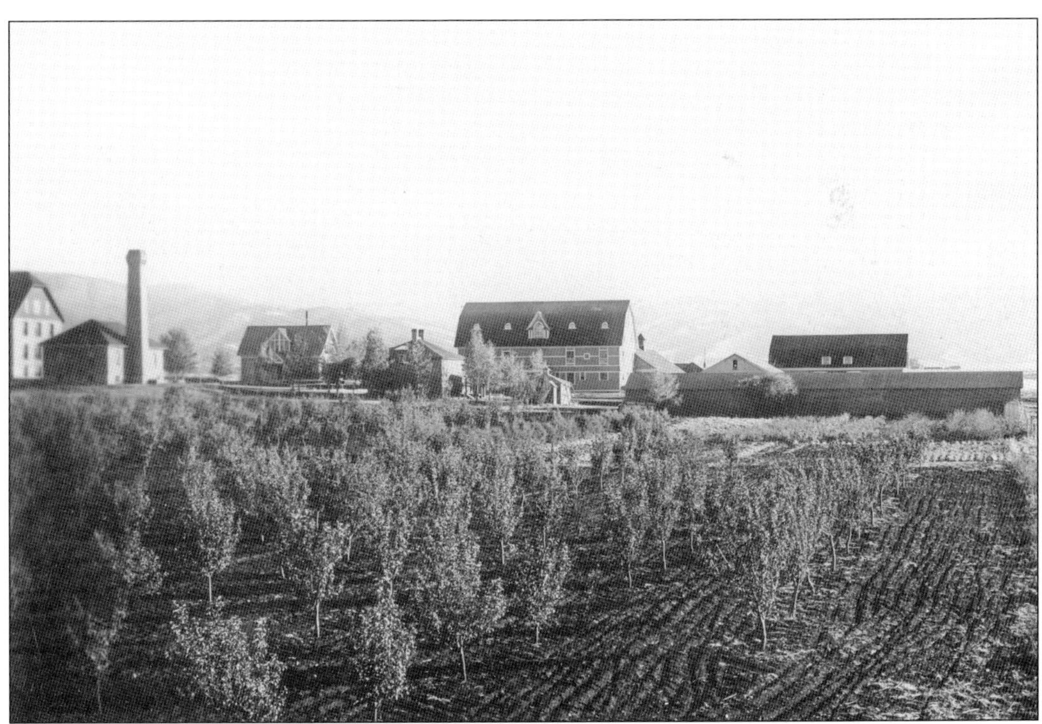

The Montana State University campus in Bozeman consists of 1,780 acres in the Gallatin Valley. Several campus buildings can be seen here with fruit orchards in the foreground. Among the buildings are the heating plant, the horse barn, and the Extension Building (later renamed Taylor Hall.)

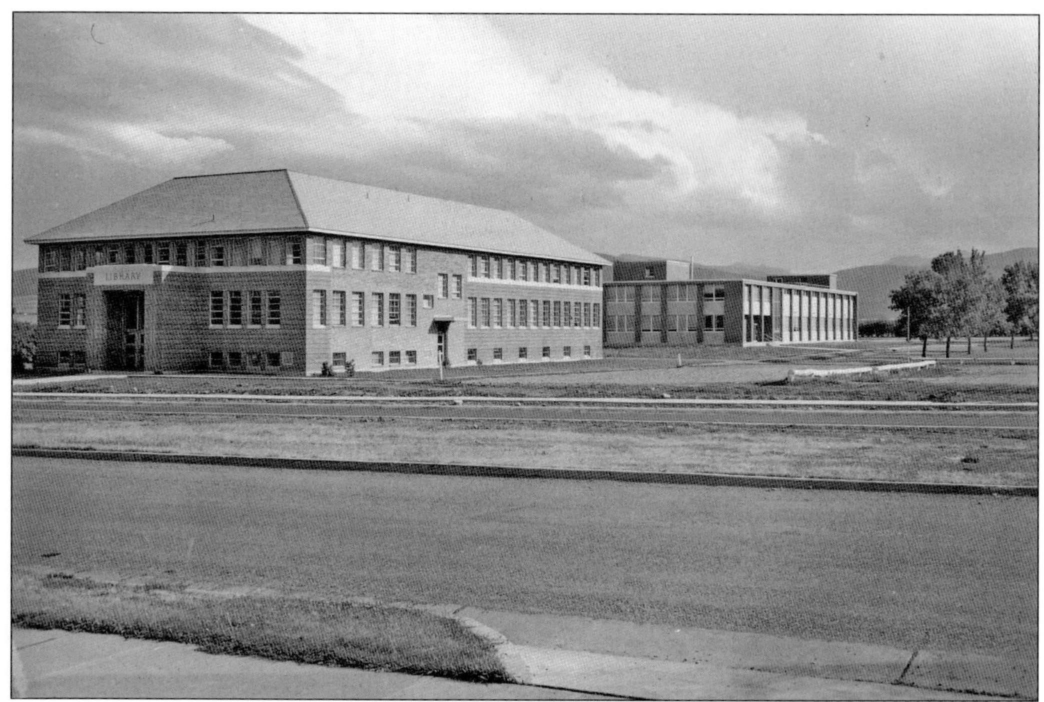

Pres. Augustus M. Ryon authorized the first order of books for the library in January 1894. The library's first permanent home was Montana Hall. In 1949, a new building was completed. As the library expanded its collections, it needed room to grow; the second and third floor were added in 1965, and the fourth floor in 1970. The library was dedicated to Roland R. Renne on October 14, 1978.

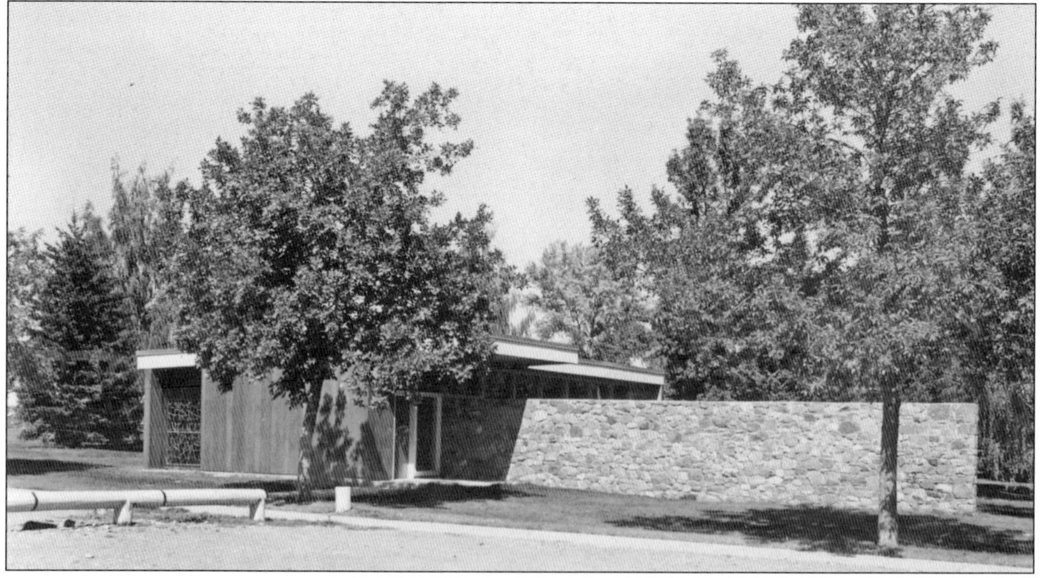

Constructed in 1952 as a quiet place for self-examination and meditation, the Danforth Chapel was built thanks to local contributions and a donation from William Danforth of the Danforth Foundation. The chapel's first services were held in May 1952. It provided a nondenominational location for religious ceremonies on campus.

Free time provides the opportunity for enjoyment. Several students are pictured enjoying some leisure time on the lawns between Renne Library and Reid Hall in 1980. One student in the foreground is carrying books, likely on his way to class.

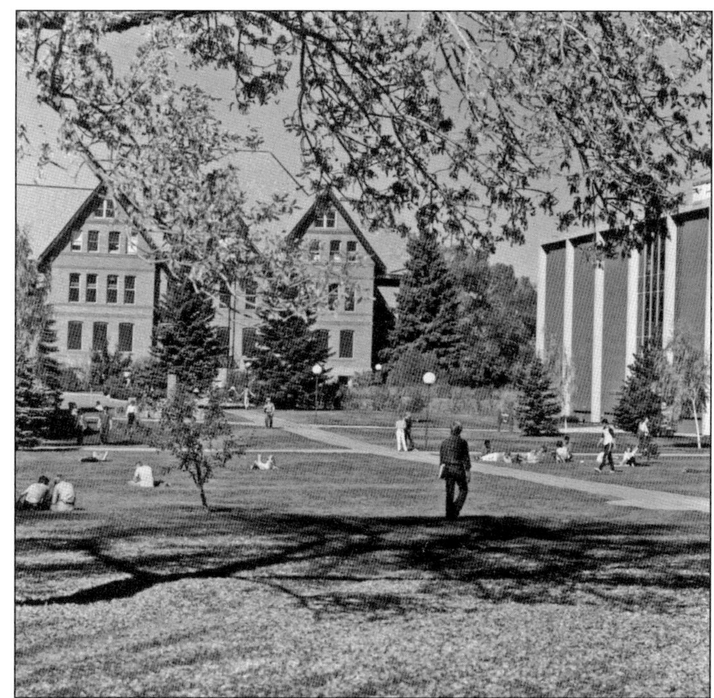

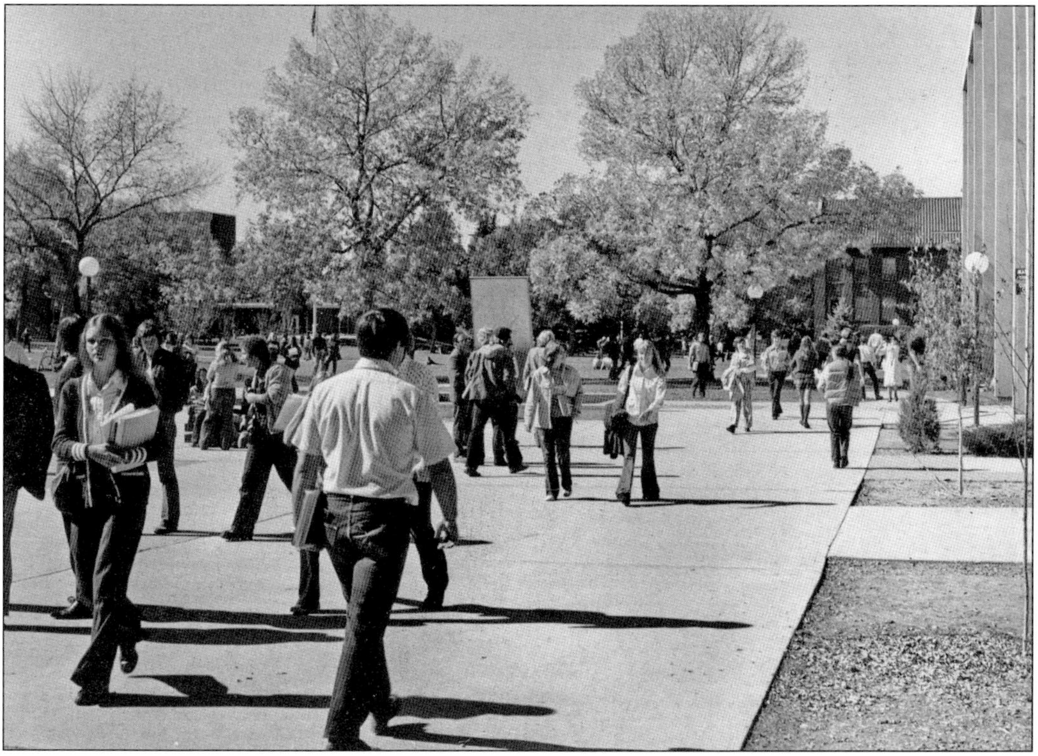

Walking on campus is a way to get to classes, but it also provides an opportunity to view the campus while visiting with friends. In 1972, several students walk along the sidewalks near Reid Hall and Traphagen Hall; others sit and visit while enjoying the scenery.

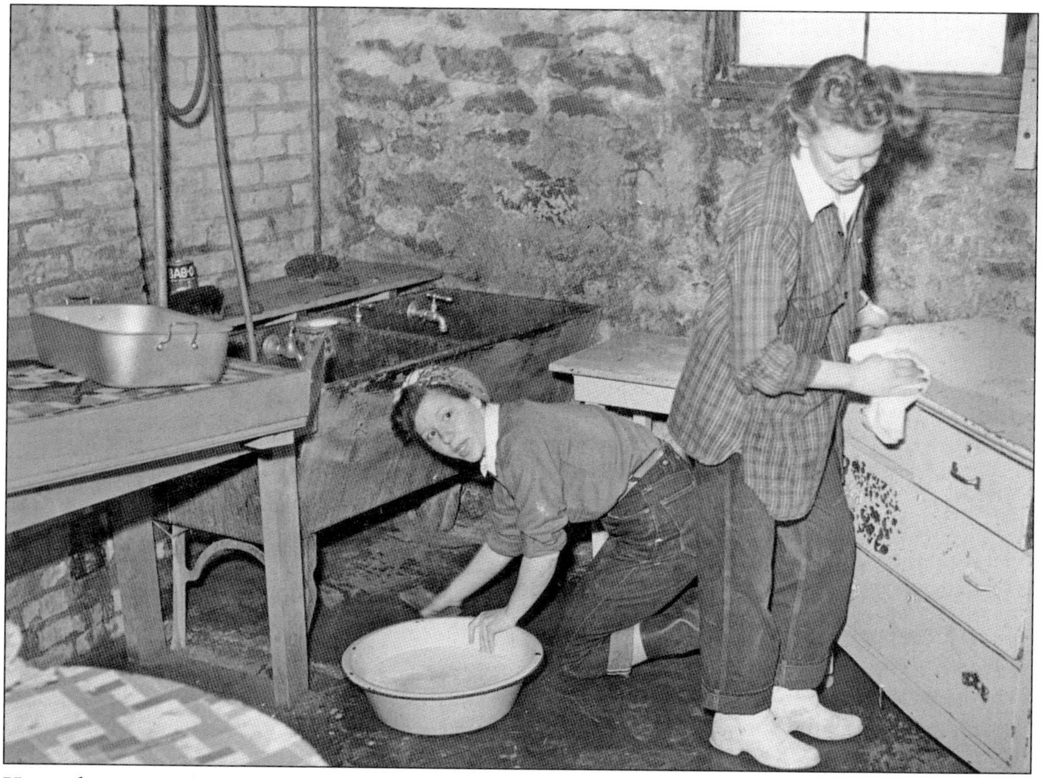

Housekeeping skills are useful in maintaining an inviting atmosphere at work, school, and home. Here, two young women work together to clean a room; while one cleans a dresser, the other scrubs the floor under the sink as part of a series of World War II defense training courses.

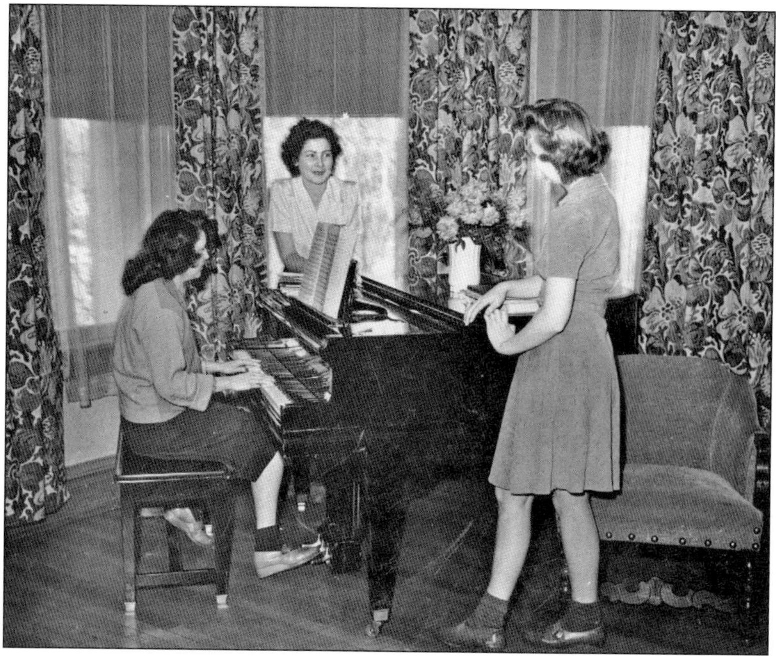

Music conveys a variety of ideas and emotions through harmony, rhythm, and melody; here three young women around a piano share their time and a song in 1944. They demonstrate a sense of community and friendship as part of a series of World War II defense training courses.

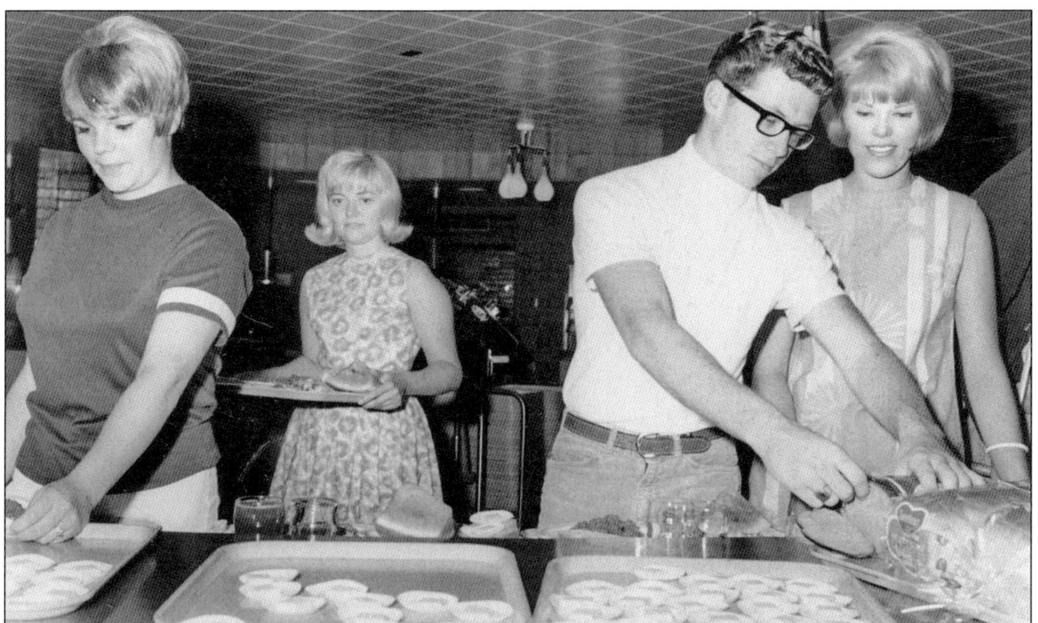

New and exciting choices make life more interesting, but providing a fresh and well-balanced meal to a large student body can prove challenging. To keep food fresh and avoid repetition, food services prepares meals in small batches from a preplanned rotation system. Several students are pictured making their meal selections in 1966.

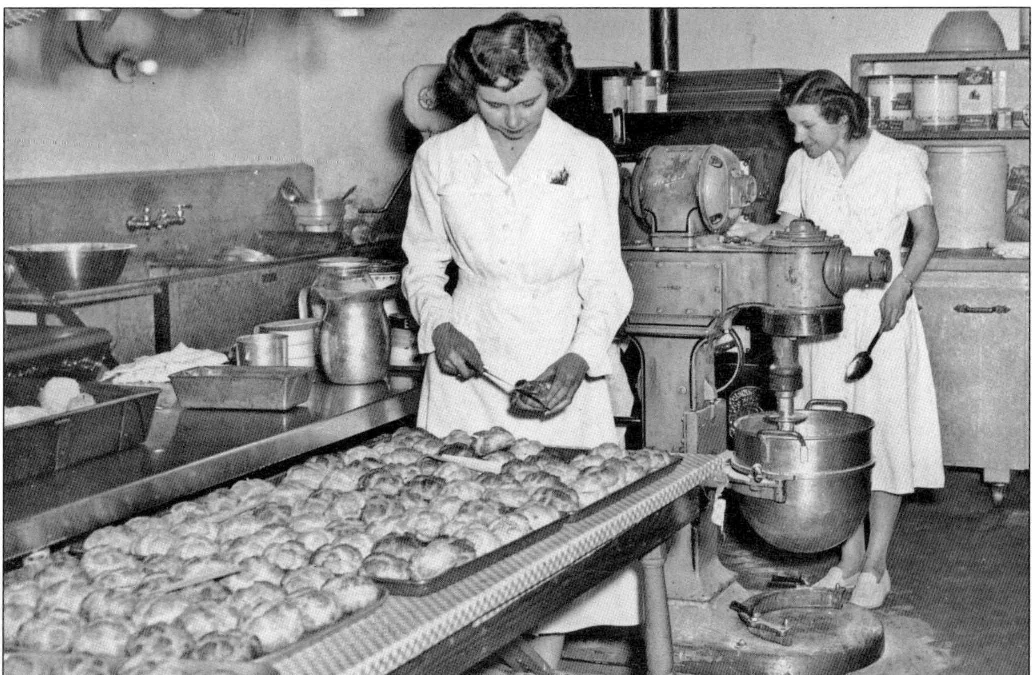

It takes a lot to feed a campus full of students. Home economics provided students in the 1950s with the opportunity for planning and preparation of meals in large numbers through large-quantity cookery classes. These two students are baking rolls in a quad kitchen for a quantity cooking class in 1950.

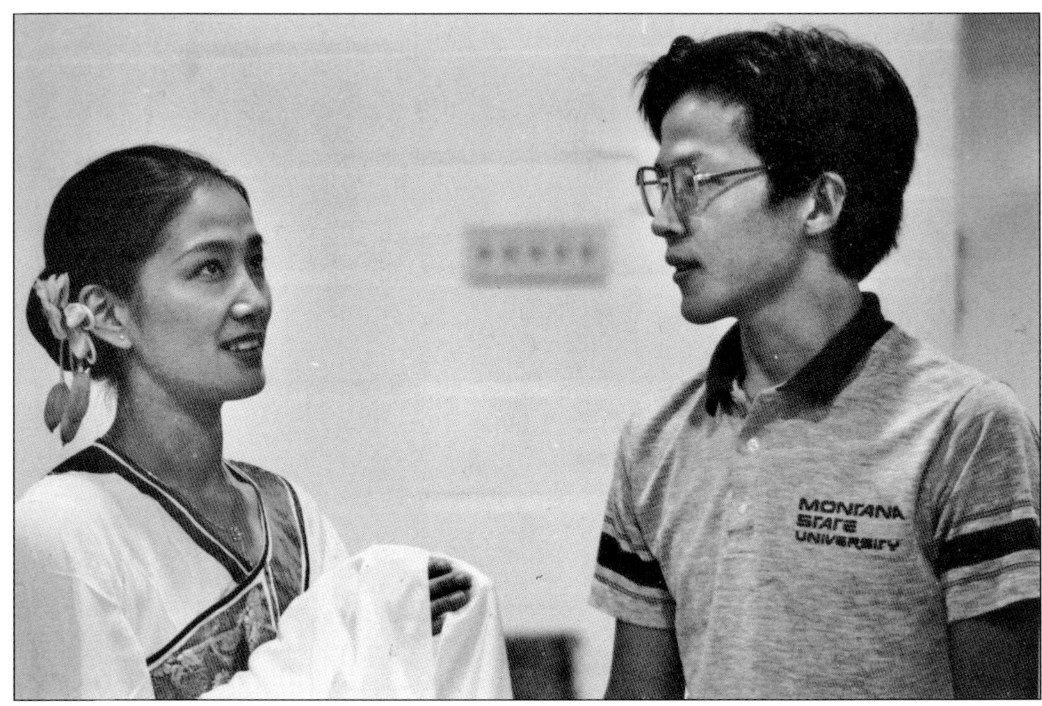

Two foreign exchange students share a cultural exchange from China in 1979. Making new friends and finding common ground is essential to help foreign exchange students bridge the gap between homesickness and a sense of belonging. The International Club provides an outlet for new students to connect and communicate as they discover commonalities.

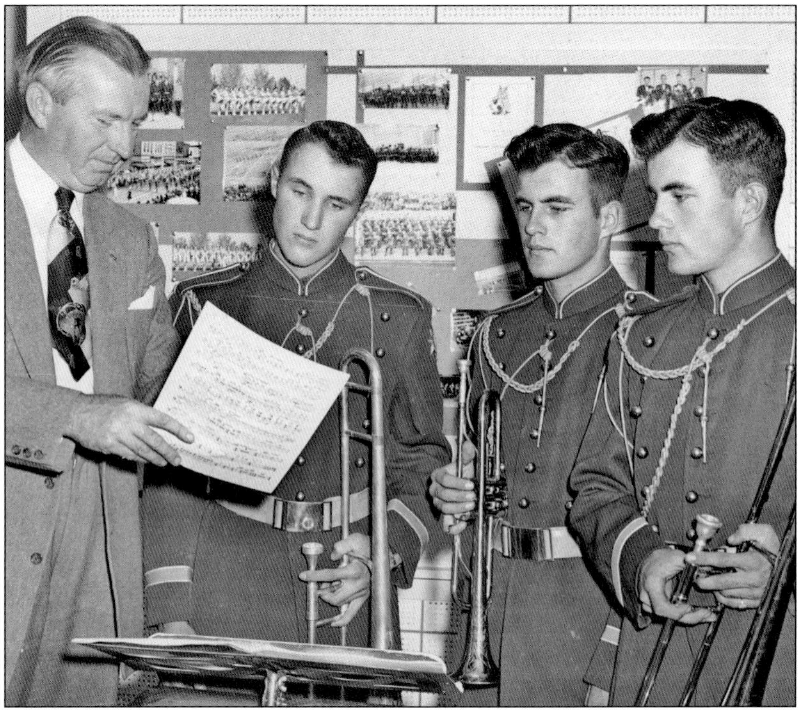

Music is a regular feature on campus—it takes the form of the symphony, marching bands, jazz bands, and symphonic bands. Seen here are Dean, Dale, and Don Knox from Kolin, Montana, with band director Ed Sedivy in 1953. The Knox brothers were the first triplets to enroll at Montana State University.

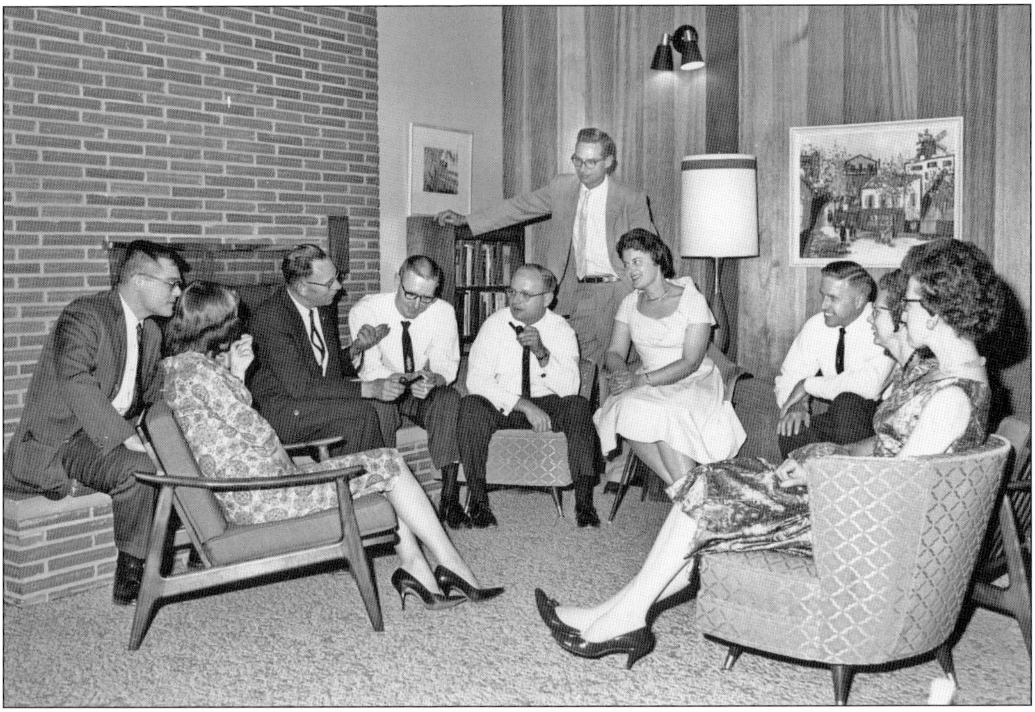

As the highest level of academic degrees, the doctorate demonstrates that its recipients have an in-depth knowledge of their discipline. Acknowledging that honor, this image shows Dr. Leon Johnson, dean of the Graduate School, at his home entertaining the Ph.D recipients of 1962 and their wives. Among the recipients is Norman Anderson, standing near the bookcase.

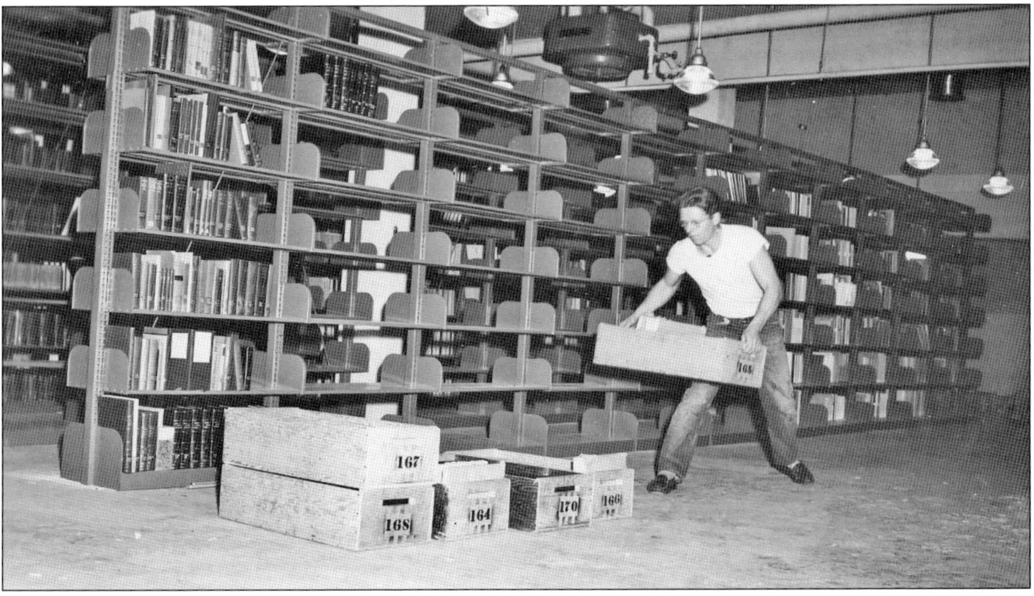

A young man moves boxes filled with books from their old home in Montana Hall to the newly constructed library in 1949. The transition involved two trucks, approximately 20 men, and around 200 moving boxes; it took place over Christmas break and was completed in time for the library to open its doors in January 1950.

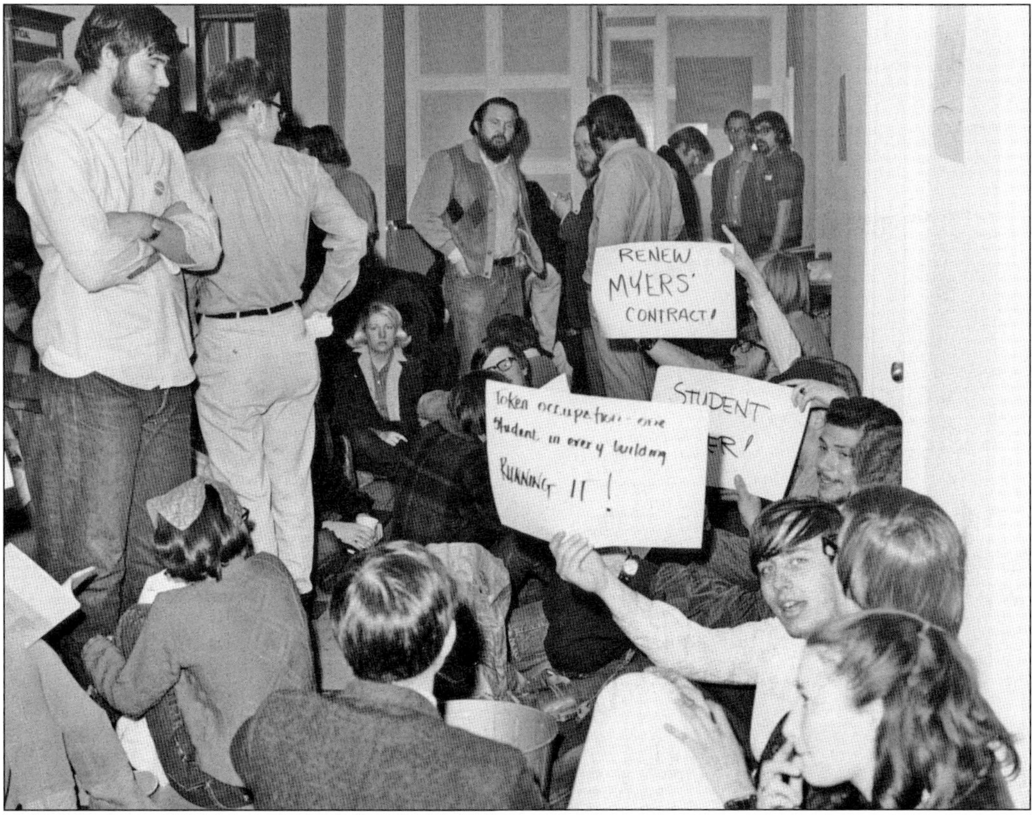

James Myers, English instructor at Montana State University, was terminated in June 1970 due to conflicts over challenges to established norms and sensitivities as well as academic freedom. These students are staging a nonviolent sit-in at Montana Hall to protest the cancellation of Myers's contract. His termination was upheld after a review hearing.

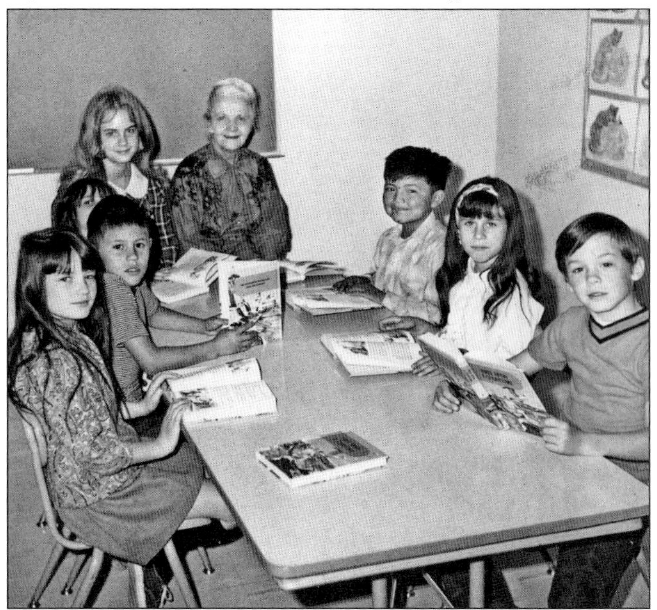

Child development courses offered students the opportunity to observe and study young children to learn how best to understand and guide them. In this image, a student is working with elementary schoolchildren as part of her on-the-job experience in the child development course at Polson High School in 1951.

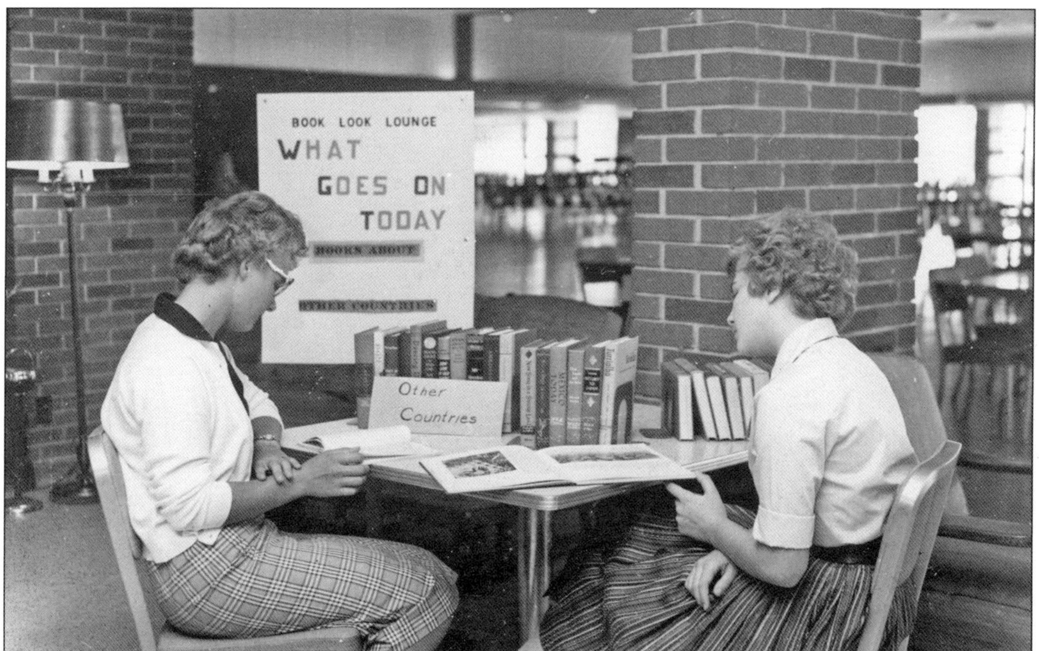

Expanding knowledge on new topics opens portals to new frontiers, and 4-H Clubs provided opportunities for Montana's youth to learn about topics ranging from food and clothing preparation to agriculture and livestock. These two students are reading books about other countries in a Book Look Lounge during a 4-H Congress in 1961.

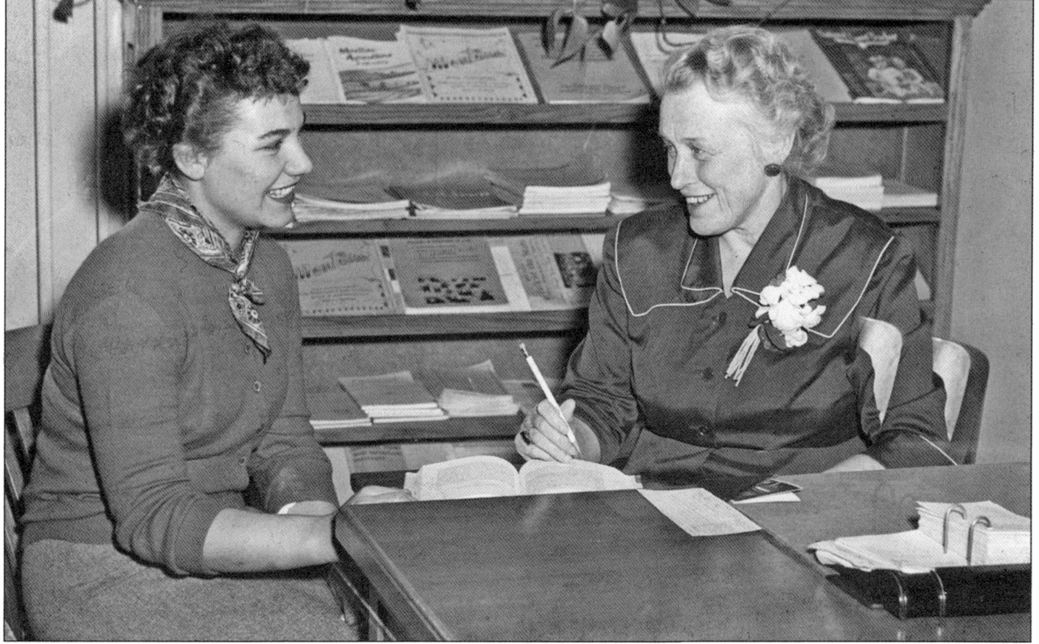

Providing students with suggestions about the best course of action is an essential administrative function. Katherine Roy, dean of the Division of Professional Studies at Montana State University from 1946 to 1959, is advising a student in 1955. Dr. Roy's division included the Departments of Applied Art, Secretarial Studies, and Home Economics.

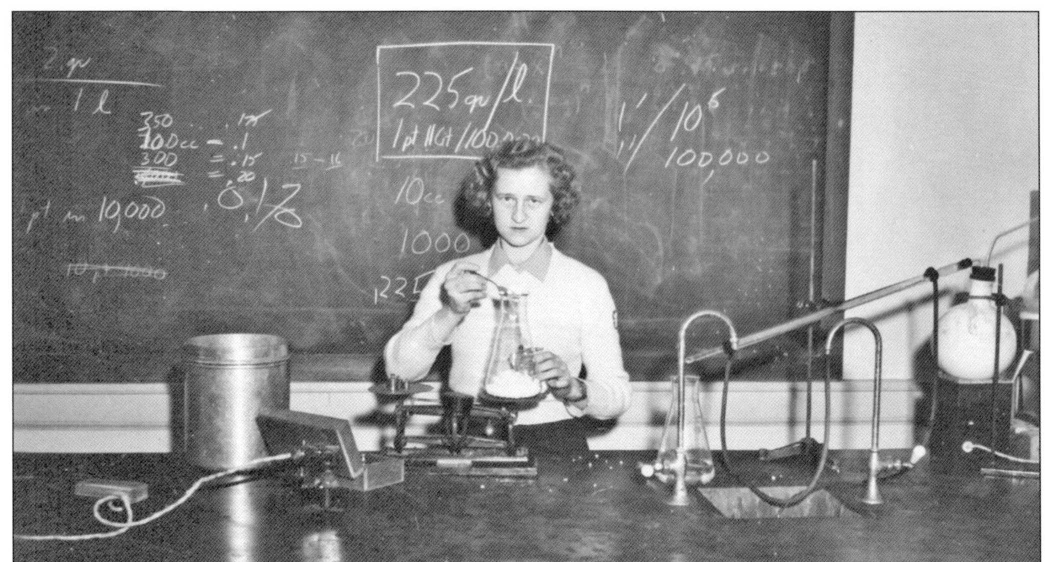

Chemistry courses provide students at Montana State University with the opportunities to investigate substances to determine how they interact and change when combined in order to prepare them for jobs in research, government service, teaching, and industry. In 1950, Maria Burger, a chemistry student, stands in front of a chalkboard adding substances to a beaker. (Photograph by MSU Office of Information.)

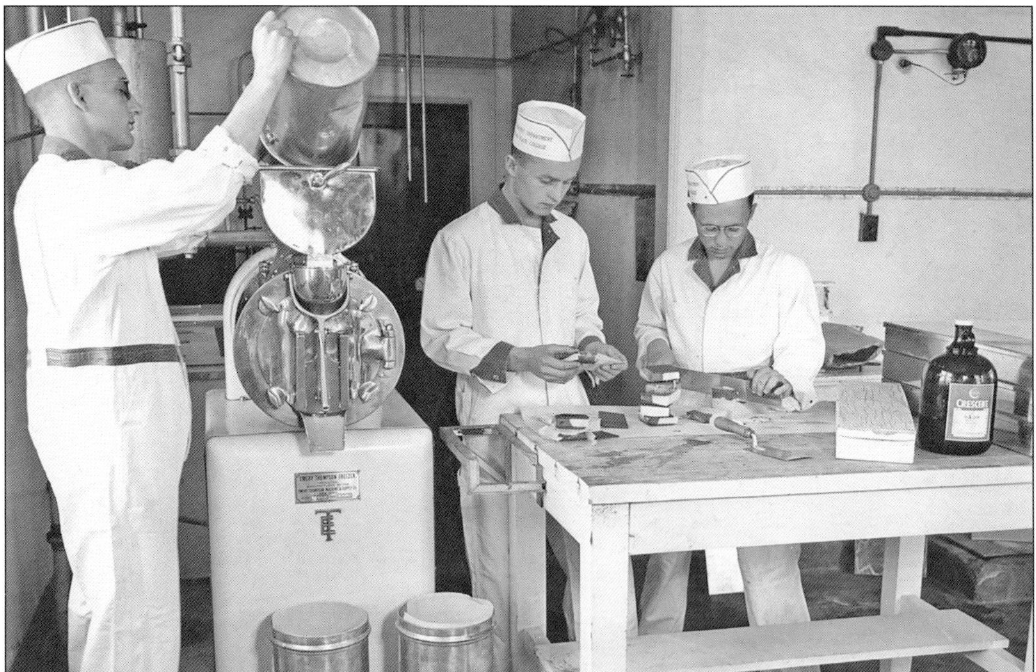

Dairy industry courses deal with the study of dairy cattle breeds; selection, breeding, and feeding; and factors pertaining to the economical and sanitary production of milk. Among the dairy manufacturing courses offered was one that provided knowledge of practical composition and quality tests for ice cream. Here, three men make ice cream sandwiches for a dairy industry ice cream course in 1958.

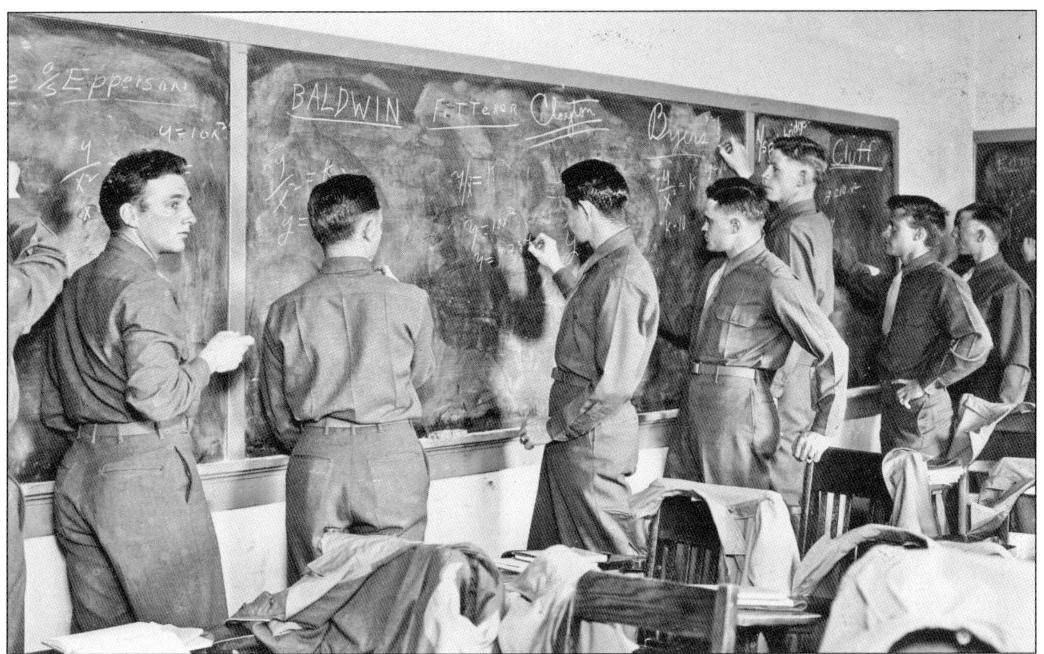

Solving mathematical equations is much more than the abstract science of numbers, quantity, and space, just as drills and the tactics of military science are not the sum of an ROTC cadet's college career. These ROTC cadets work to solve math equations as part of their regular curriculum in 1944.

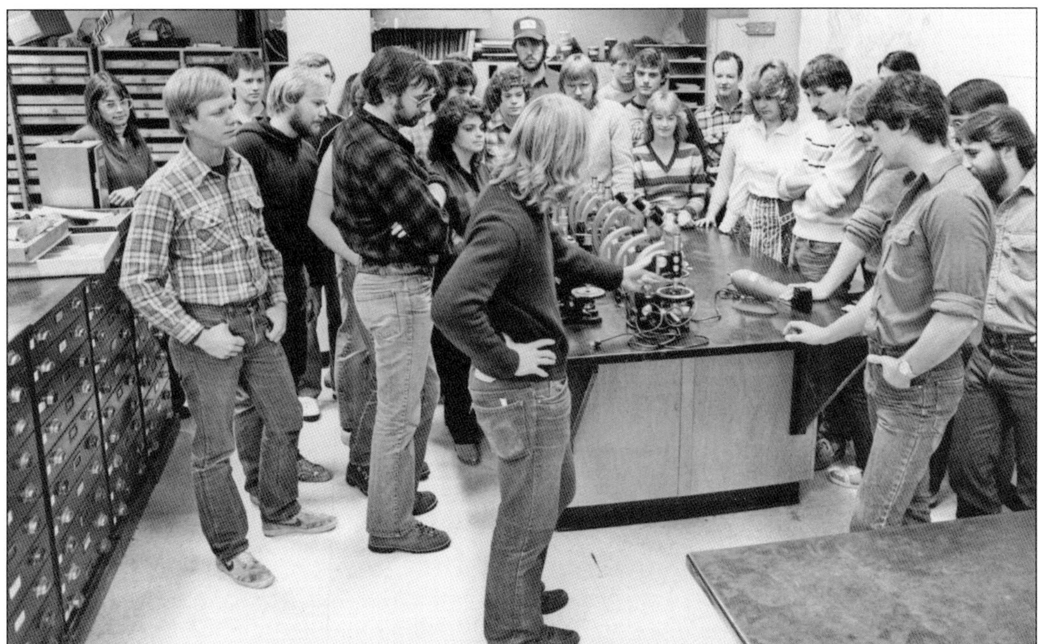

Microscopes enable students to view the features and physical structure of rocks and soil. Geology courses at Montana State University open doors to careers in mining, petroleum, avalanche study, hydrology, and geochemistry. In 1985, several students surround a table arrayed with microscopes in a geology laboratory.

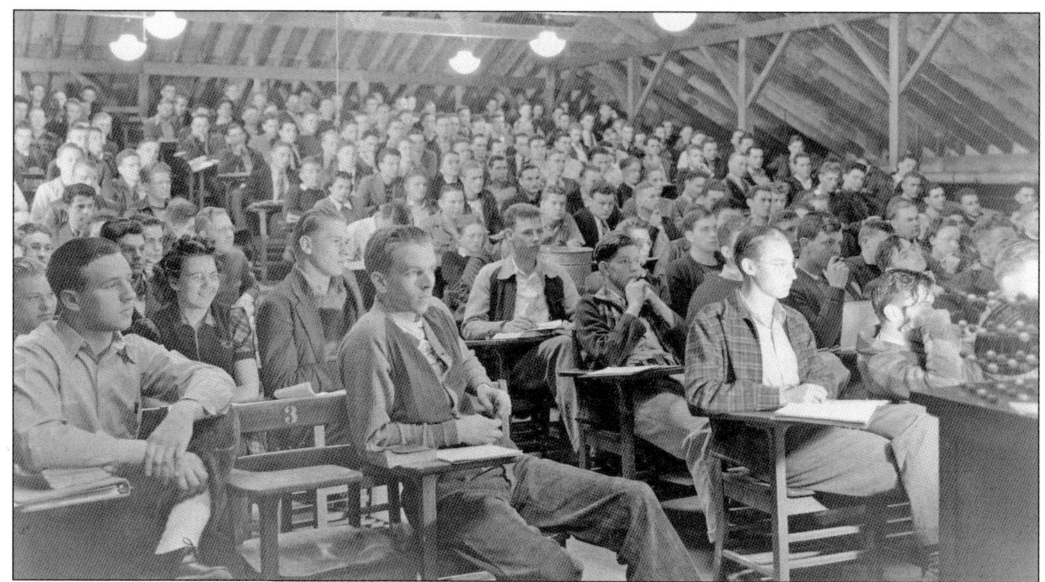

Montana State University's chemistry lecture halls provide students with the large space and tiered seating that focuses their attention and allows the professor to reach a larger audience. In 1949, several students listen to a professor provide instruction on topics that might include the application of organic chemistry, quantitative analysis, elementary glass blowing, or dairy chemistry.

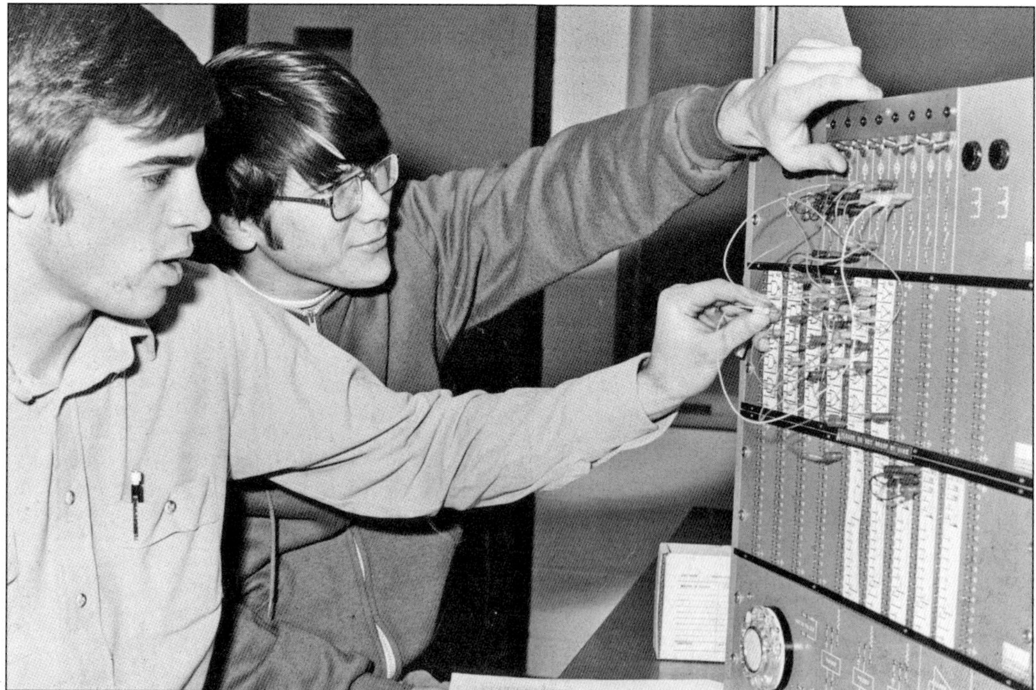

Two students study a circuit panel in 1980 as part of their laboratory practice for a degree in electrical and electronic engineering technology. Courses in electronics provided students with knowledge of an assortment of electrical apparatus that included biasing circuits, device models, signal amplifiers, power supplies, and analog and digital systems.

Three

SPORTS AT MONTANA STATE UNIVERSITY

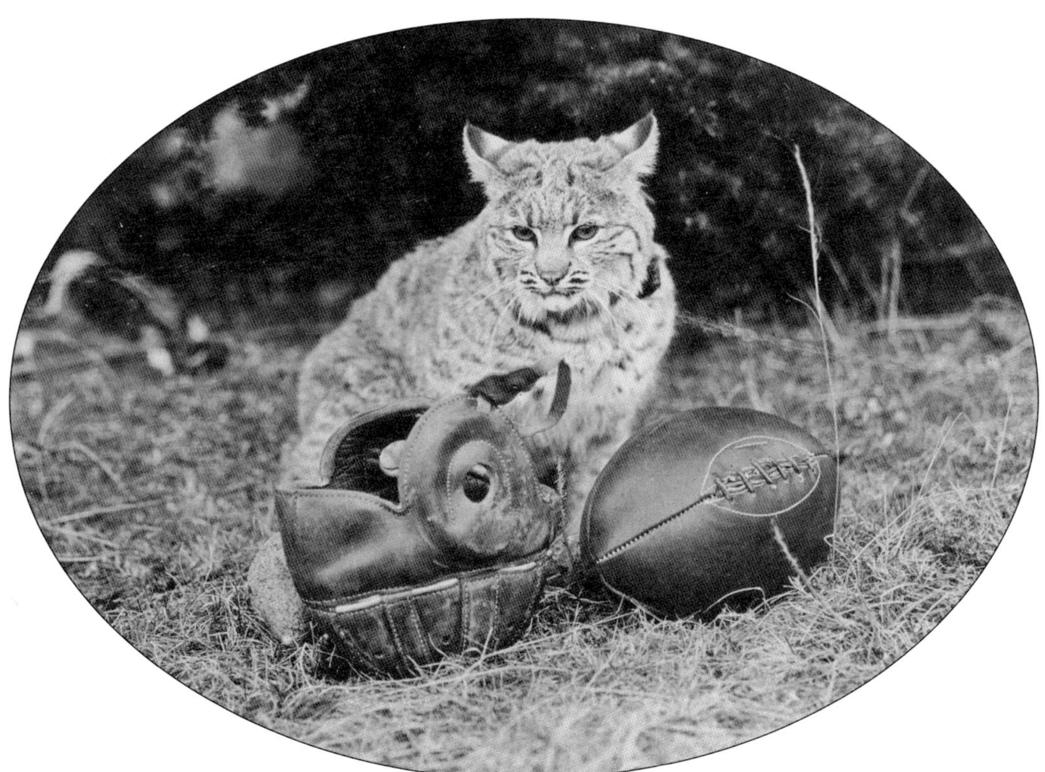

Montana State University needed a team name for its athletes that carried a trace of the mountains, and a mascot that reflected that name. In 1916, the school selected a crafty animal that lived in the mountains of the West to fill this role. The Bobcats named their mascot Spirit. The MSU bobcat urged his teams on with gleaming eyes and meaningful growls.

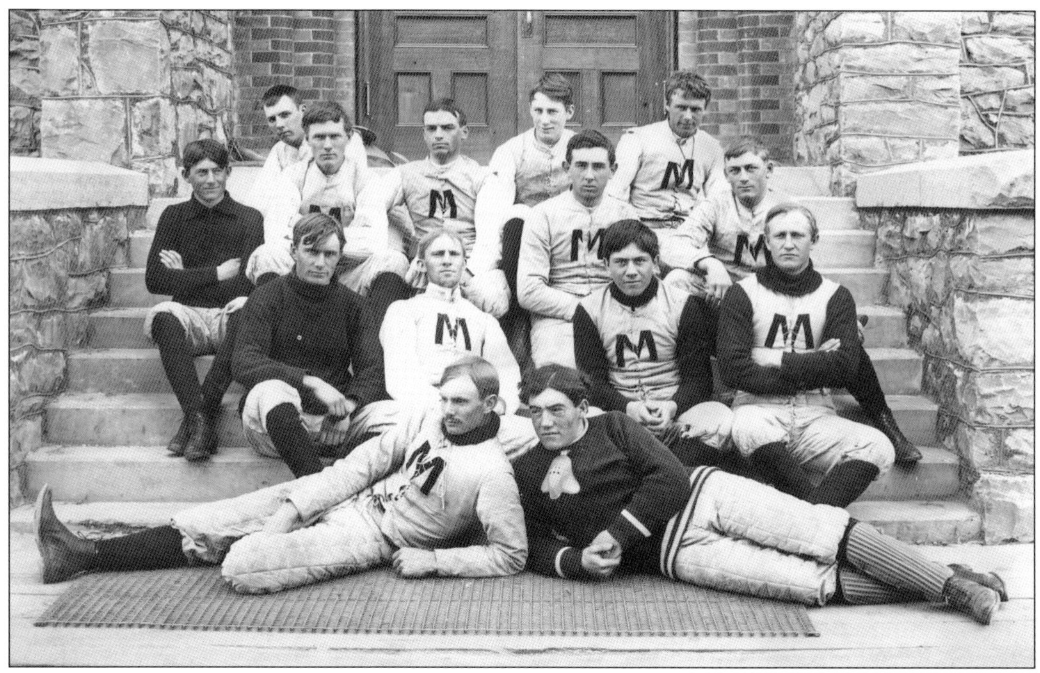

The first football team was formed in 1897. From left to right are (first row) quarterback C.D. Flaherty and right end John Peat; (second row) right halfback Harry Patterson, right end Will Flaherty, left guard John Seyler, and right tackle Tom O. Caldwell; (third row) left end Jim Arnold, left halfback Scott Mills, center Ralph Boyles, right tackle Reno H. Sales, fullback Herman Waters, right guard Ellie Moore, left guard Irvin Cockrill, and left halfback Will Brandenburg. Not pictured are center Sam H. Sharman and quarterback Clarence Jeffers.

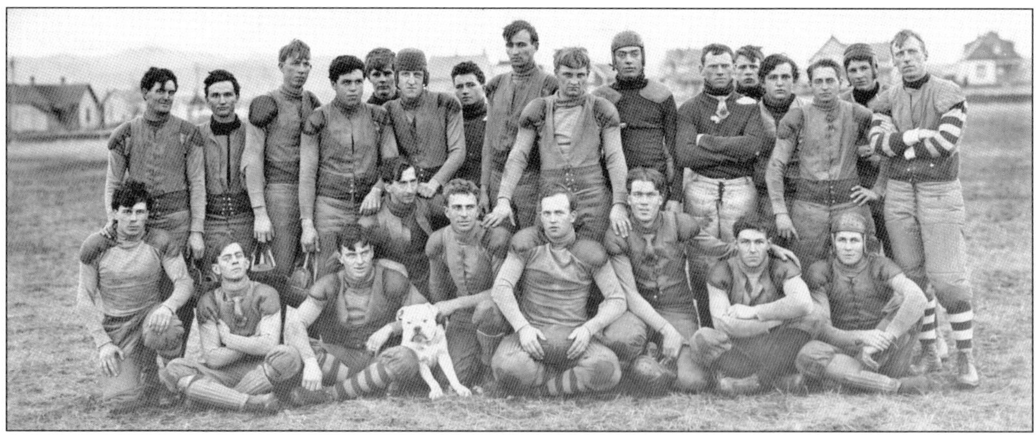

The 1908–1909 football team is, from left to right, (first row) Elmer Williams, Sam Pound, Court Sheriff, Fred Walchli, Walter Smith, Tom Norton, Gilbert Hansen, William G. Tremper, and Louis K. Pool; (second row) Bert Hind, Jim Drinville, J.C. Taylor, Ralph Cooley, John Edward Hodgskiss, Archie Brown, Cassius Kirk, J.S. James, Charles Framsham, W.A. Dutle, John McGraw, Archie Wade, Harold Wolpert, Lyle Henderson, Brooke Hartman, and coach John McIntosh. The dog's name is Tuck.

Richard Roman was a football player for the Montana State Bobcats from 1936 to 1937. Roman, who went by "Rick," had also been a member of the freshman football team, known as the "Bobkittens," in 1935. In addition, he played the role of Balthasar in the MSU production of *Romeo and Juliet* and was a member of Sigma Chi.

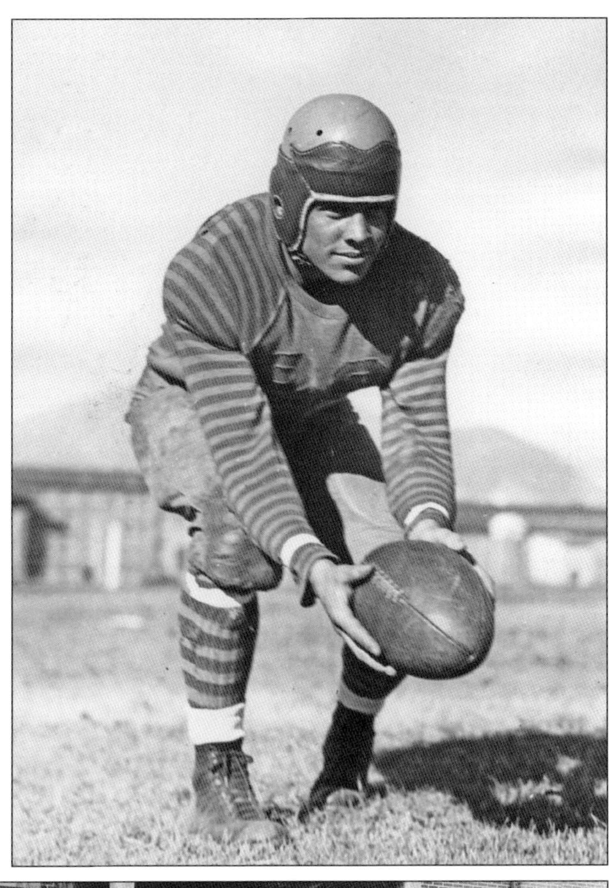

The 1938 Bobkittens team was used to develop and train new recruits for the varsity team. A majority of players went on to play for the Bobcats. In 1935, the Bobkittens and Bobcats met on the field, and while they held the varsity team to just 12 points in the first half, the Bobkittens eventually lost 45-6.

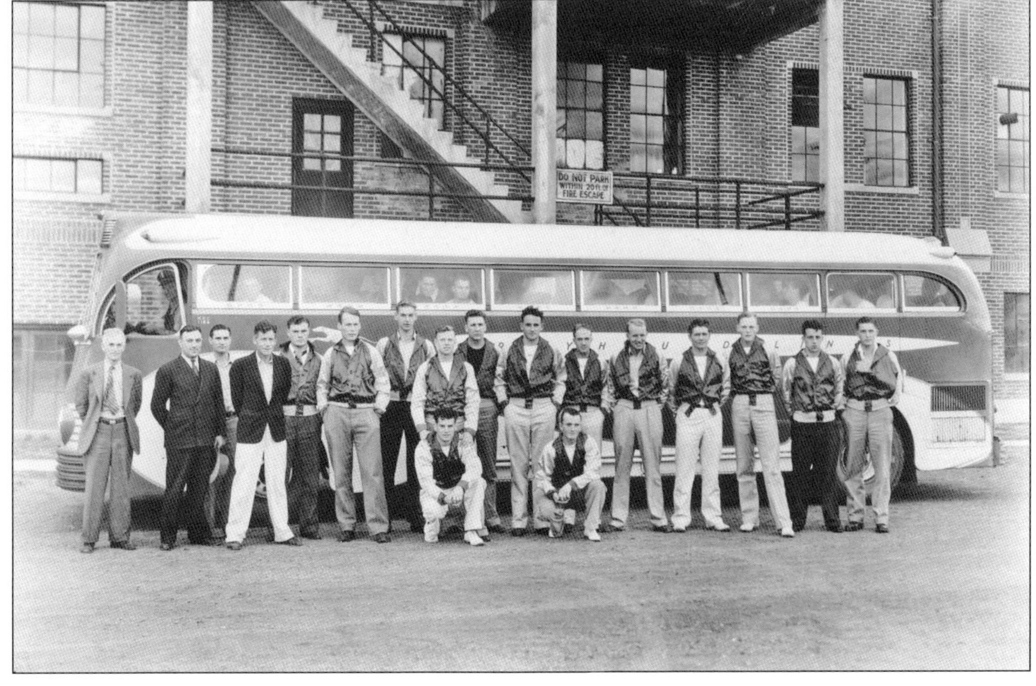

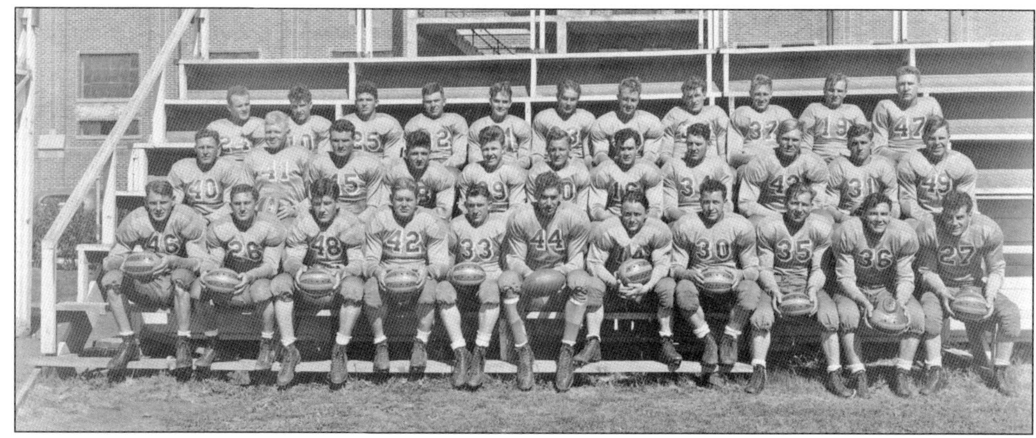

The 1940–1941 football team is pictured here. Many team members traded in their football uniforms for those of the military. Of the players who went off to fight in World War II, 11 of the full- or part-time starters on the MSU varsity team did not return.

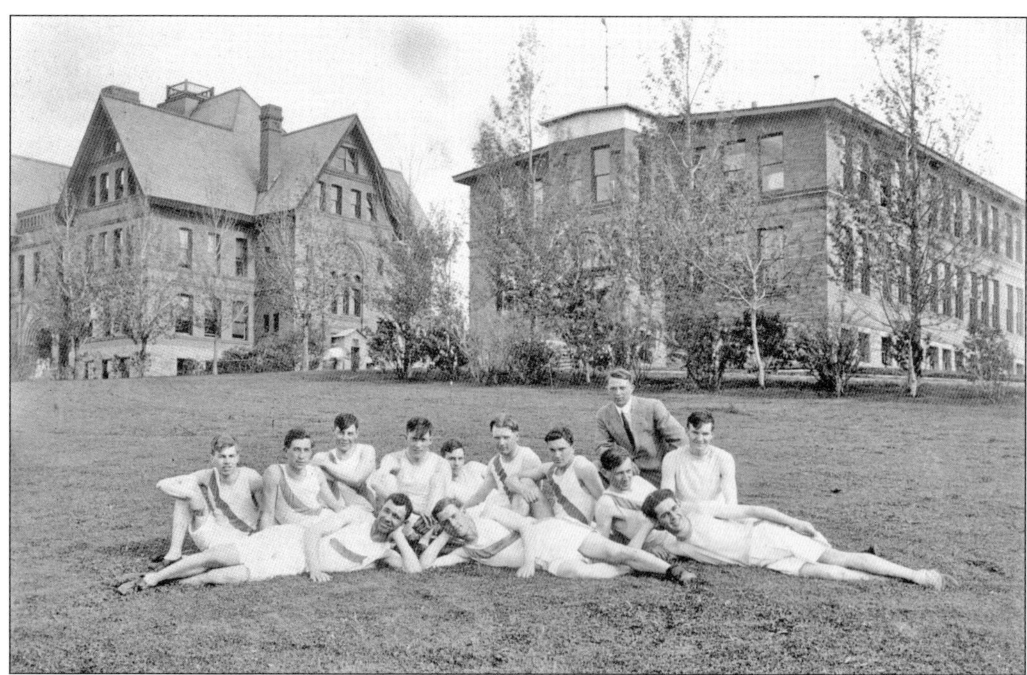

The men's track team is pictured with the chemistry building and Montana Hall in the background. The photograph was taken between 1900 and 1916, when the chemistry building pictured was destroyed in a fire. Track is one of the few sports with both men's and women's teams over a 100-year history at MSU.

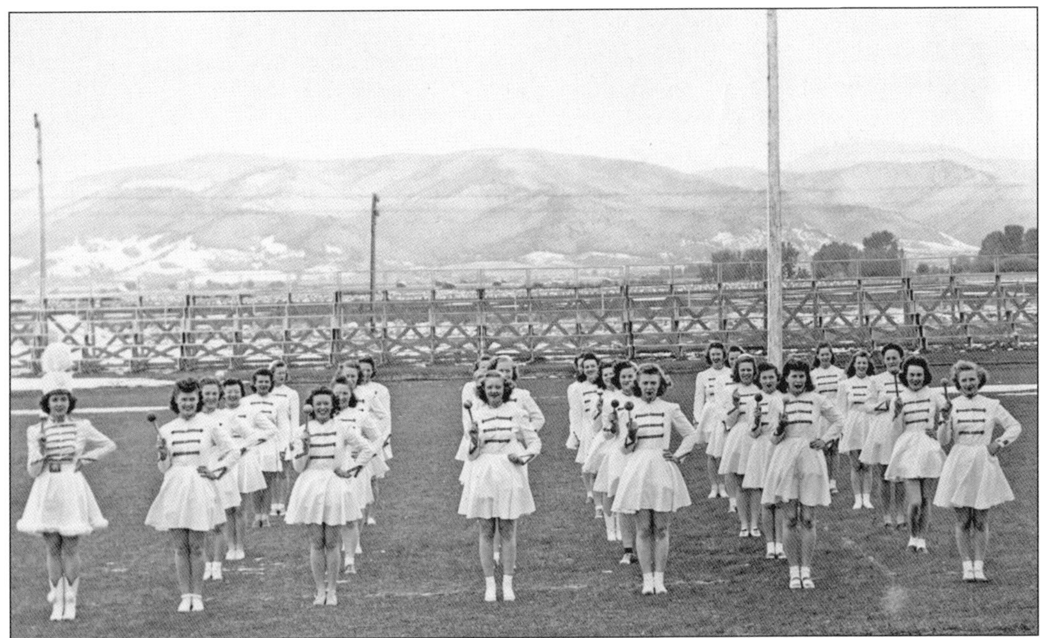

The majorettes practice on Gatton football field in 1941. The head majorette, Mildred "Mickey" McKinley, is pictured along with seniors Betty Batch, Margaret Cline, Betty Reed, and Margaret Smith. Three of the graduating women listed their majors as secretarial and the fourth as physical education. Currently, MSU does not offer degrees in secretarial studies.

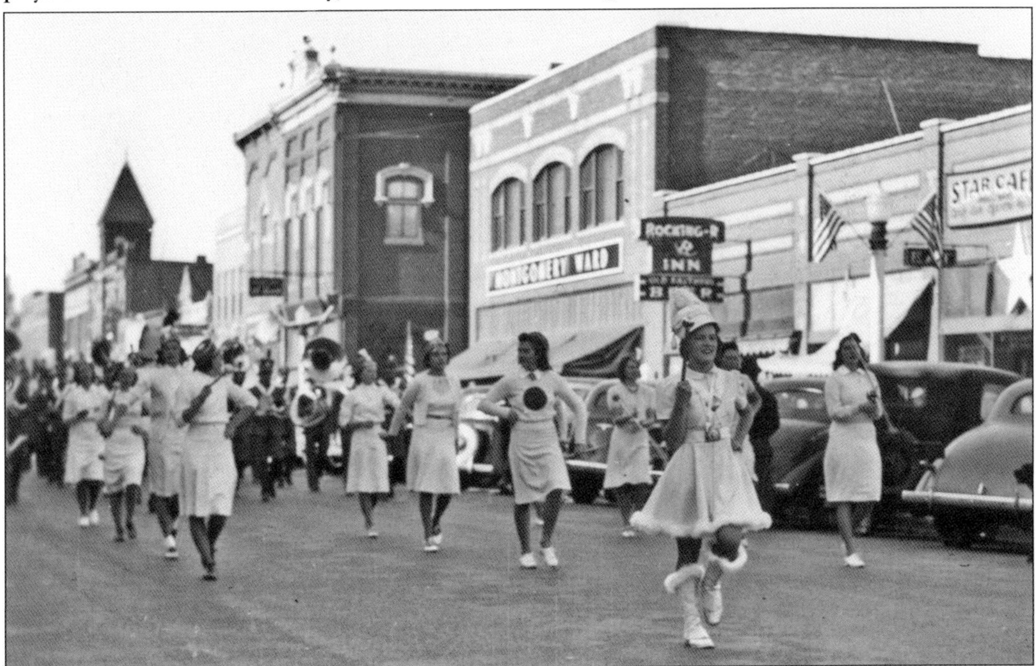

The 1939 drill team marches down Main Street in Bozeman. In the background are the Montgomery Ward building and the Rocking R Inn. The Montgomery Ward building was constructed in 1928, and while still standing, it holds new businesses. The Rocking R is still a place to grab a beer and burger in downtown Bozeman.

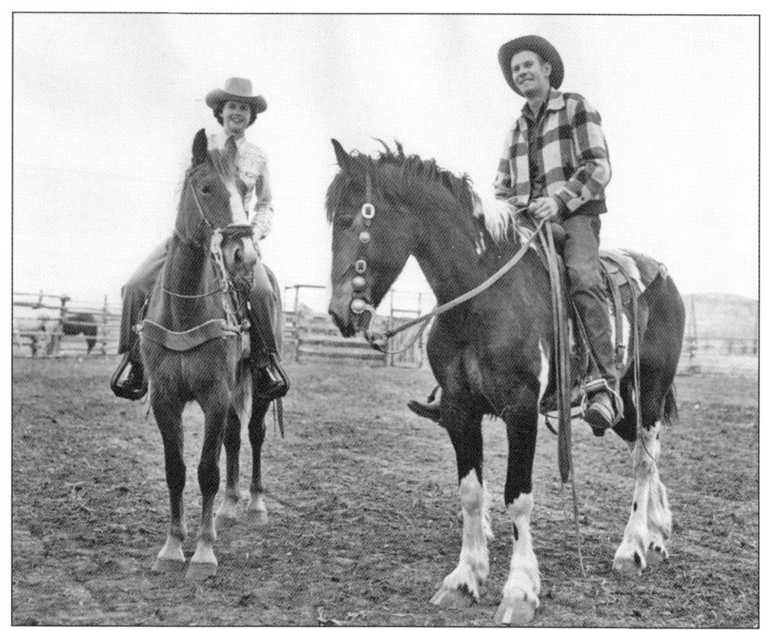

Outdoor activities come in many forms for faculty, staff, and students at Montana State University. In this photograph, taken between 1950 and 1962, Ed Atkins and Olleen Korell are riding horses. Atkins was a Montana Cooperative Extension Service agent for McCone County (1950–1952), Madison and Jefferson Counties (1952–1956), and Beaverhead County (1956–1962).

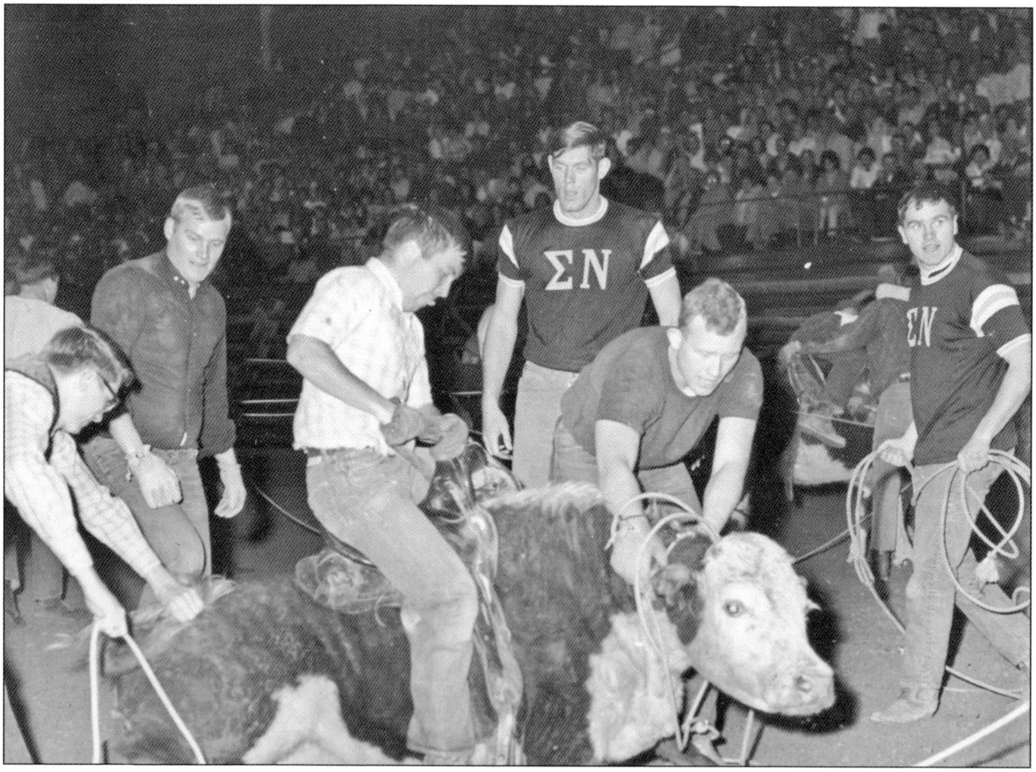

A group of Sigma Nu members attempt to ride a cow. The fraternity cow ride was a traditional feature of the annual intercollegiate rodeo. Bobcat rodeo is one of the great, storied programs in the history of the National Intercollegiate Rodeo Association. MSU rodeo teams have claimed eight national team titles, 32 individual national championships, and a multitude of Big Sky Region crowns.

Montana State University rodeo gained its spurs in 1947, when then–Montana State College students held an all-school event at the Bozeman fairgrounds. Construction of the fieldhouse in 1957 provided a venue for the rodeo in which student J.B. Anderson is pictured in 1969 while bull riding. Later, the fieldhouse served as the annual site for the College National Finals Rodeo from 1970 to 1996. (Photograph by Denny Rathbun.)

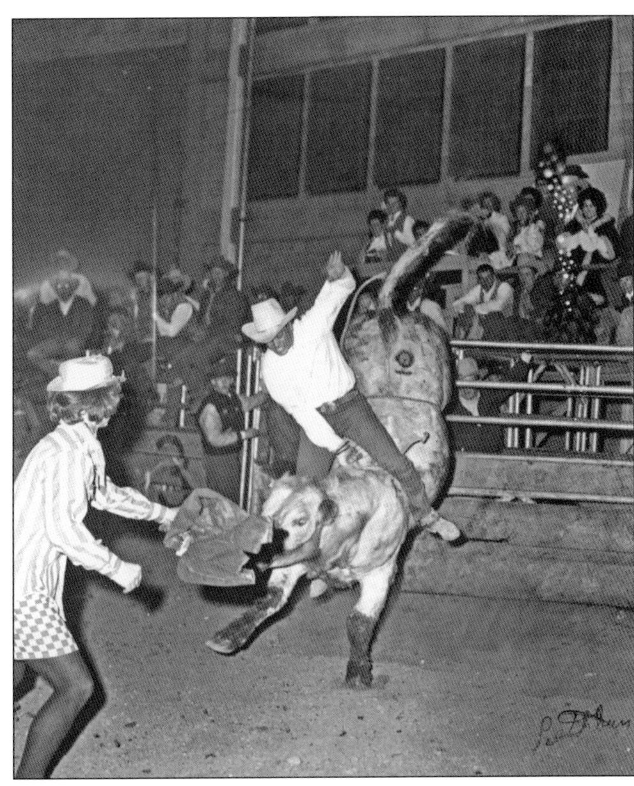

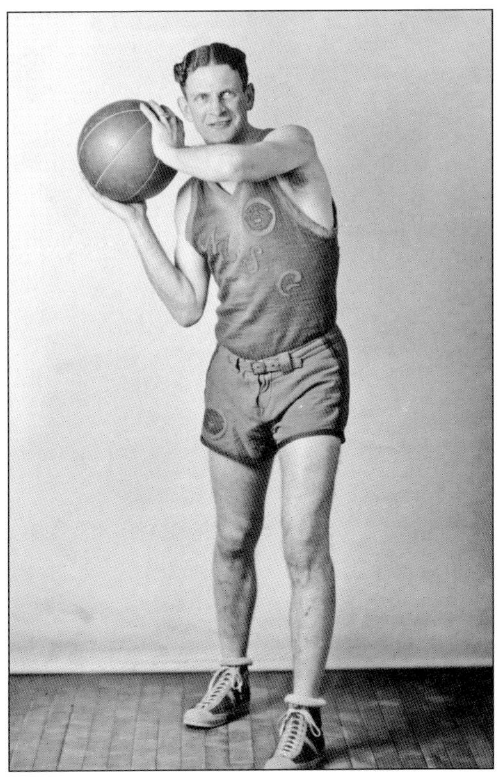

Herbert "Herb" Winner was an all-around athlete. Pictured in his basketball uniform, he also played football and was the commissioner of athletics for the student council. In the 1926–1927 season, he led the Bobcats to a 10-0 victory against the rival Wyoming Cowboys through his "brilliant and outstanding" performance on defense, according to the 1927 *Montanan* yearbook.

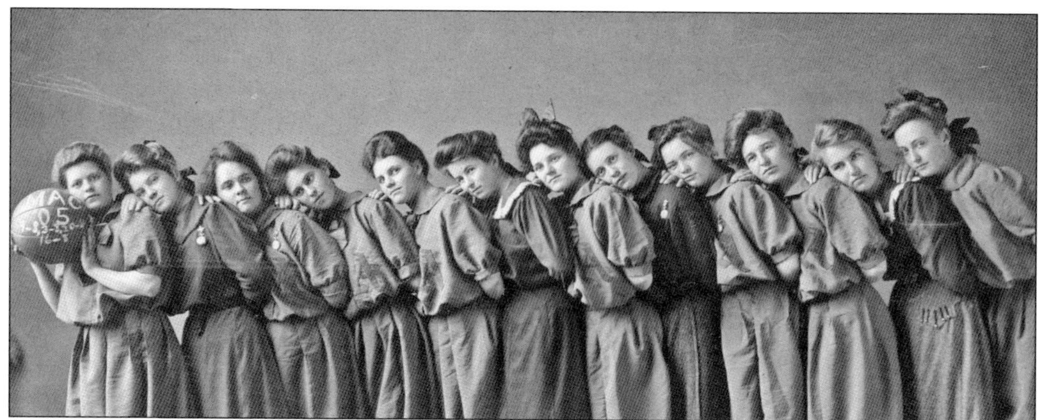

The women's basketball team is pictured in the winter of 1904–1905. From left to right are Annie Brenneman, Ethel Hutton, Agnes Mountjoy, Anna Krueger, Belle Osborn, Mamie Alward, Flora Carmichael, Phoebe Morgan, Lucile Mountjoy, Anna Elgin, Eva Bower, and Edna Tracy. Women's basketball has a long history at MSU. The coach as of 2018, Tricia Binford, is a former WNBA player whose tenure since 2005 has been the team's winningest period.

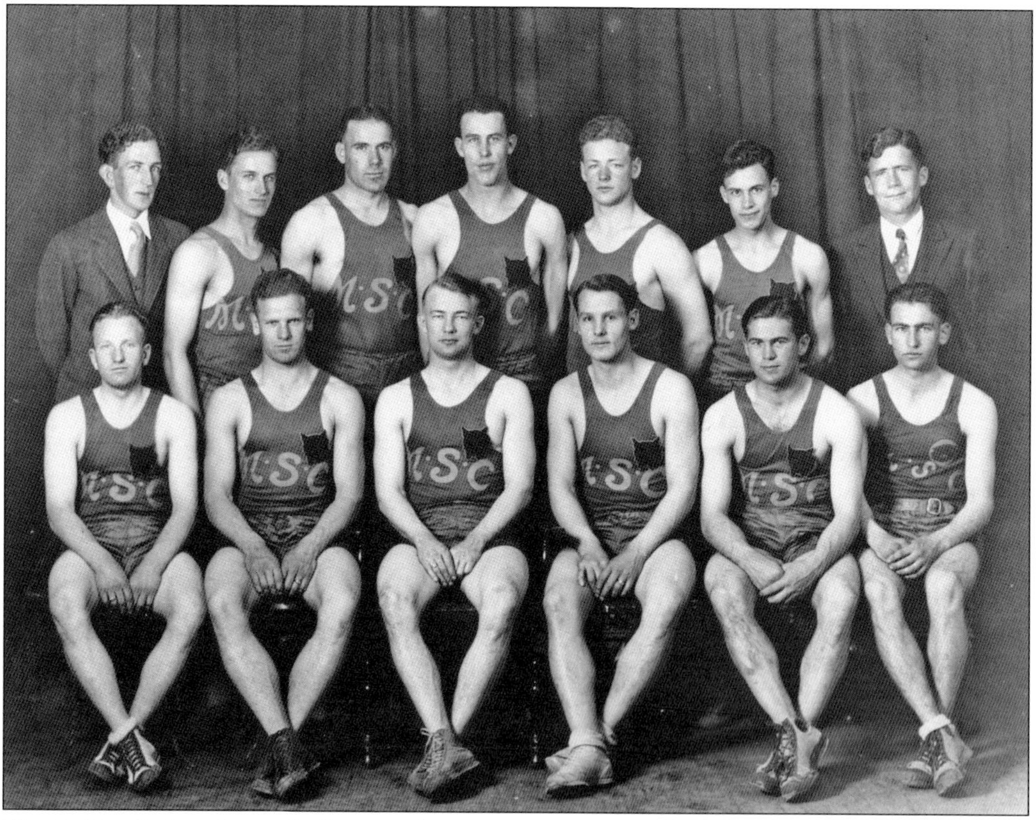

The Golden Bobcat basketball team of 1928–1929 is pictured here. From left to right are (first row) guard Fred "Red" Browning, Ott Gardner, forward "Tommy Cat" Thompson, forward Orland Ward, "Peck" McFarland, and Roy Homme; (second row) manager Clifford Swanson, Ed Buzzetti, guard John "Brick" Breeden, center and team captain Frank Ward, guard "Max" Worthington, Harold Sadler, and coach Schubert Dyche.

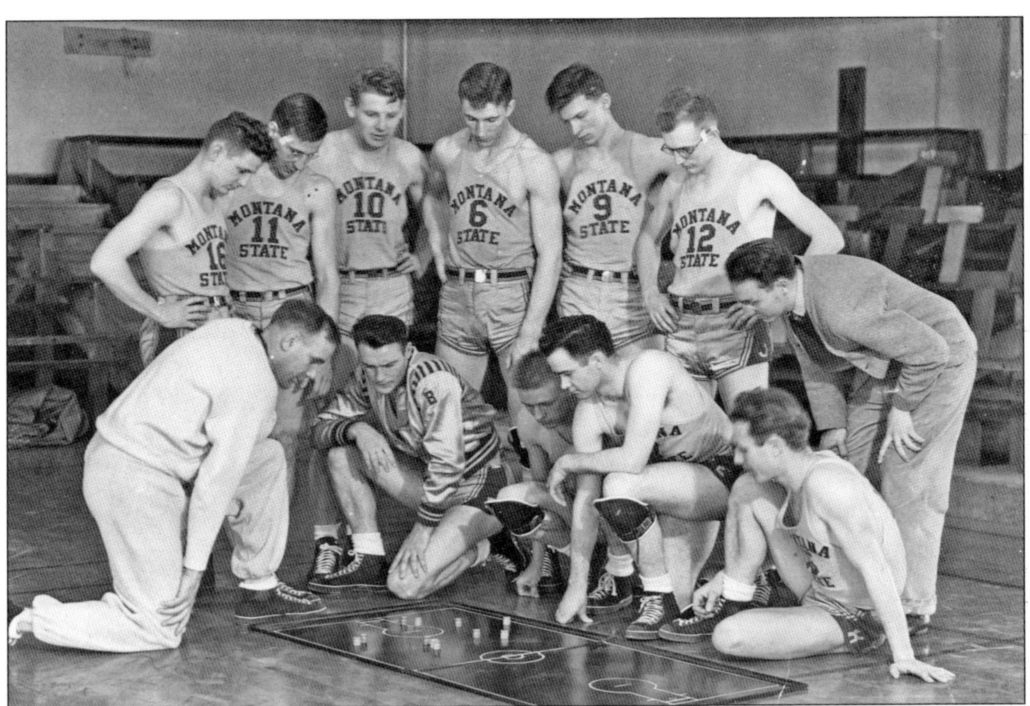

Coach John "Brick" Breeden of the 1939 men's basketball team demonstrates plays using a model of the court. Brick, who also played for the team in the 1920s, led the team to 283 wins as coach between 1935 and 1954. The fieldhouse was later named in his honor.

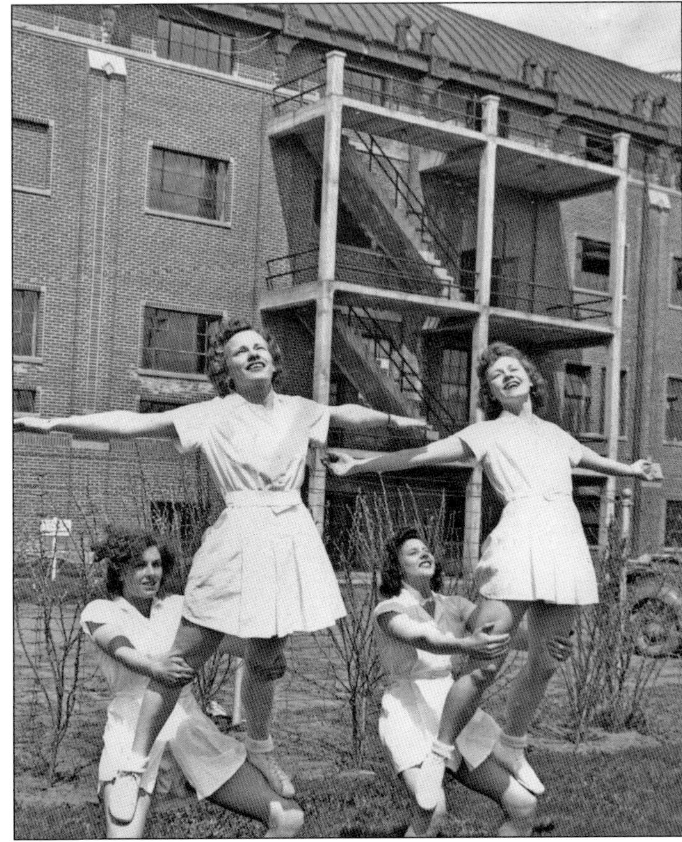

Built in 1922, Romney Gymnasium at Montana State University included facilities for handball, basketball, swimming, dancing, and more, but exercise was not always limited to inside the gymnasium. In this photograph, a group of four women practice their tumbling between 1940 and 1960 behind Romney Gymnasium.

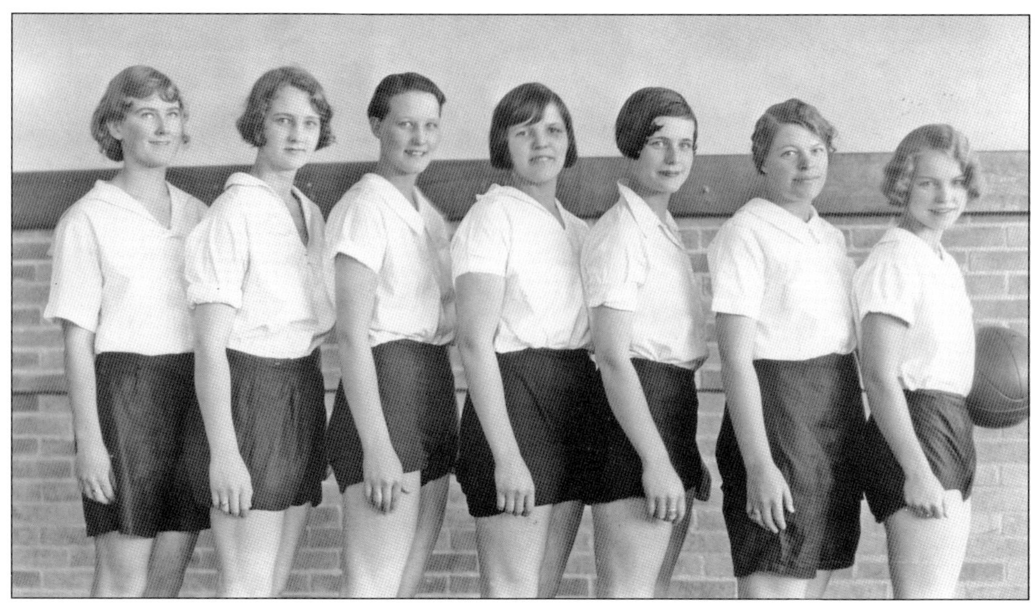

The 1931 intramural volleyball team is, from left to right, Jane Murdock, Ruth Nelson, Ortell Ward, Helen Albrecht, Anne Harrington, Mary Weider, and Pauline Wirak. The caption for this photograph in the 1931 *Montanan* reads, "The intramural system has created a greater interest in volleyball among co-eds in general." The winning team for the year was that of Alpha Omicron Pi.

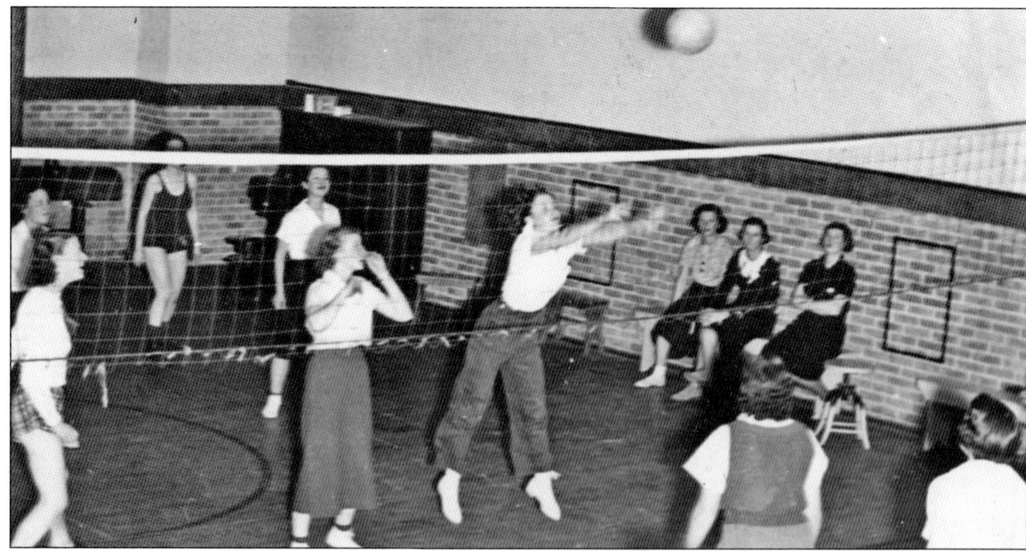

Young women play a game of volleyball in 1938. While not an official sport, volleyball was part of women's athletics, led by Katherine Crissman and the Women's Athletic Council. Other sports women could participate in included badminton, gymnastics, basketball, hiking, and archery. The 1938 yearbook states "It may be possible that in future years a degree in Physical Education will be offered for women students."

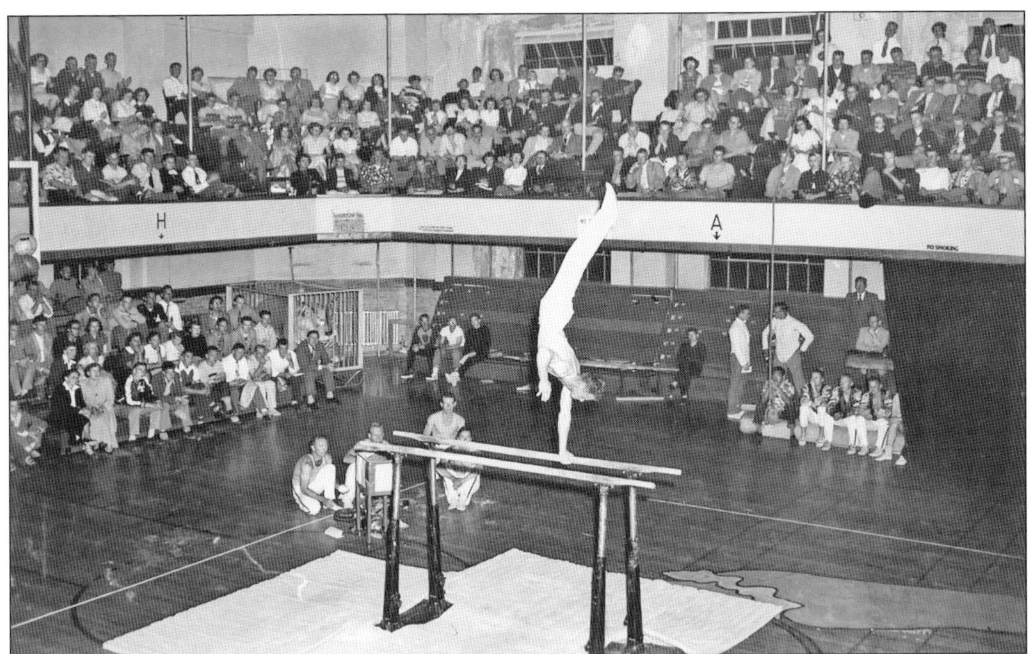

Men's and women's gymnastics have been both club and officially sanctioned sports in the past. While funding for women's sports was cut after World War I, it was finally reinstated in the 1960s, and a new women's team was created. All gymnastics teams were dropped in the late 1980s due to funding limitations.

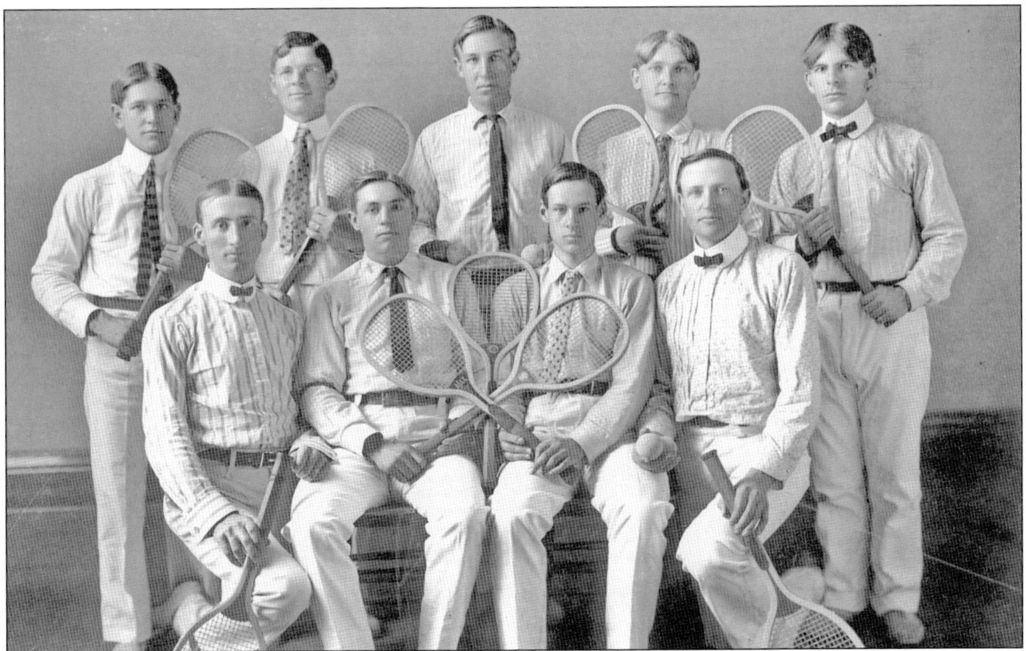

The 1905 tennis squad poses with their rackets. From left to right are (seated) Stanley Yergey, Clyde C. Penwell, Howard Flager, and Warren Griffith; (standing) Carl Widener, Will Hartman, Clinton Wylie, Clyde W. Penwell, and Tom Quaw. Tennis is still played by men's and women's teams at MSU.

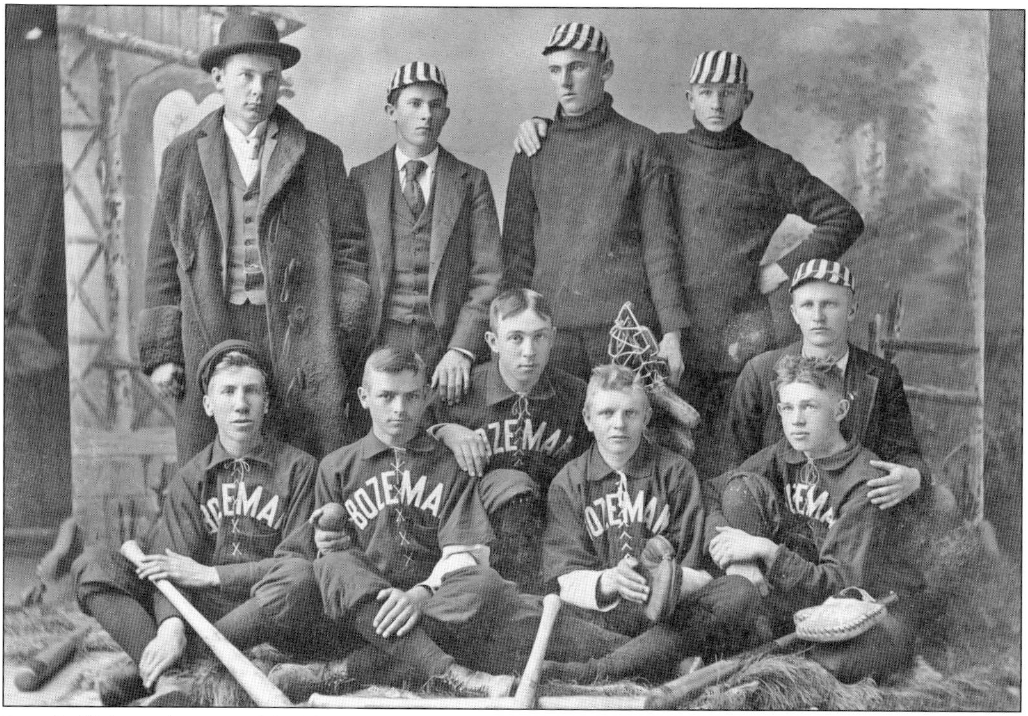

Baseball, bicycling, and field-day sports were important in the early history of the university. The 1896 baseball team, pictured here, proved to be a strong squad. From left to right are (first row) Charles "Gus" Lundwall, Reno H. Sales, Russ Hodges, and Fred F. Willson; (second row) Nathan J. Sperling and Tom Caldwell; (third row) Tom McKee, Allen Cameron, Louis Krueger, and ? Dodgeworth. (Photograph by R. Dawes.)

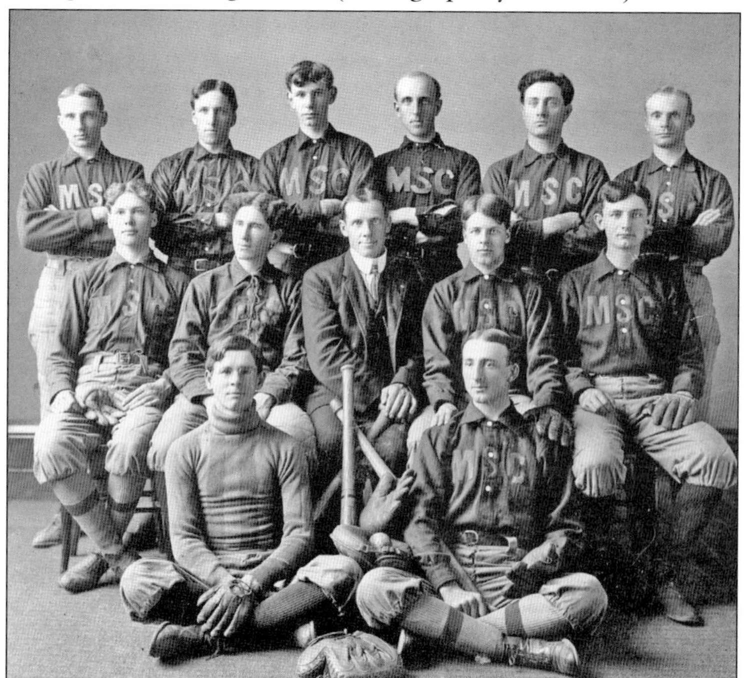

The 1903–1904 baseball team poses for a formal studio portrait surrounding their coach. From left to right are (first row) Will Hartman and Stanley Yergey; (second row) Jerome Locke, unidentified, William McKee, O.P. Chisholm Jr., and Nert A. Hapner; (third row) James Flaherty, two unidentified, Arthur M. Stevenson, Fred Ervin, and Charles D. Flaherty. While no longer an official sport, the tradition is kept alive through the baseball club.

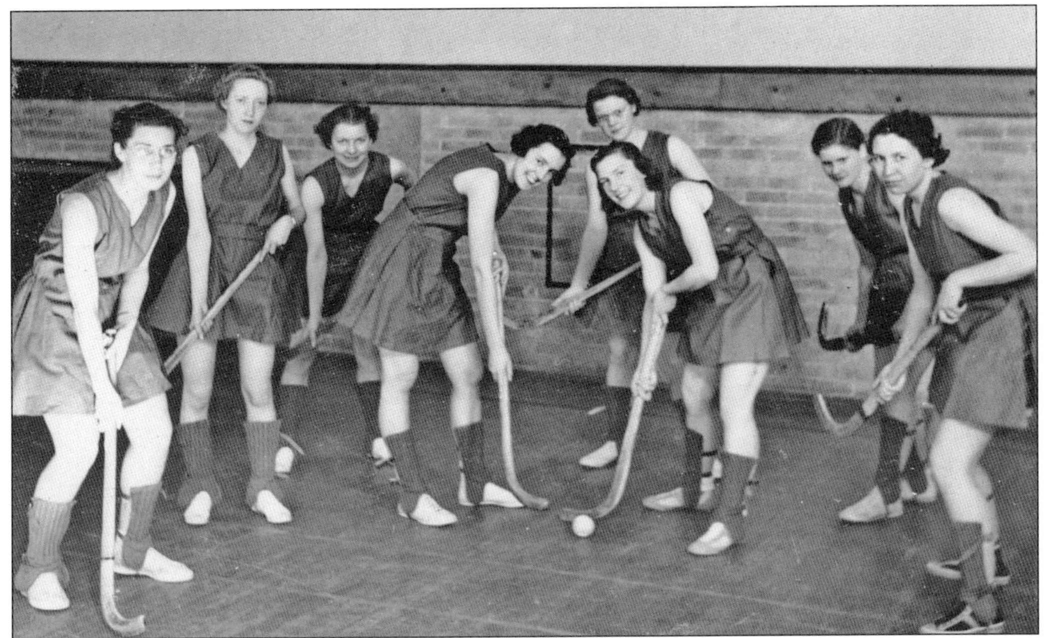

The women's hockey team is pictured in 1936–1937. The team was part of an honorary athletic fraternity for junior and senior women. The 1937 yearbook describes it as an organization where "no men are allowed" and "coeds forget their inhibitions." Members included Ruth Krumholz, Margo Seamans, Florence Jane Buchner, Marjorie Petrie, and Marie Simkins.

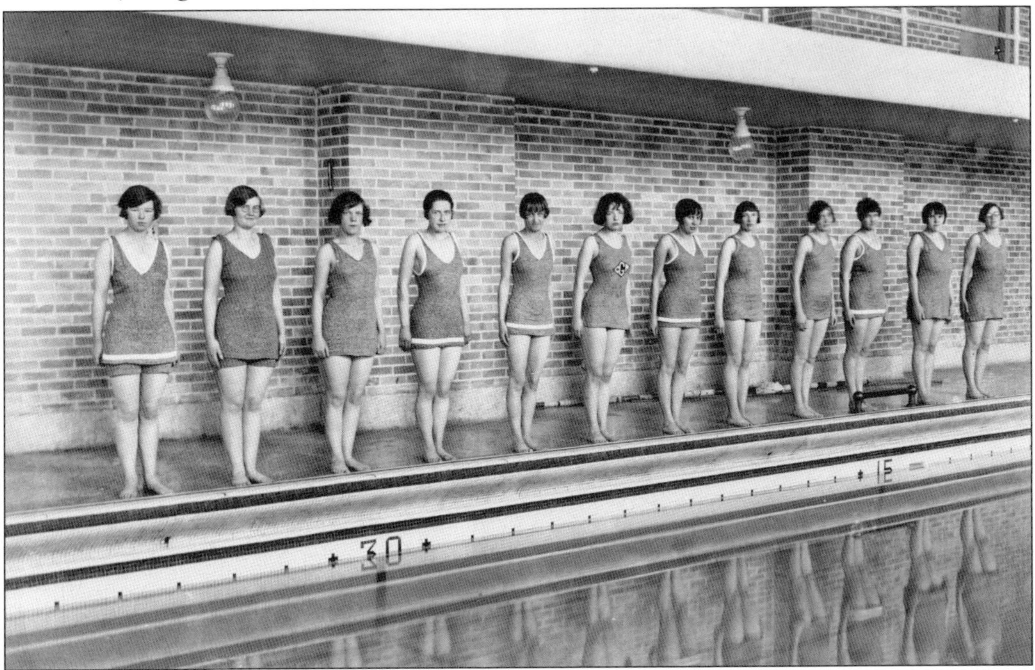

Women stand next to a swimming pool in Romney Hall. While not an official sport at MSU, swimming has been part of the physical education curriculum, student clubs, and recreation since the first pool was built on campus. The current pool is located in the Marga Hosaeus Fitness Center, just across the street from Romney Hall.

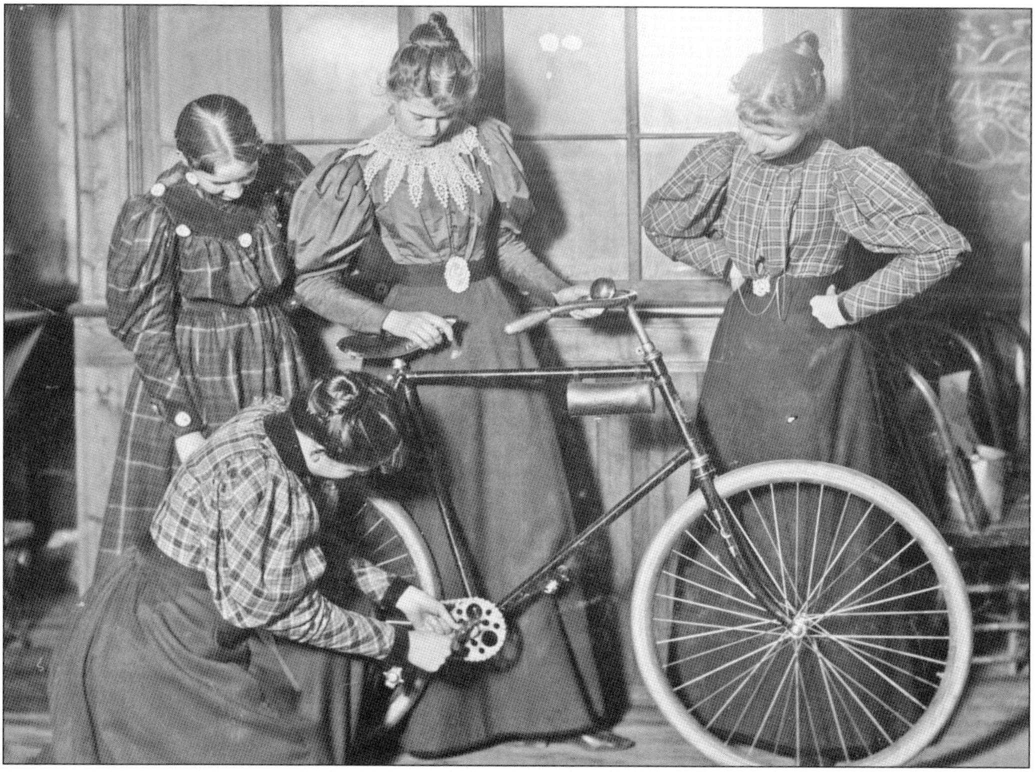

A young woman works on a bicycle while three others watch. Biking has a long history as a club sport and form of recreation as MSU. The current club sponsors races and represents the university at intercollegiate events.

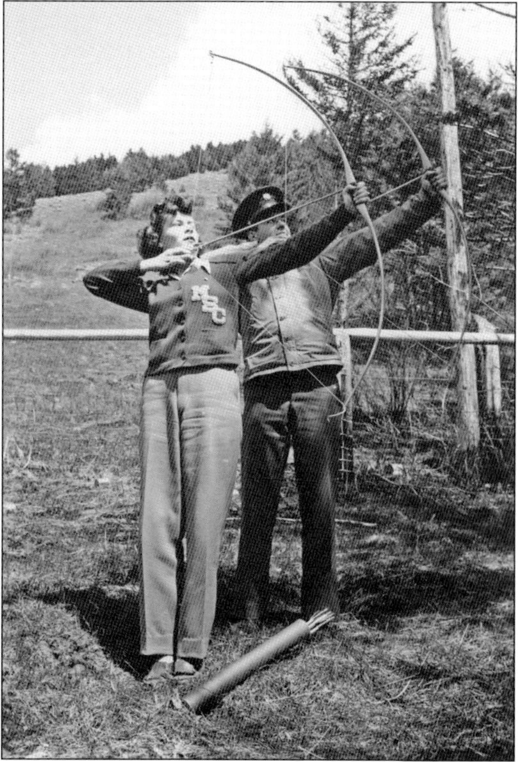

Two students practice archery with wooden bows. MSU students have practiced and taught archery through 4-H events on campus and as members of the MSU archery club. This photograph dates from the 1940s and shows a woman wearing a Montana State College sweater and a man in a military uniform.

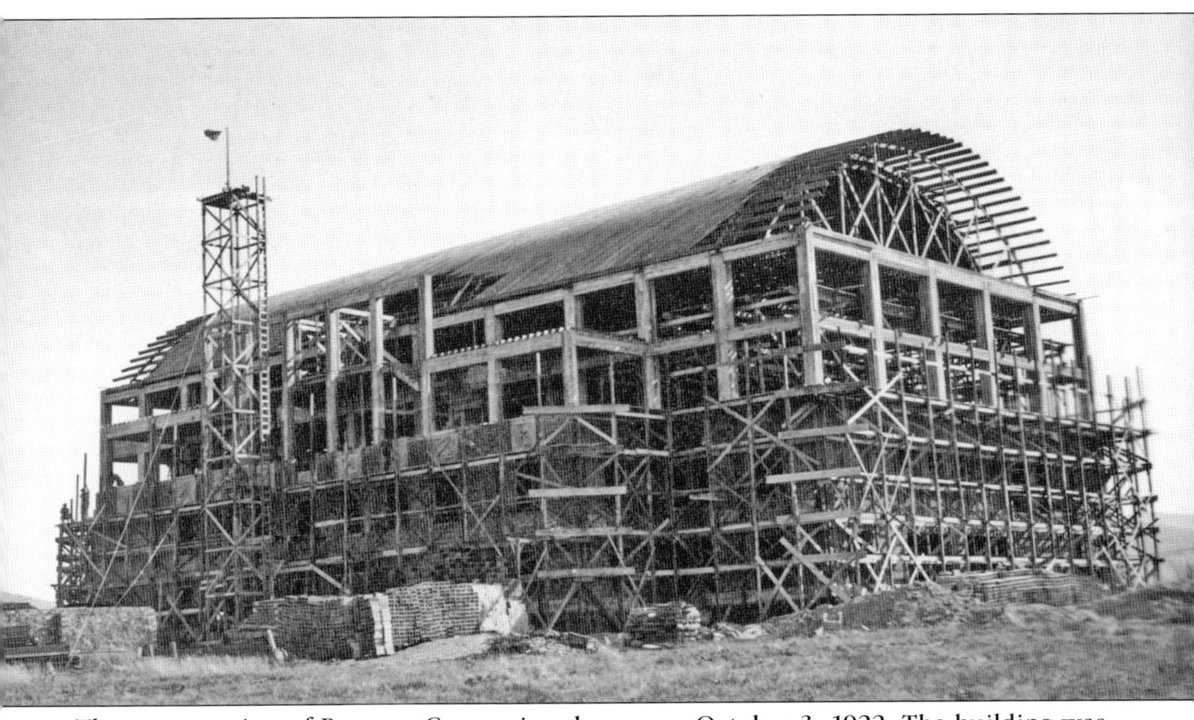

The construction of Romney Gymnasium began on October 3, 1922. The building was completed in 1926 and included handball courts, a running track, a swimming pool, and a gymnasium that seated 3,000. The building allowed Montana State University to expand its physical education and sports programs and served as the center for athletics from 1922 to 1958. It was officially named for G. Ott Romney, former basketball coach and director of physical education, in 1973. Romney is currently home to the College of Education, Health, and Human Development's offices and labs. The building also sports classrooms used by university departments in the College of Education, Health, and Human Development and Gallatin College. Growth on campus and a need for building improvements have brought a desire to renovate Romney from a nonfunctional gym into a modern, vibrant space equipped with innovative learning technologies.

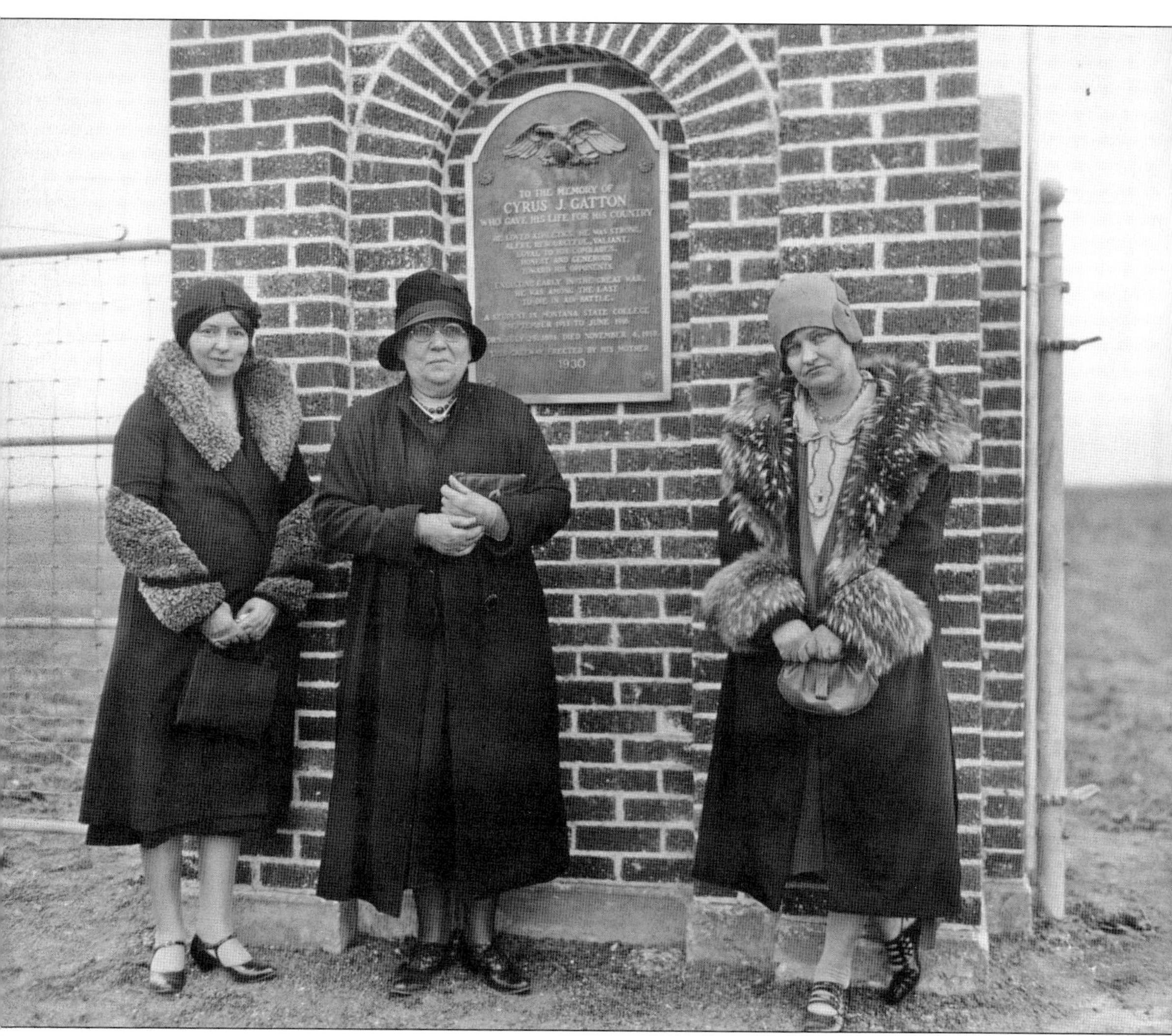

Gatton Field was named for Cyrus J. Gatton, who was a student from 1913 to 1916 at what was then Montana State College. Cyrus served as captain of the 1915 Bobcat football team. He enlisted and fought in World War I and was killed in 1918 in one of the last air battles of the war. From left to right are Laura Gatton (sister of Cyrus) and Marietta Gatton (mother), both of Seattle, and Mrs. C.A. Scheytl of Maudlow (sister). Gatton Field hosted many of the university's athletic events, including football and practice for MSU majorettes, and served as a gathering place for students and practice grounds for ROTC and the Bobcat marching band. Gatton Field no longer hosts athletic events; instead, the field has transitioned into a memorial to one of MSU's most memorable sports figures.

Four

Art at Montana State University

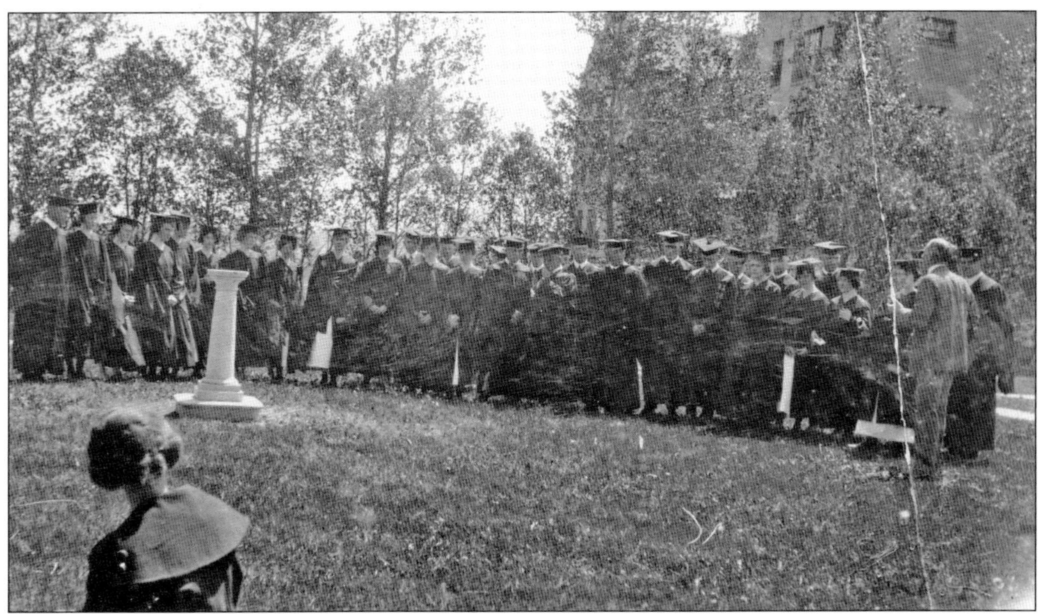

The class of 1920 presents a sundial at Montana State University. The sundial was located in a small courtyard known as the Iris Garden. While the original has been lost, it has been replaced with a modern sculpture, and the Iris Garden is still a place of beauty and solitude on campus.

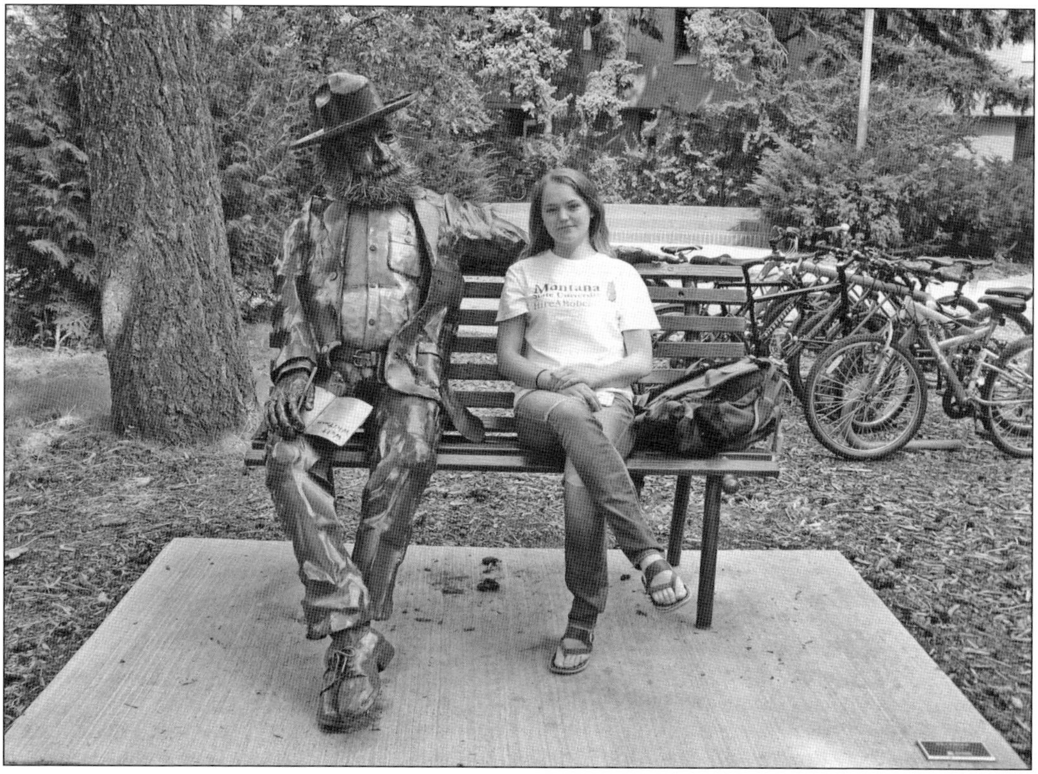

A young MSU student relaxes on the Walt Whitman bench, which sits in the Wilson courtyard and is a popular meeting place for students. Donated to the university by local artist Jim Dolan in 2009, it was placed in the courtyard partly because of the many humanities programs housed there and the connection to Whitman's works. (Courtesy of James J. Thull.)

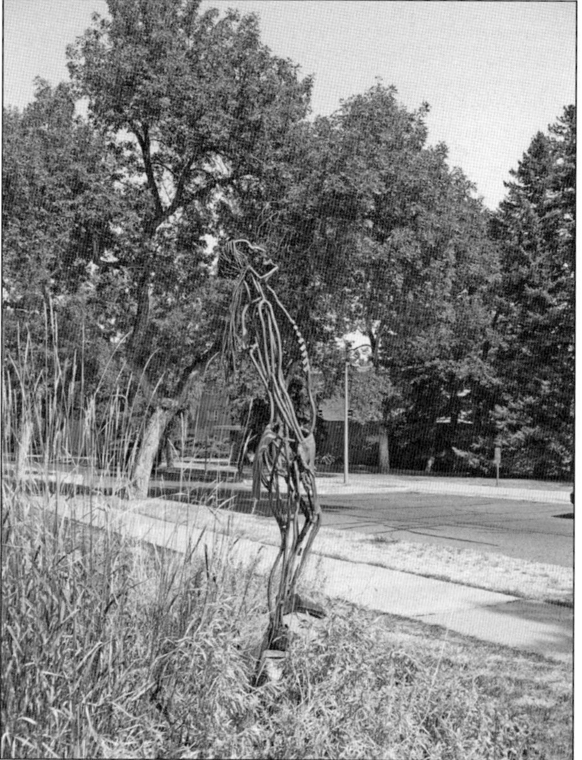

Black Elk was donated to the university by metal artist Jim Dolan in 2012. He faces east to greet the rising sun each day and resides just southeast of the Native American Studies Department. Black Elk was a holy man of the Lakota Sioux whose famous biography was published in 1932 by John Neihardt. (Courtesy of James J. Thull.)

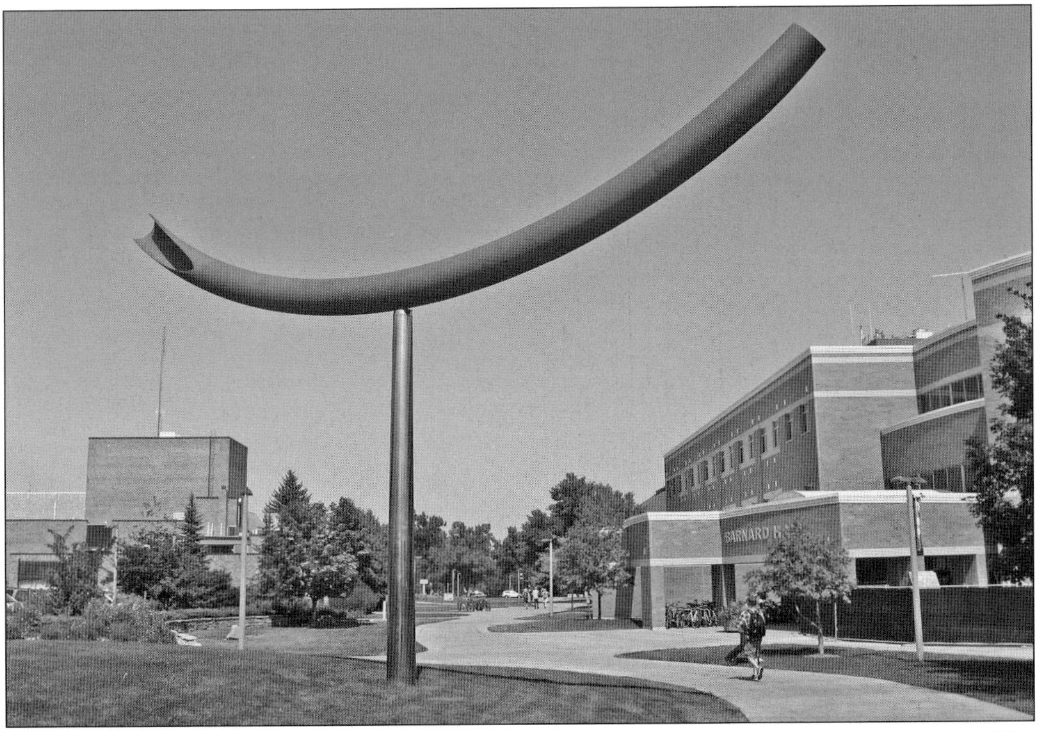

The Wind Arc has been a feature on campus since it was installed in 2002. It was created by artist and MSU alum Gary Bates under the Montana Arts Council Percent for Art Program. Commonly referred to as "the Noodle," it moves in the breeze and is meant to echo the curves of the mountains in the distance. (Courtesy of James J. Thull.)

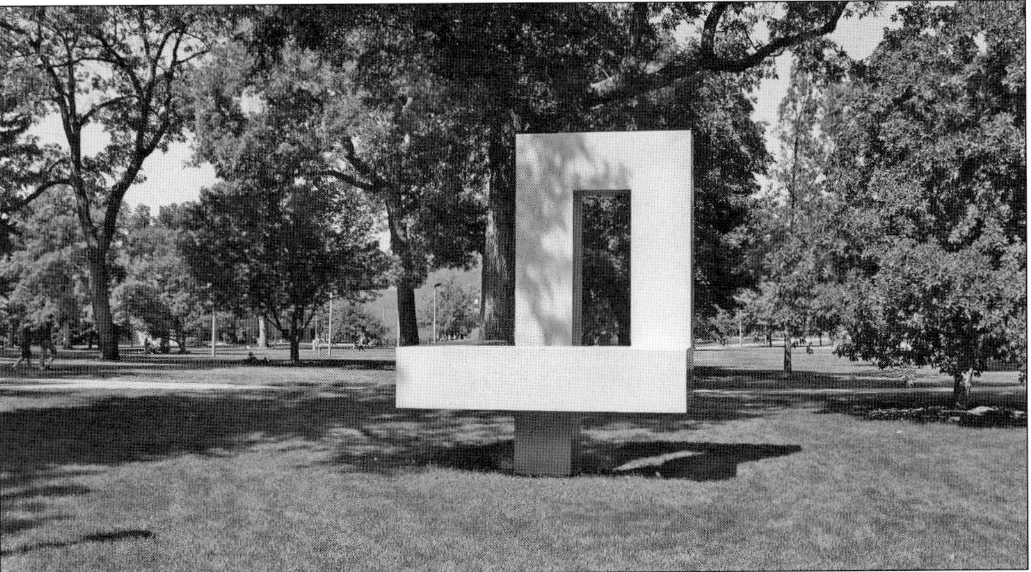

The Big Yellow Piece is located between Romney Hall and Renne Library. It was created by artist Gary Bates while he was a student. Bates won a student art competition and designed this piece for the space in which it would reside. Commonly called the "Four," students often relax near it, taking advantage of the shade it provides. (Courtesy of James J. Thull.)

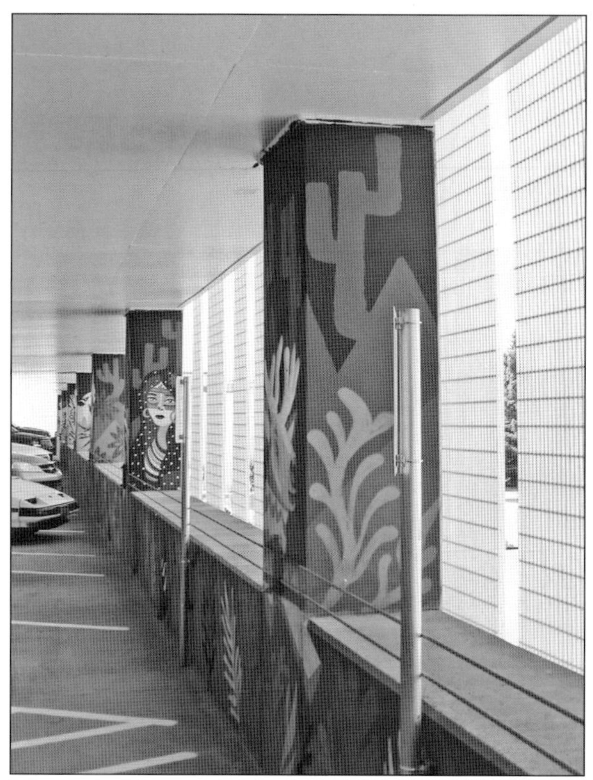

The interior of the parking garage recently built in conjunction with the new Norm Asbjornson Hall is filled with spray-painted art on the columns and short walls of all three floors. This work from the second floor was created by Columbian street artist Le Dania. She integrated local wildlife, MSU symbols, and Native American culture into her brightly colored murals, which she said are a visual representation of the Americas. (Courtesy of James J. Thull.)

A bobcat done in spray paint by Argentinian graffiti artist Marina Zumi can be found on the second floor of the parking garage. The South American graffiti muralist with an international following used more than 200 cans of spray paint to transform the first floor of the new Montana State University parking garage into a massive mural. (Courtesy of James J. Thull.)

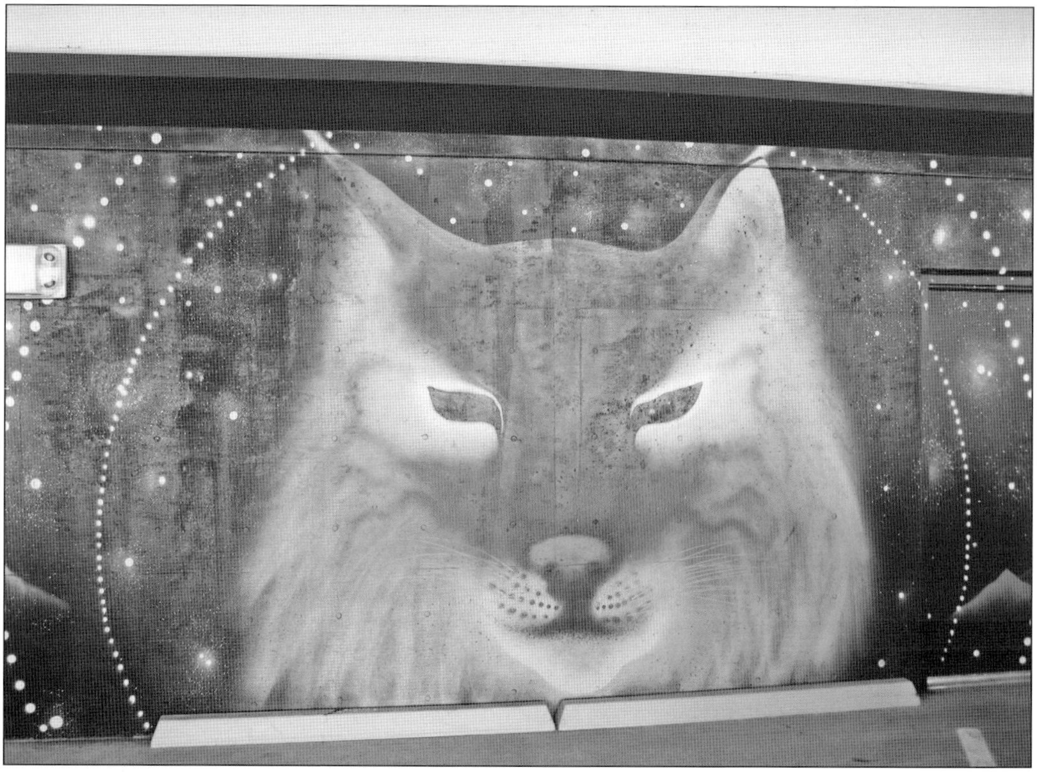

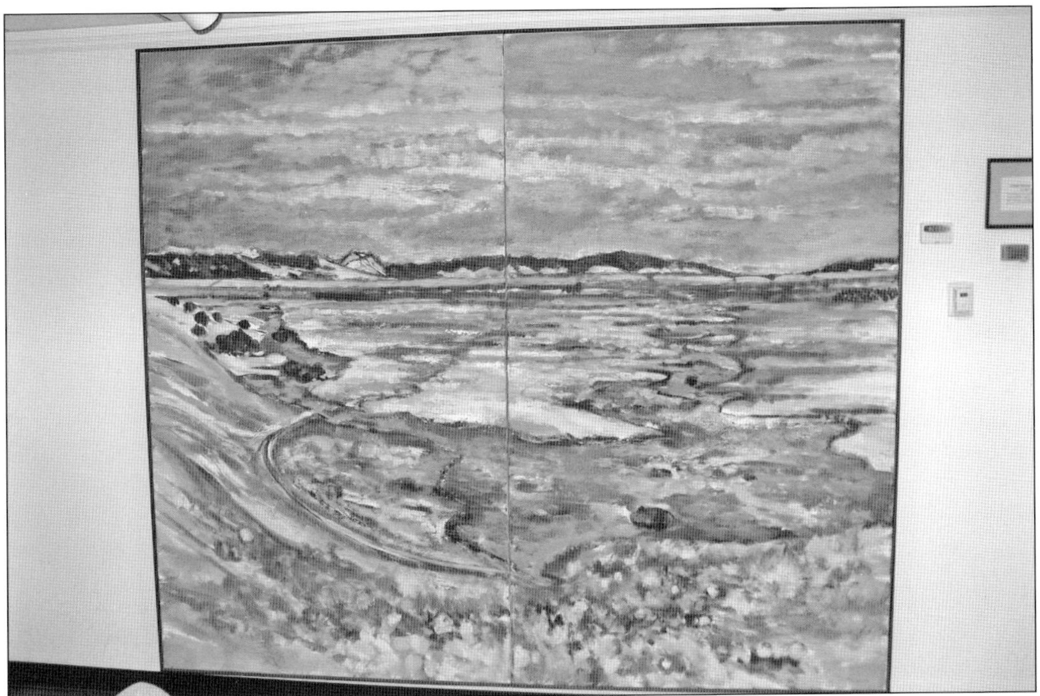

O'Dell Spring Creek, by Mari Lyons, is on permanent display in the MSU Special Collections Library and was donated by her loving husband, the writer-publisher Nick Lyons. The painting was done in 1995 and inspired by time spent near Ennis, Montana. The library also holds the archival papers of Nick and his publishing company. The subject matter relates directly to the library's world-class trout and salmonid collection. (Courtesy of James J. Thull.)

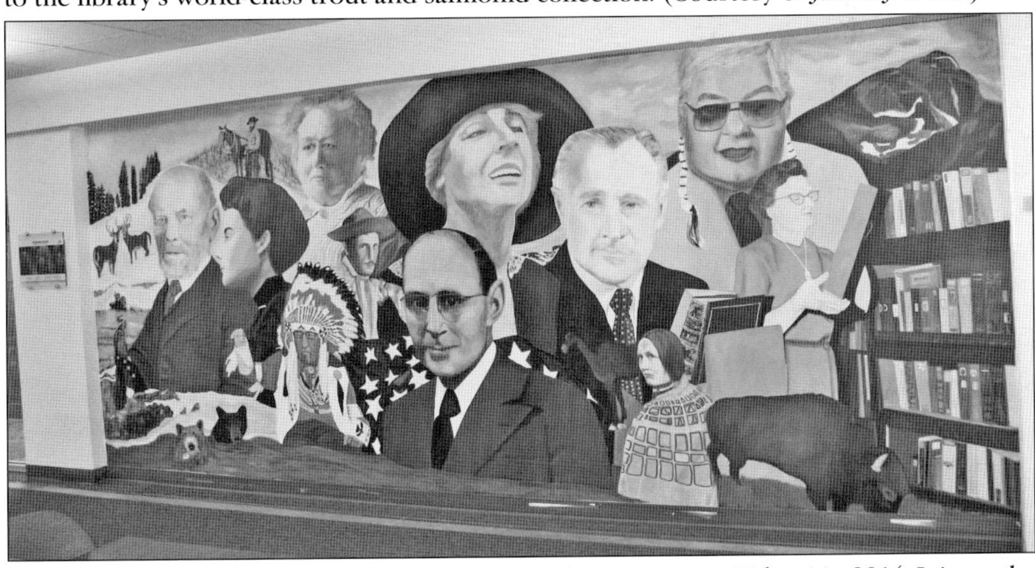

Uncommon Ground is a mural done by MSU student artist Lara Valenti in 2014. It is on the second floor of Renne Library and incorporates significant figures from Montana's history, including Barney Old Coyote, Minnie Ellen Paugh, Sacagawea, Peter Koch, and Merrill Burlingame. The work is dedicated to the memory of the artist's father, Giuseppe. (Courtesy of James J. Thull.)

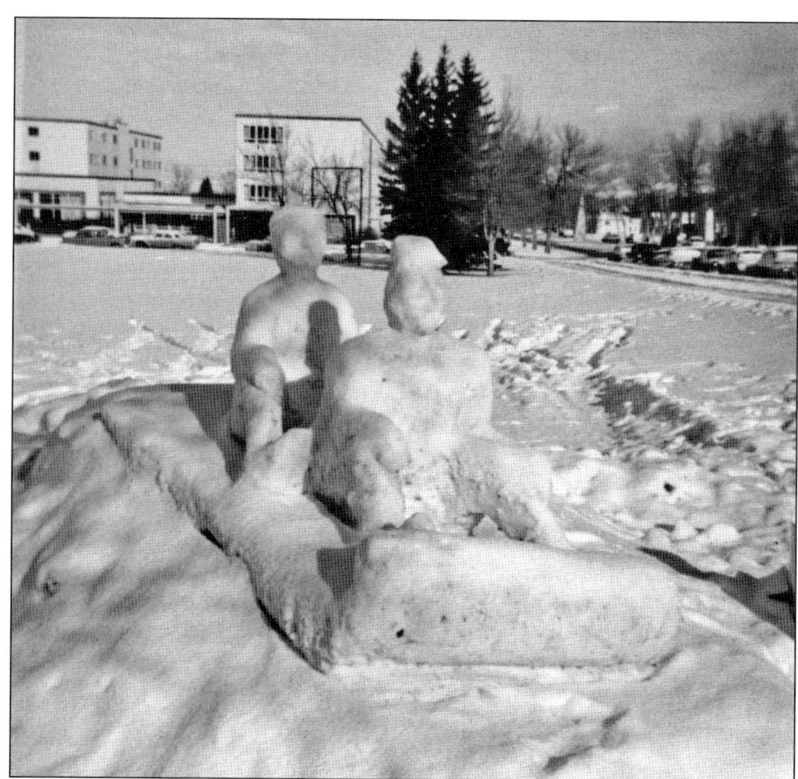

Not all art is meant to last. This snow sculpture depicting two riders on a sled was created by students in 1964. Of course, this was created in Montana, so it could have been sculpted almost any month of the year.

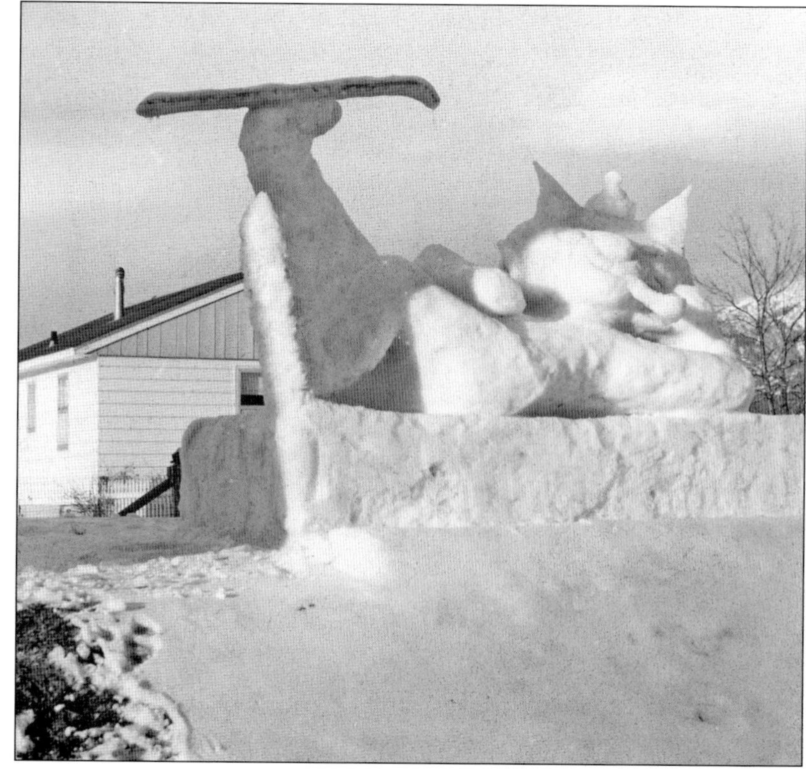

Another snow sculpture created by students in the winter of 1964 depicts a crowned figure reclining with an upraised ski and smoking a pipe. Skiing is a favorite pastime of many MSU students and often one of the reasons they chose to attend school in Bozeman. The area is famous for its abundant access to skiing and other winter sports.

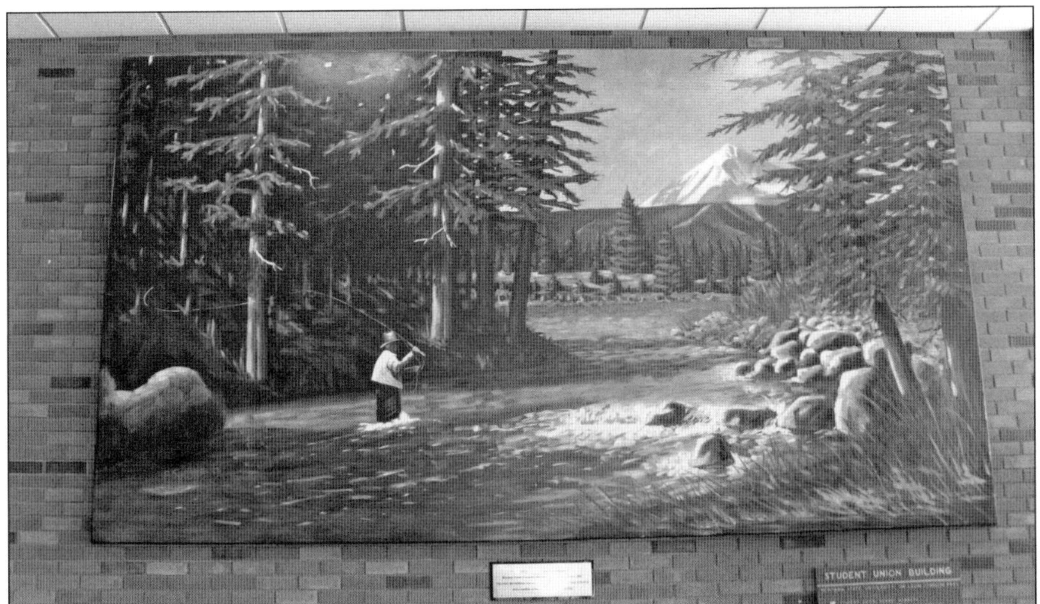

The Gallatin's West Fork was commissioned by the Montana Power Company and donated to MSU in 1965. The artist, Bill Spillane, depicts a popular fishing, rafting, and swimming destination on the blue-ribbon trout waters of the Gallatin River, which flows just north of Bozeman. The river meets the Jefferson and Madison Rivers in nearby Three Forks to form the Missouri River. (Courtesy of James J. Thull.)

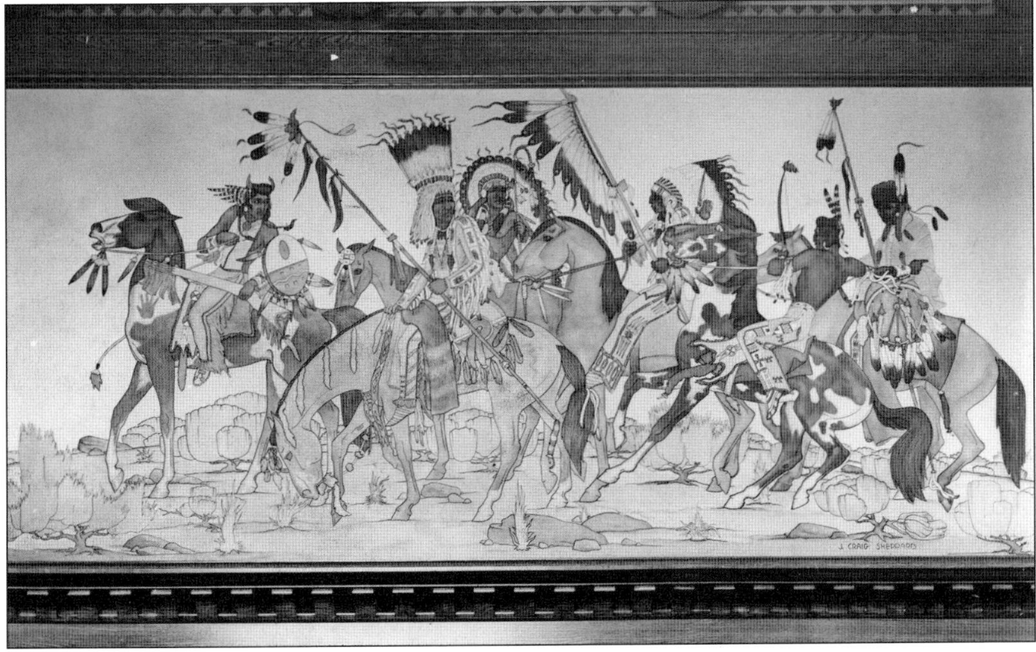

This painting of Native Americans on horseback is by artist J. Craig Sheppard (1913–1978), who specialized in Western themes. A native of Lawton, Oklahoma, he was a cowboy and rodeo rider in his youth. This work hangs in the Leigh Lounge in the Strand Union Building. The lounge is named in honor of Mildred Leigh, director of the building from 1940 to 1967.

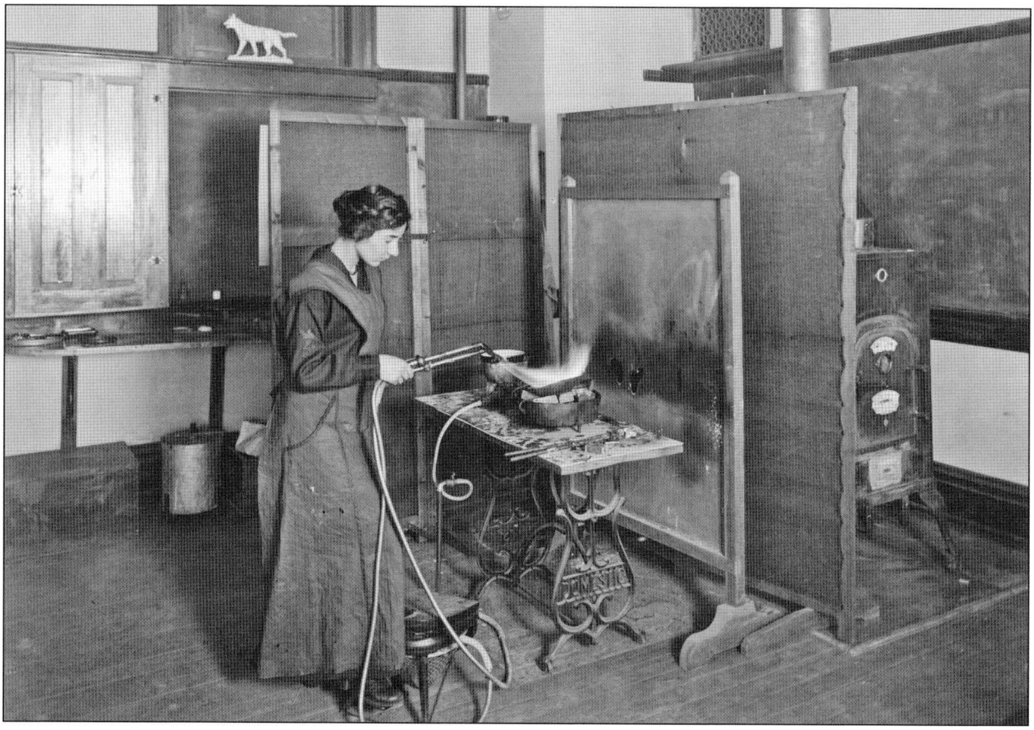

A woman works with a welding torch in the art department. She is operating a torch that is fed through a gas line and operated with a foot pedal controller. Metalworking has long been a feature of the curriculum at MSU, and so has the display of indoor and outdoor sculpture done in metal.

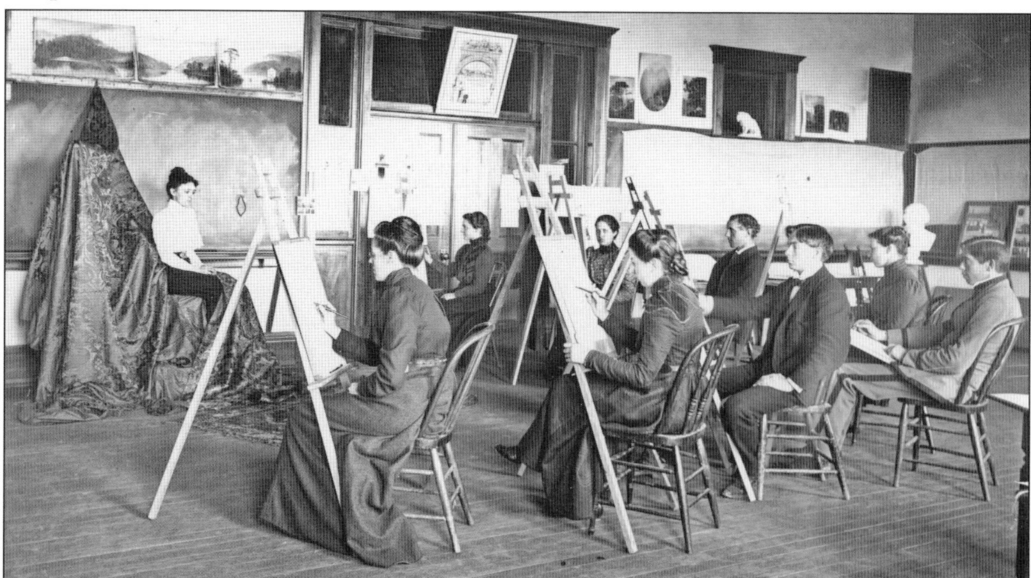

A class of eight students sketch a seated woman between 1900 and 1920. Small sculptures and some artwork can be seen in the background. Art has played a role in the education of MSU students since the school's inception. In 1911, the school employed 12 faculty members in the Department of Art and Music.

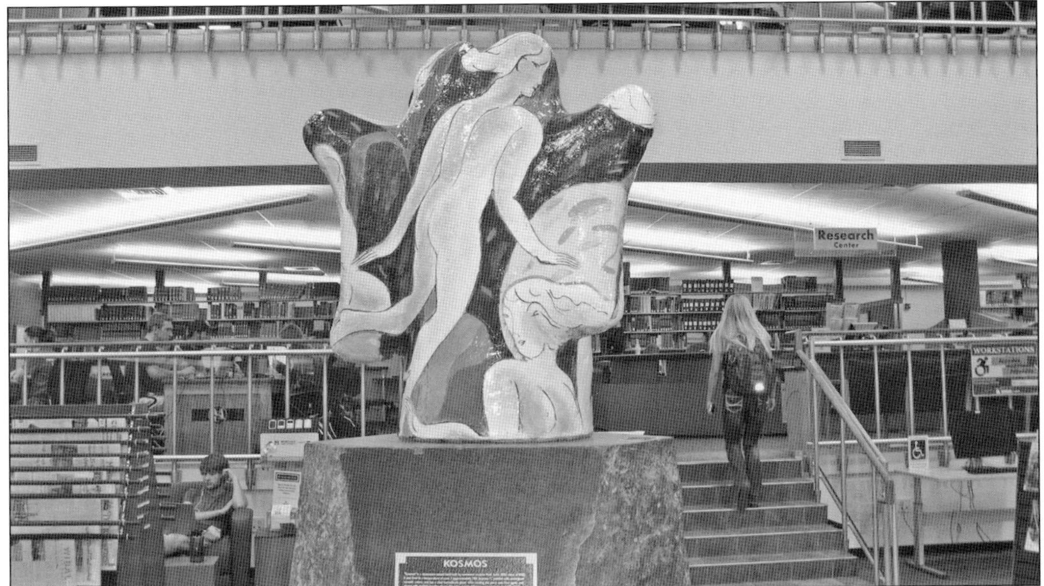

Kosmos is a stoneware vessel hand-built by sculptor Rudi Autio. The artist was a member of the 1950 graduating class of what was then Montana State College. Named after the artist's favorite restaurant, in the center of Helsinki, Finland, the piece sits on a stone base in the courtyard on the library's first floor. (Courtesy of James J. Thull.)

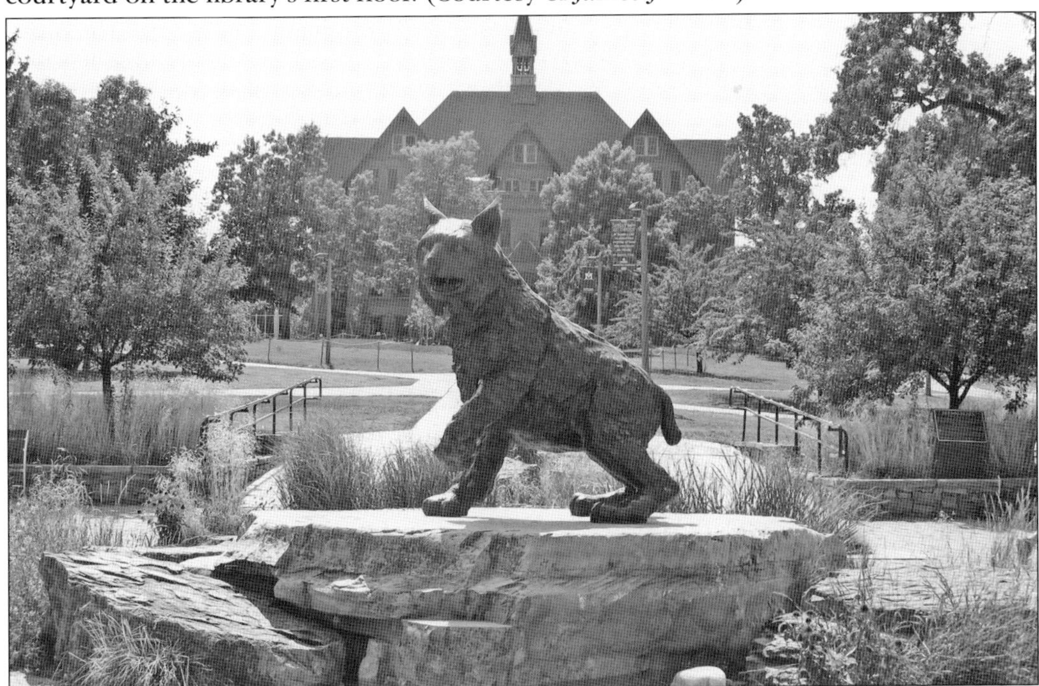

Spirit sits on a walkway north of Montana Hall and greets visitors coming to campus from that direction. A popular spot for visitors and graduating students to take photographs, the statue is named for the first live bobcat mascot. The name "Bobcat" was first used in 1916, when two editors at the school paper decided the sports teams should be named after a fierce animal. (Courtesy of James J. Thull.)

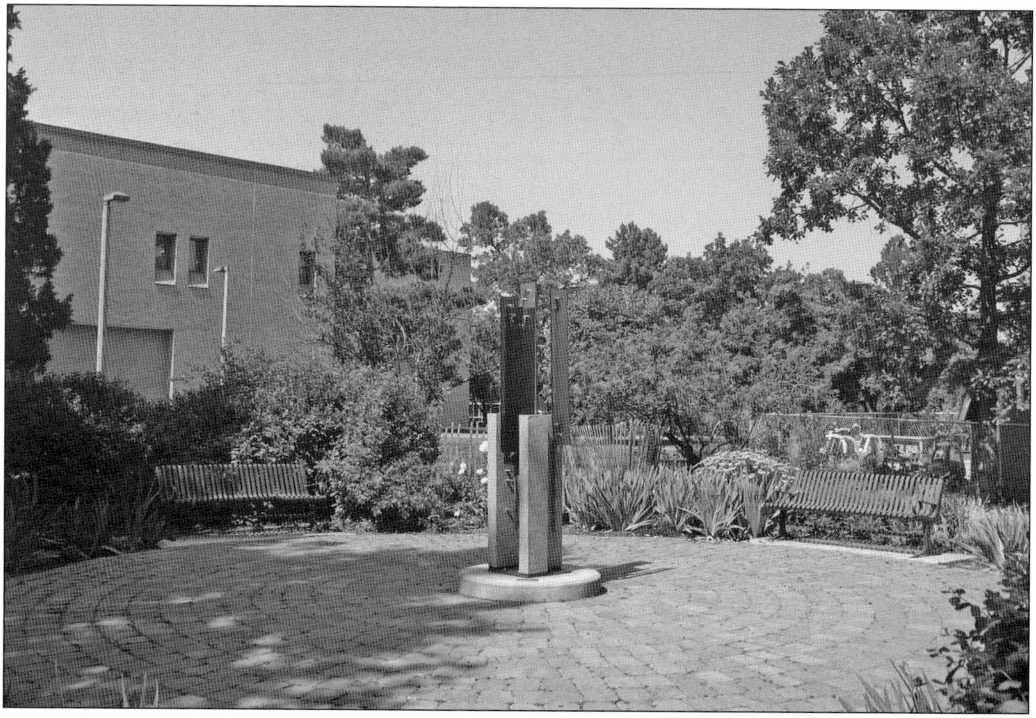

Four Seasons is a piece by MSU faculty member and artist Heath "Tad" Bradley. Commissioned by students for Danforth Park in 2010, the piece sits where the original sundial was placed by the graduating class of 1920. The panels, in various colors, are meant to represent the changing of the seasons. (Courtesy of James J. Thull.)

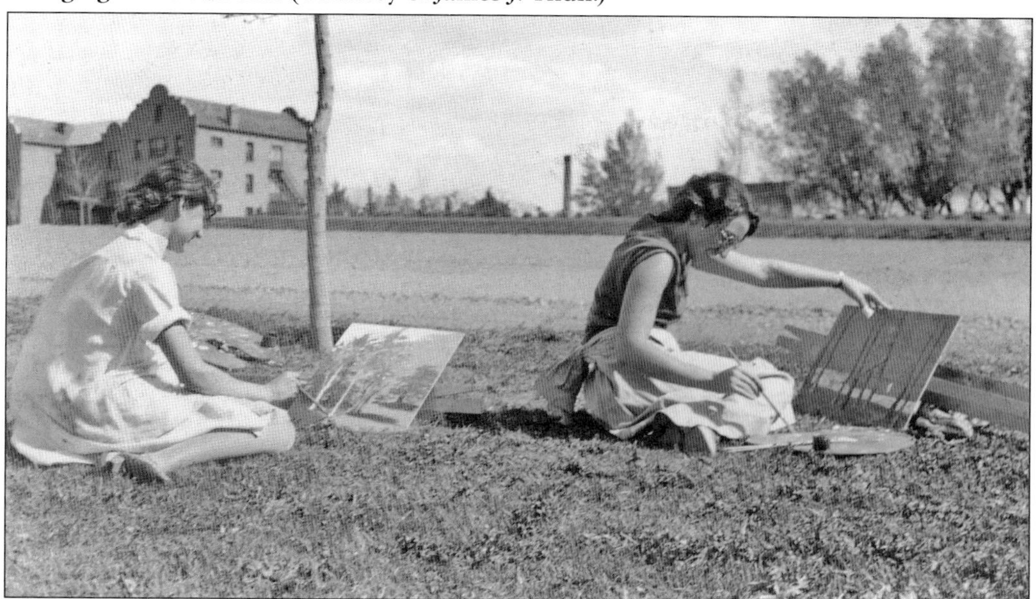

Two women paint landscapes while sitting on the lawn outside Montana Hall in the spring of 1930. Hamilton Hall can be seen in the background. Originally designed in 1910 as a women's dormitory, Hamilton was eventually converted into offices and currently houses the Gallatin College programs, as well as Army and Air Force ROTC programs.

Students are pictured in the spring of 1930 on a lawn near Montana Hall painting trees. The 1930 *Montanan* spoke to the value of art: "Modern industry is dependent upon artists for many things. They are necessary in the design of clothing and of many other articles, but in the field of advertising they have probably become most essential."

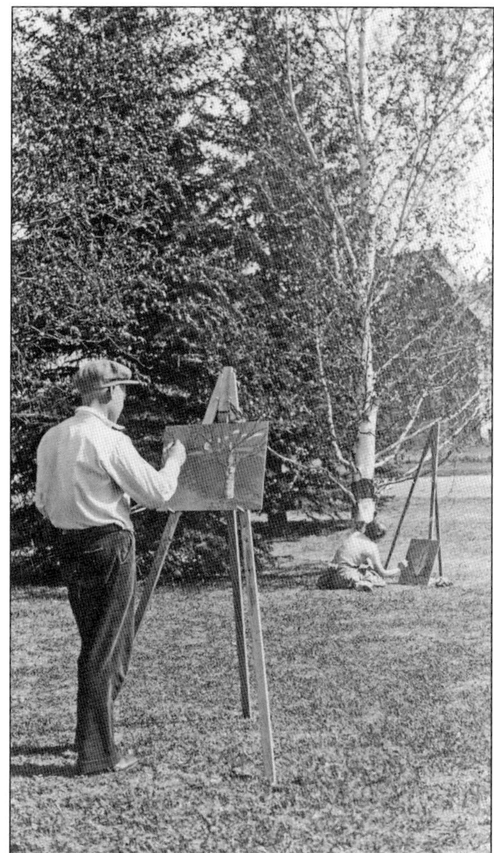

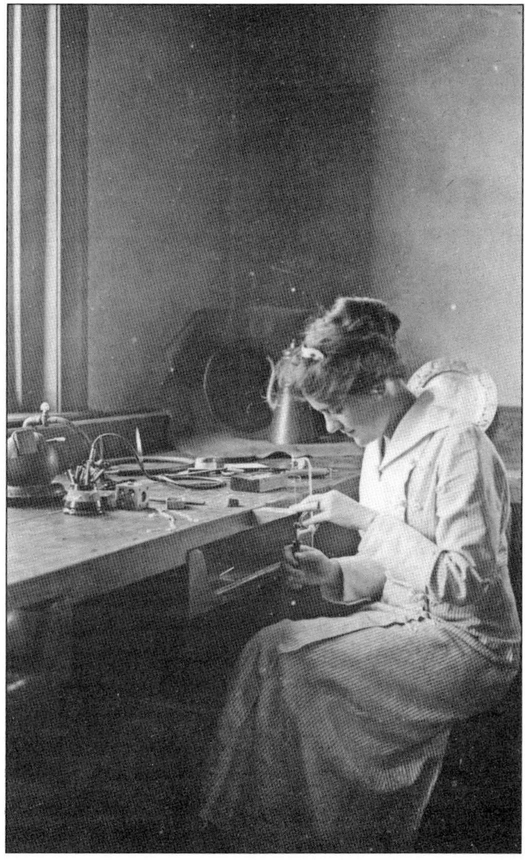

A woman creates jewelry with a small torch, vice, and saw. On the table, there is a short piece of delicate chain for a necklace or bracelet, and in the background, a silver plate and coffeepot can be seen. The world of the artist is varied, and students at MSU have historically been given leeway in expressing their artistic visions.

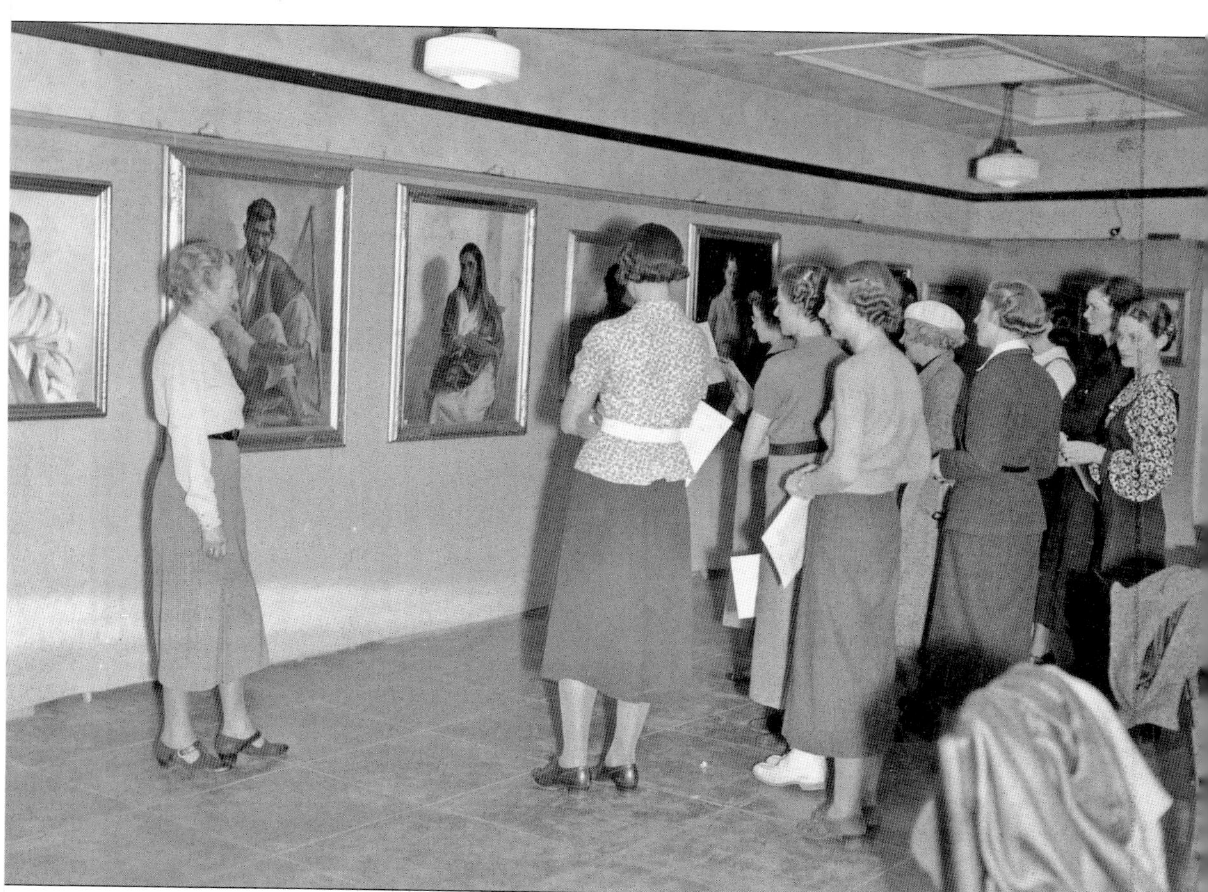

The School of Art at Montana State University was established in 1893 and conferred its first graduate degree in 1932. The curriculum revolves around subjects including art history, ceramics, jewelry, metalsmithing, painting, drawing, and sculpture. Art education at MSU is not limited only to the classroom; experiencing the atmosphere of a local gallery's display is also important. MSU's School of Art provides such a venue in the form of the Helen E. Copeland Gallery. In this image, a group of students view an art exhibit in 1939. Most of the paintings depict non-Caucasians and offer a world view of art. Many local Montanan students had little opportunity to travel outside of the country or meet people like the ones portrayed in these paintings. As true then as now, art can help connect to people and places one may never see in person.

Five

Montana State University American Indian Council Pow Wow

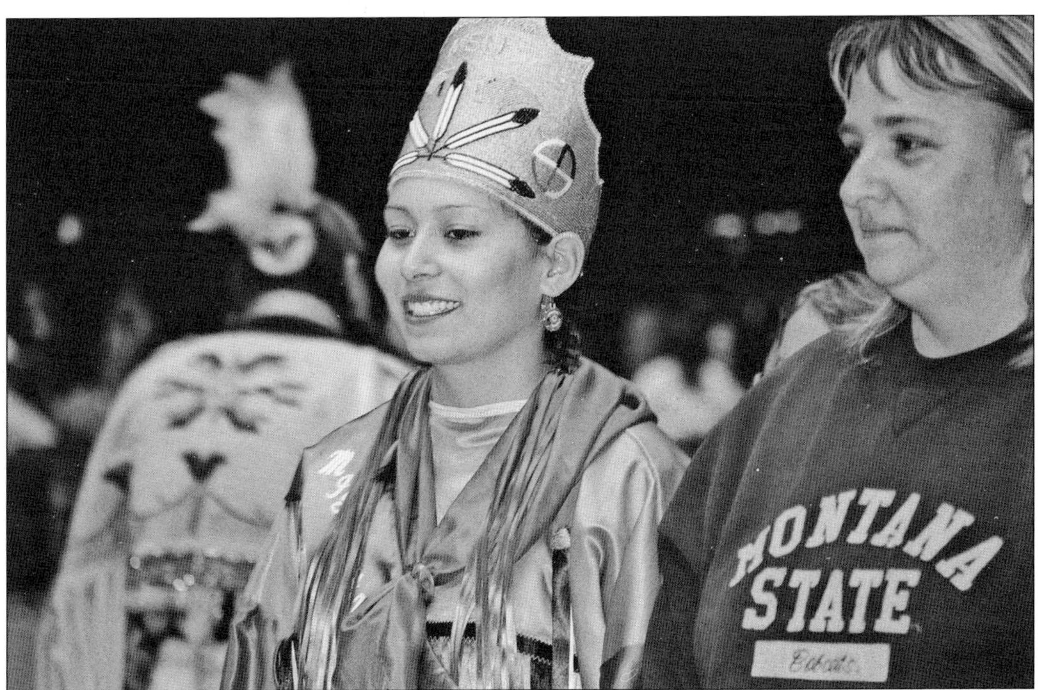

Two women enjoy the 2004 American Indian Council (AIC) at Montana State University. The AIC-MSU Pow Wow is one of the largest annual college pow wows in Montana and always free of charge. The term "pow wow" is a mispronunciation of the Algonquian word *pau-wau*, which originally indicated a ceremony conducted by spiritual or religious leaders. (Courtesy of MSU Native American Studies Department.)

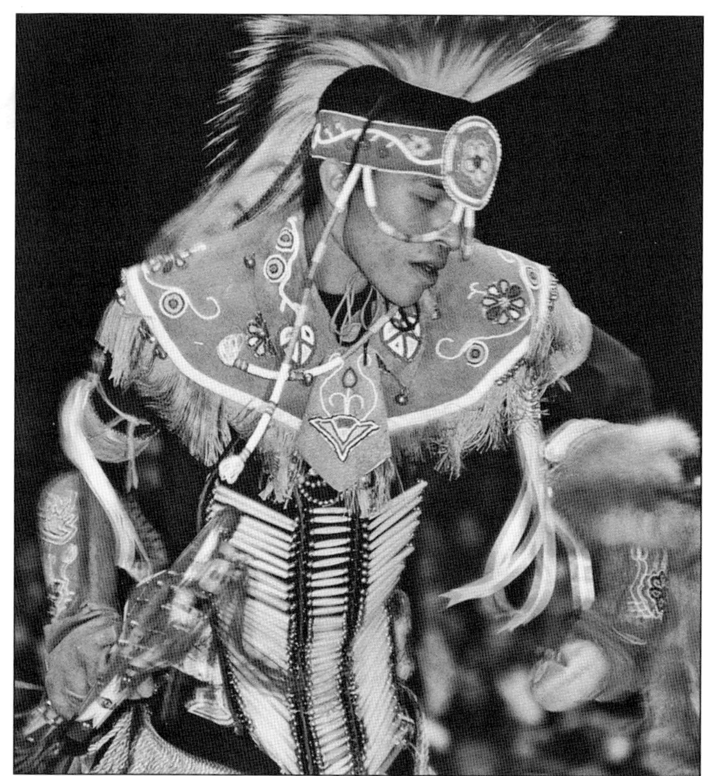

A young male dancer wears a traditional bone breast plate and porcupine roach headdress at the 2004 pow wow. Native American tribes developed an impressive amount of defensive technology, including armor made of bone and leather. Historically, breast plates were worn in battle by many Plains tribes; today, they are often worn at pow wows and ceremonial events. (Courtesy of MSU Native American Studies Department.)

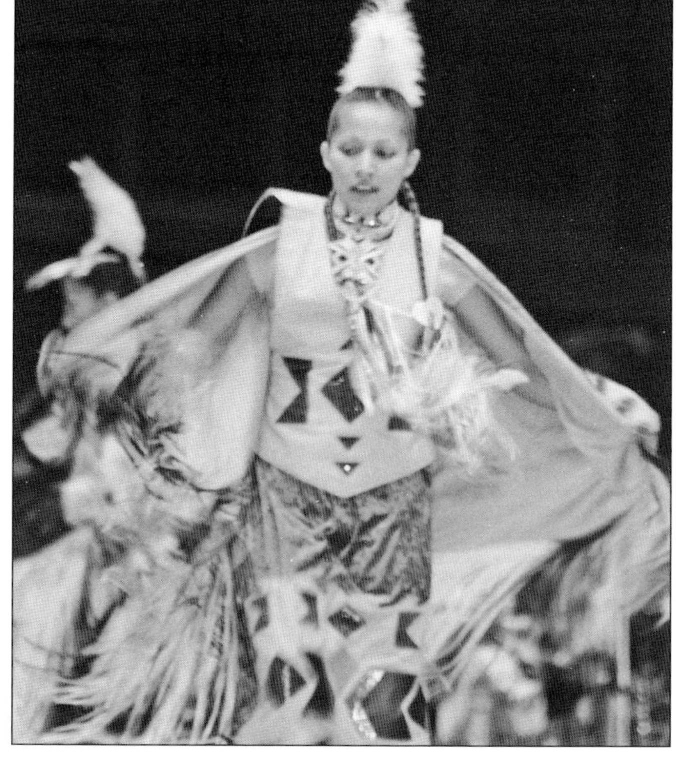

A young woman dances at the 2004 pow wow. The history of the pow wows are somewhat vague, and it is unclear when exactly the first one occurred. For much of the recent past, Native American gatherings were banned on reservations, so it is likely the tradition goes back much further than the records available. (Courtesy of MSU Native American Studies Department.)

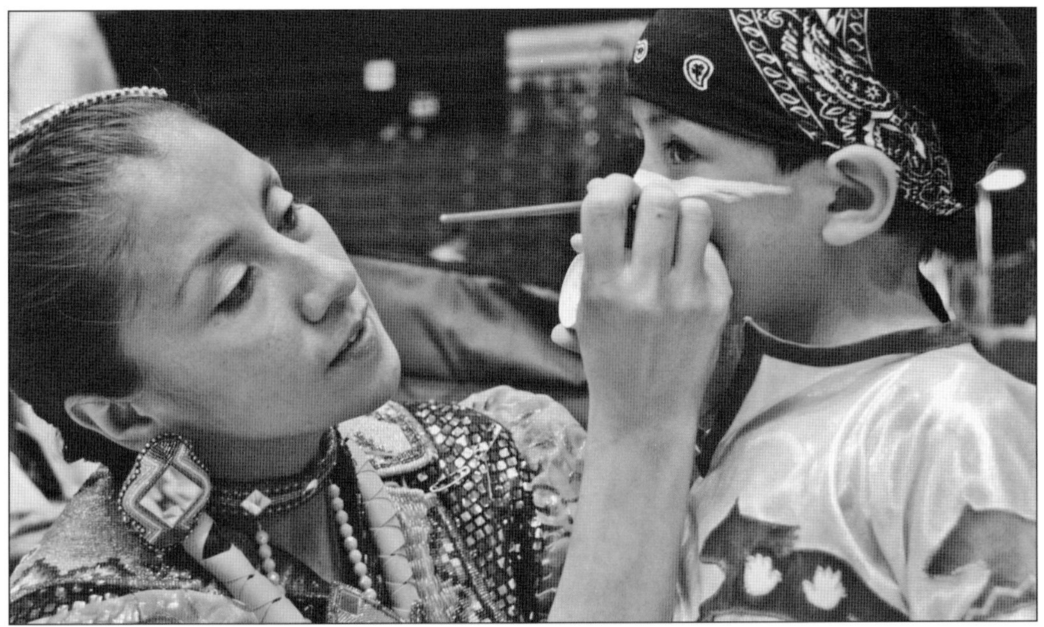

A young woman applies face paint to a child at the 2004 pow wow. Face painting and body decoration is practiced by indigenous peoples the world over. Tattoos have been found on mummified bodies from over 5,000 years ago, and face painting has been used by societies from India to Peru to prepare for battle and mark sacred events. (Courtesy of MSU Native American Studies Department.)

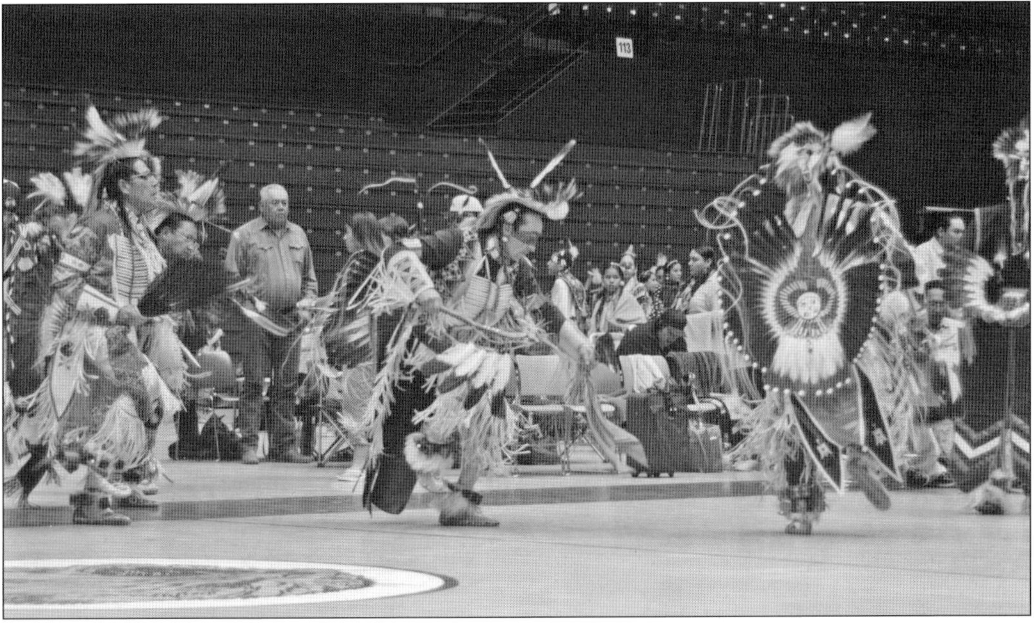

Male dancers at the 2004 pow wow are dressed in a traditional manner, wearing headdresses and bone breast plates and carrying feather fans. Pow wows serve to bring friends and family together to celebrate elements of a common culture and compete in dancing and singing. Participants come from near and far to partake in the events. (Courtesy of MSU Native American Studies Department.)

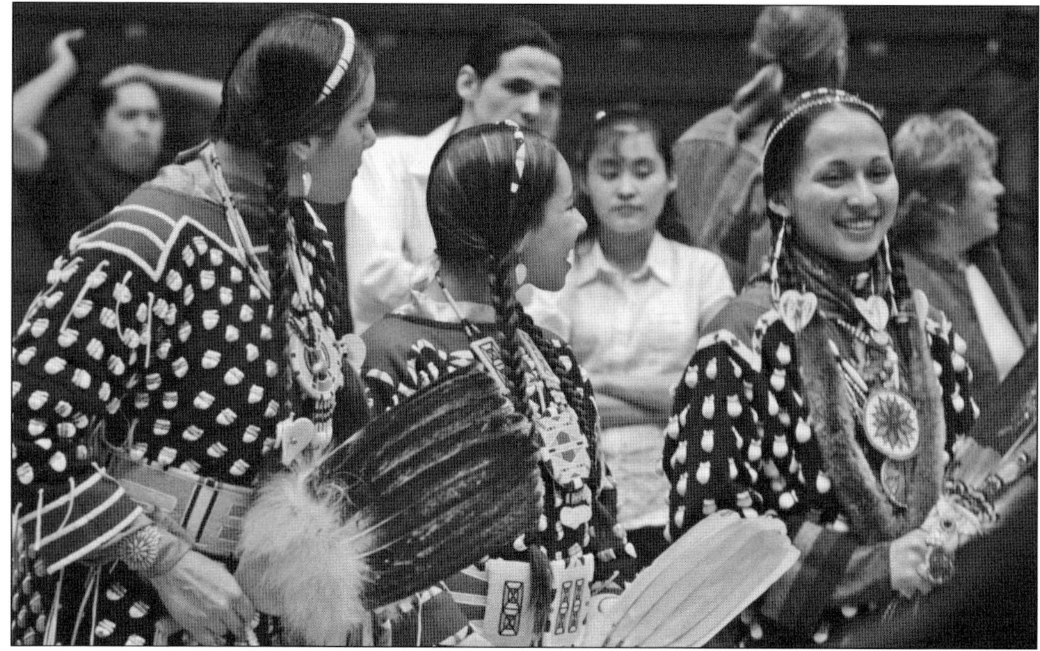

Young women dancers share a laugh at the 2004 pow wow. Their dresses are decorated with elk teeth, they are wearing beadwork, and they carry feather fans. The tribes' longest traditions all connect to locally found or harvested items, like the feathers of the fan and the elk teeth that are often sewn onto dancers' clothing. (Courtesy of MSU Native American Studies Department.)

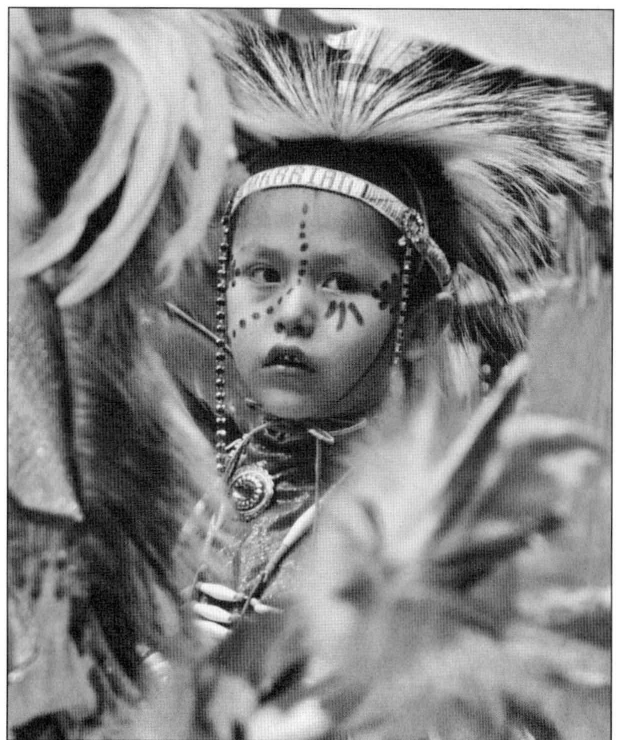

A young boy is pictured at the 2004 pow wow with face paint, a breast plate, and a roach. Face painting is a cultural tradition with personal, family, and spiritual meanings. Many tribes painted not only their bodies for special events but also often their horses, tipi (not all tribes used these), and shields. In many places, they created rock art through painting and carving. (Courtesy of MSU Native American Studies Department.)

A young woman dancer at the 2005 AIC-MSU Pow Wow is wearing a dress decorated with elk teeth and is holding a feather fan. Men and women often have specific dances that are a mix of history, culture, tradition, grace, and beauty. Dances can be divided by age and experience. (Courtesy of MSU Native American Studies Department.)

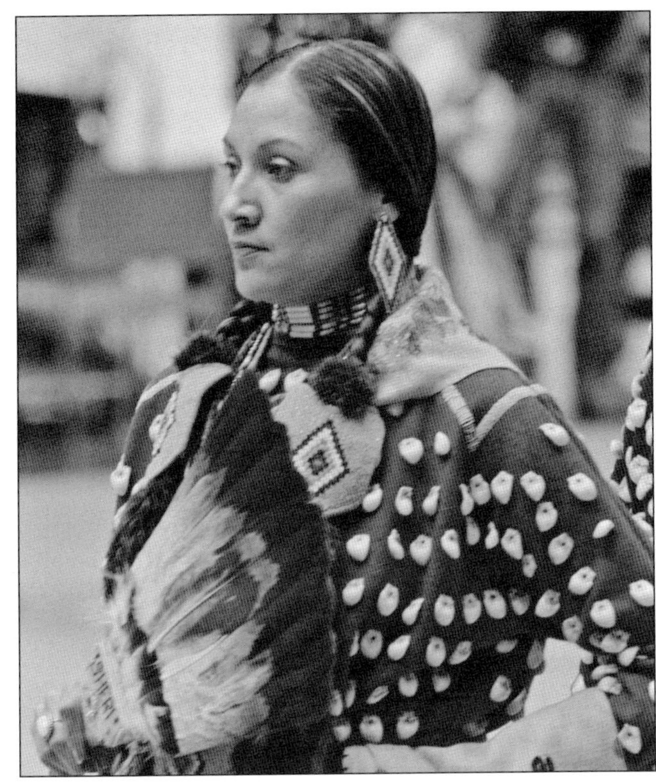

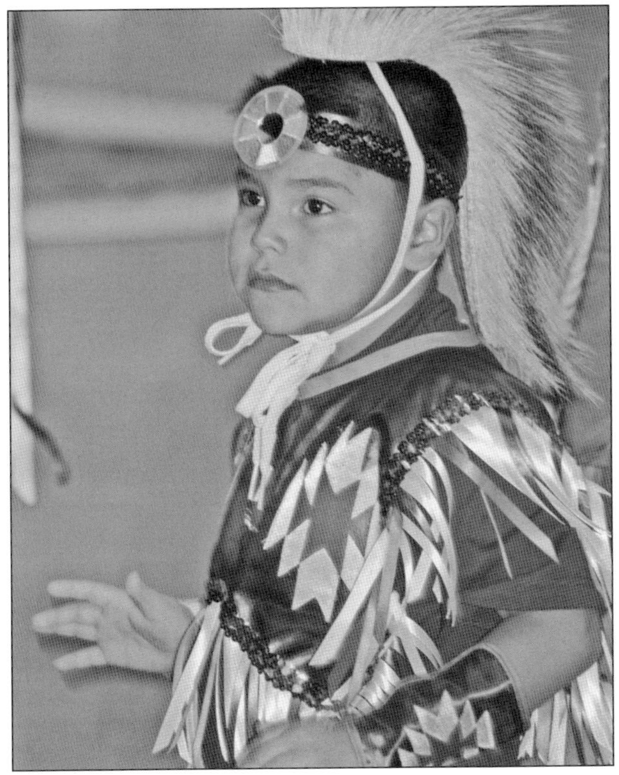

A young boy is pictured at the 2005 pow wow. Today, pow wows are held all across North America, in small towns like Bozeman and large cities like Albuquerque, where there can be thousands of dancers attending. While they do vary, dancing, drumming, and singing are always central features of the events. (Courtesy of MSU Native American Studies Department.)

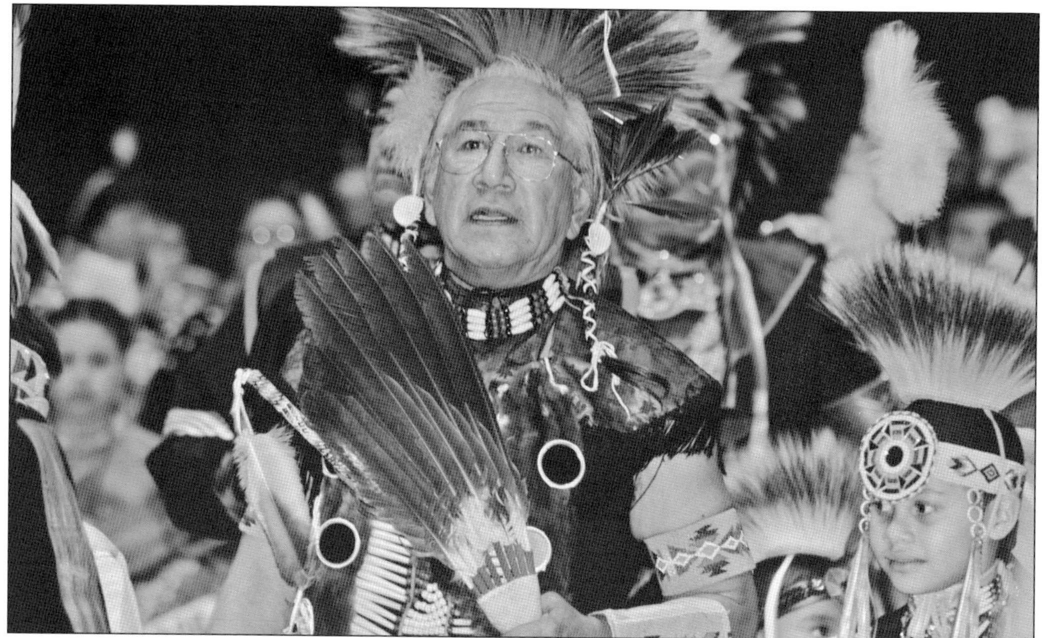

An elder dances and carries a feather fan while surrounded by young dancers in traditional dress at the 2005 pow wow. Native American cultures passed stories, history, life lessons, and morals through storytelling, dancing, and songs. Indigenous oral traditions, while often dismissed by Western cultures, were a complex, personal, and detailed way of passing information from one generation to the next. (Courtesy of MSU Native American Studies Department.)

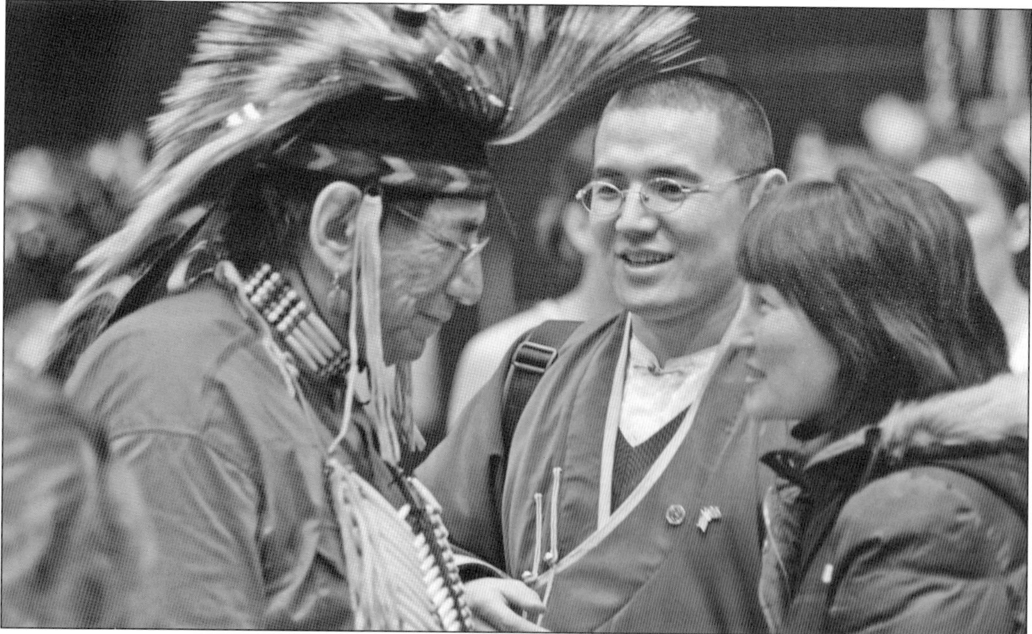

An elder speaks with a woman and a Buddhist monk at the 2009 AIC-MSU Pow Wow. The pow wow is open to everyone. All cultures, tribes, races, and religions are welcome to participate and enjoy the festivities. People from around the world have visited Bozeman to attend and help celebrate the event. (Courtesy of MSU Communications.)

Native American members of the military march during the 2009 pow wow. Native Americans have a long history of military service in all branches of the armed forces. Statistically, they serve at a higher rate than any other group of people and have served with distinction in every war for the last 200 years. (Courtesy of MSU Communications.)

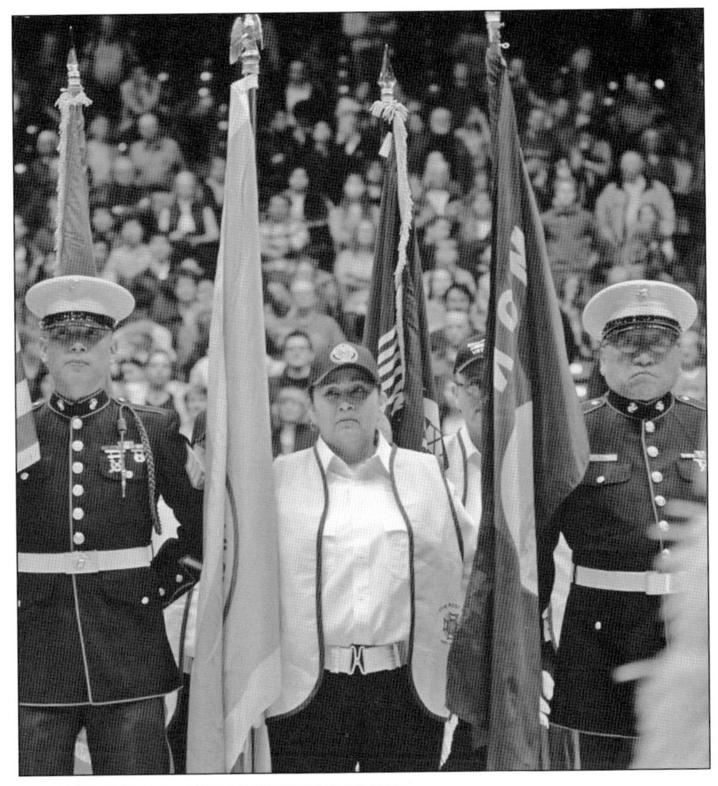

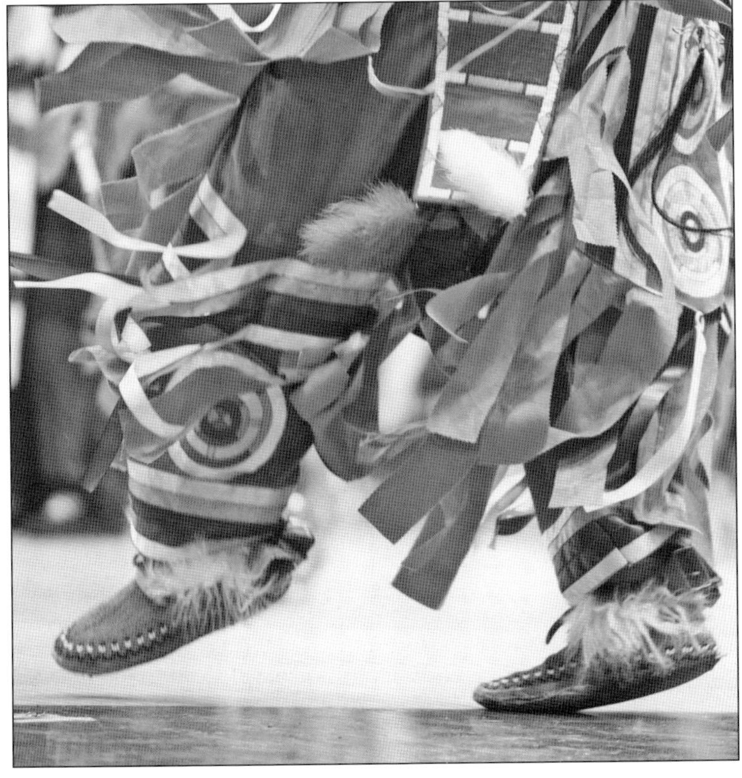

A dancer wears traditional moccasins at the 2010 AIC-MSU Pow Wow. That year's event began with a grand entry honoring retired MSU president Geoff Gamble. Gamble had been supportive of the Native American Studies department and stated he wanted MSU to be the university of choice for all Native American students. (Courtesy of MSU Communications.)

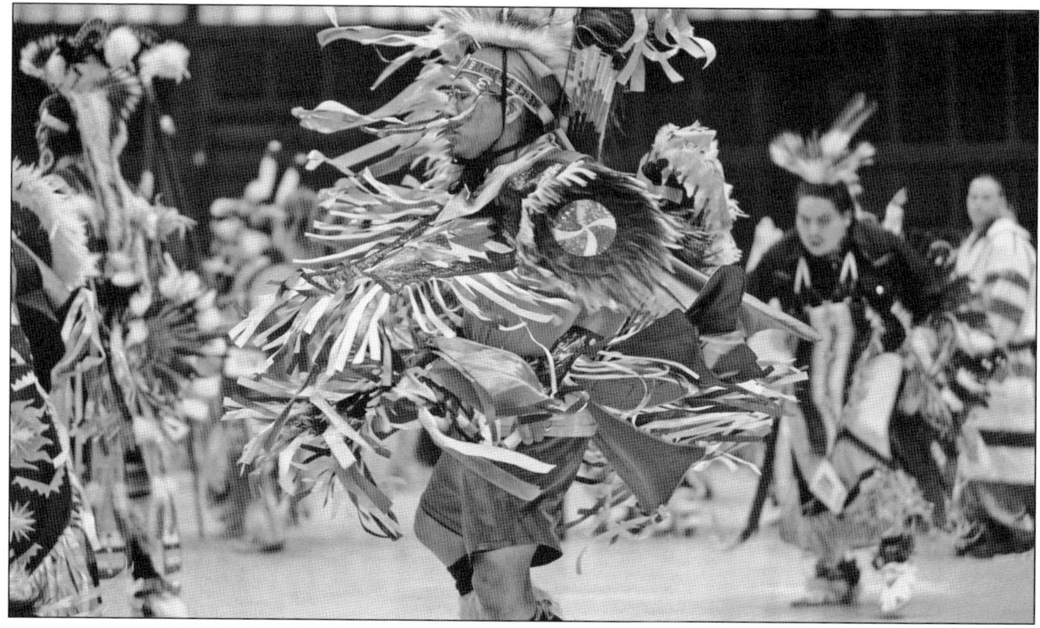

Male dancers participate at the 2010 pow wow. MSU's Department of Native American Studies houses the American Indian and Alaskan Native Student Support Services and will accommodate the planned Native American Student Center. Native American students are the largest minority population at MSU. In 2010, a record 105 Native Americans were awarded bachelor's and master's degrees during MSU's 114th commencement ceremonies. (Courtesy of MSU Communications.)

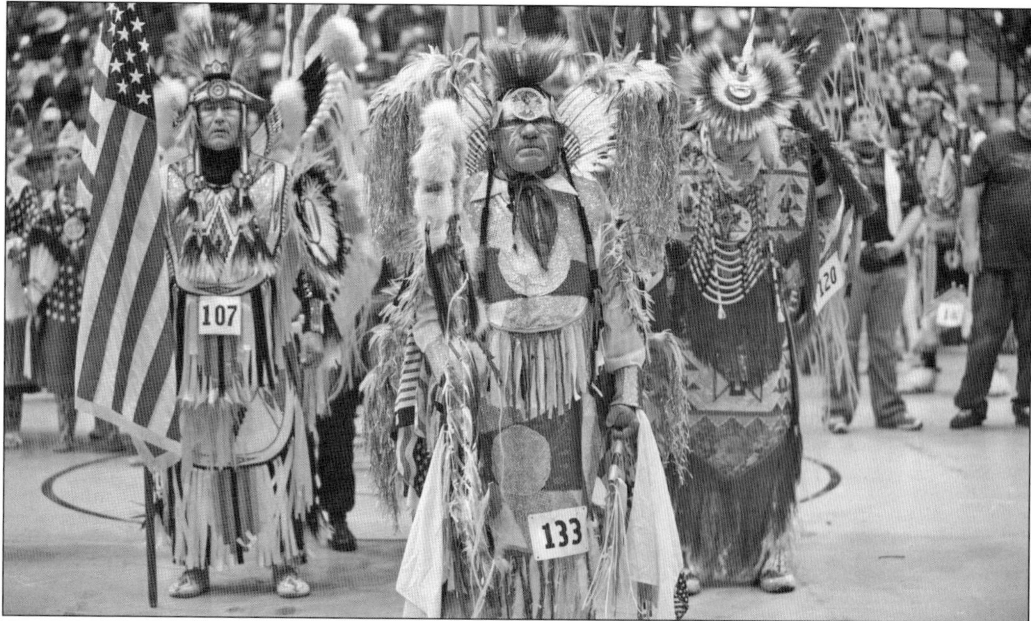

Male elders wear traditional dress at a grand entry during the 2010 pow wow. The grand entry is a common feature of pow wows across North America. At the AIC-MSU Pow Wow, there are typically one or two grand entries each day. The dancers in the grand entry represent tribes from all over the United States and Canada. (Courtesy of MSU Communications.)

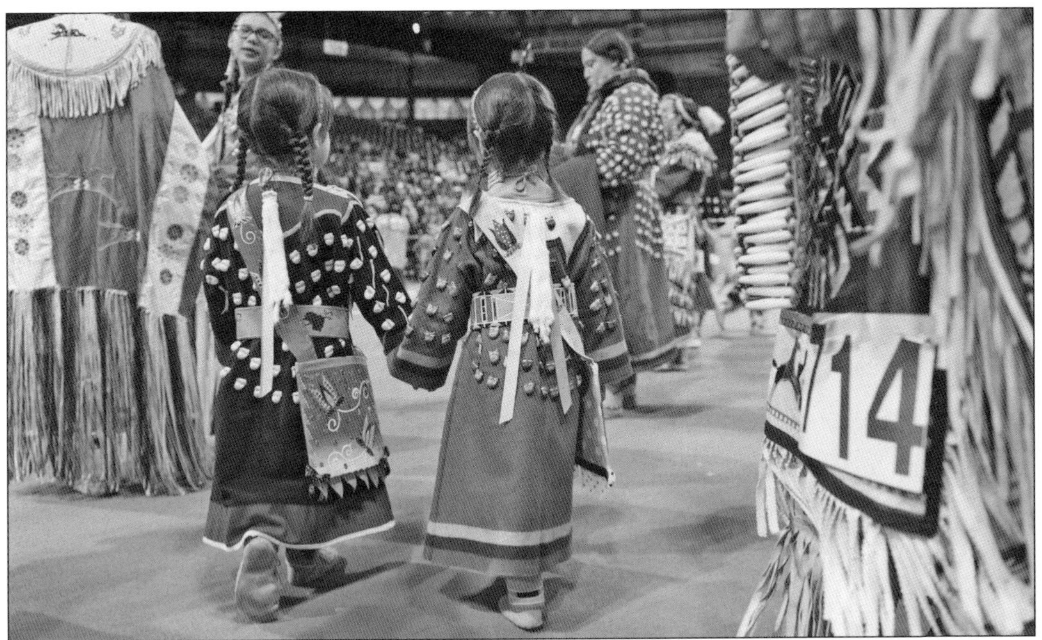

Two young girls walk hand-in-hand at the 2016 AIC-MSU Pow Wow. The American Indian Council chooses a Miss Indian MSU, a Miss Teen MSU, a Junior Miss Indian MSU, and a Miss Tiny Tot MSU each year. The 2016 selections were Miss Indian MSU Alexa Longknife, Miss Teen MSU Joleigh Old Elk, Junior Miss Indian MSU Alyona Morsette-Spoonhunter, and Miss Tiny Tot MSU Mika Rose Funmaker. (Courtesy of MSU Communications.)

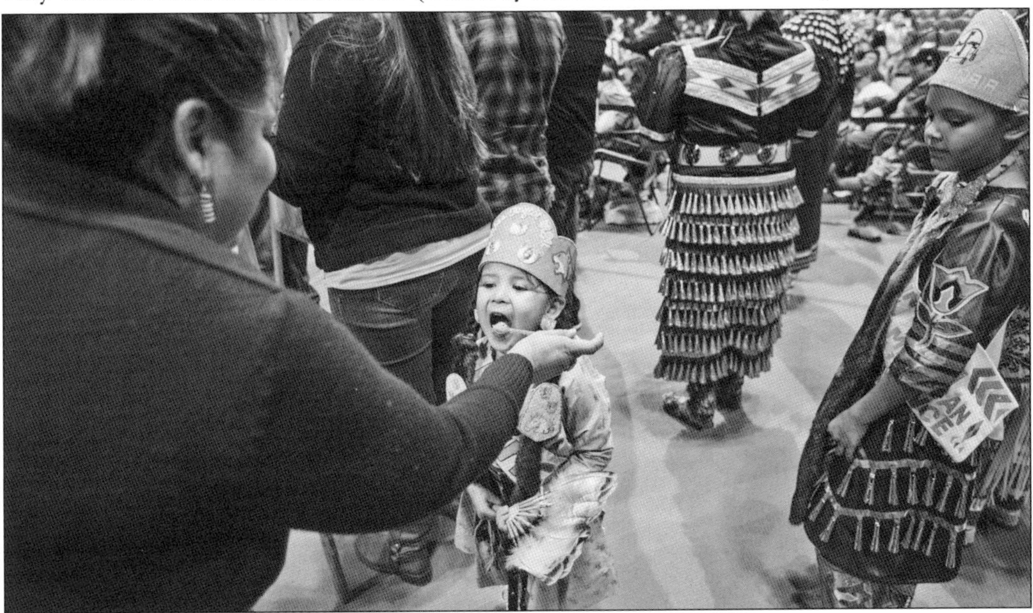

A young girl enjoys a snack at the 42nd AIC-MSU Pow Wow in 2017. A celebration of traditional foods is a mainstay and an important cultural feature of the annual pow wow. Fry bread, Indian tacos, and chili are often featured. While individual recipes vary, Indian tacos are often a combination of ground beef, chopped lettuce, sliced tomato, and shredded cheddar cheese served directly on top of Indian fry bread. (Courtesy of MSU Communications.)

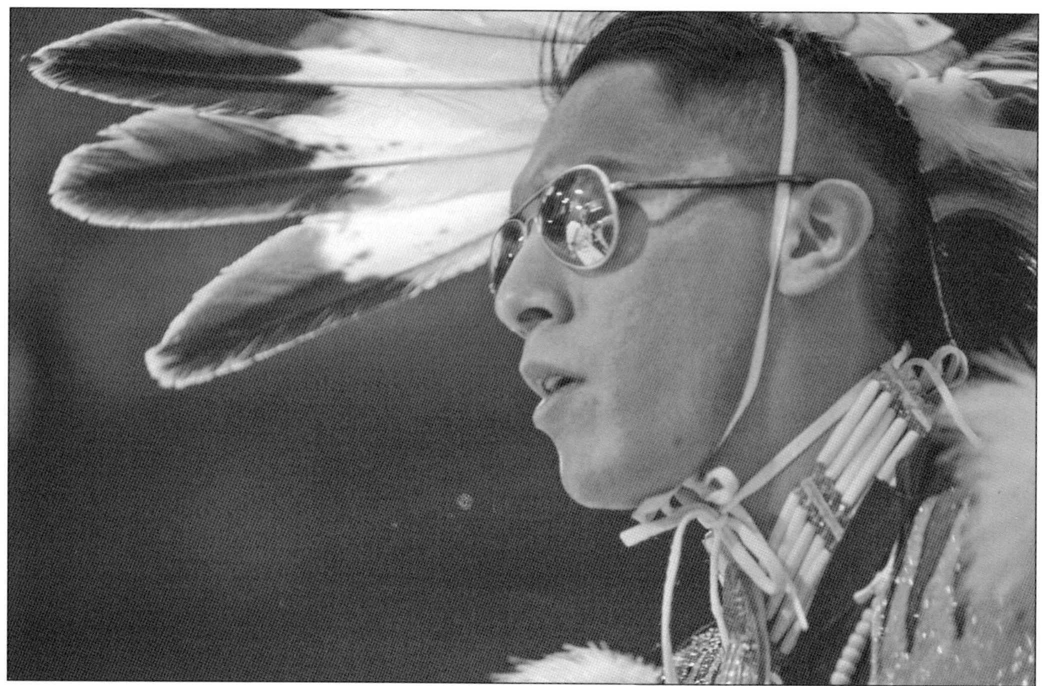

A male dancer wears a feathered headdress, bone choker, and aviator-style mirrored sunglasses. As with all cultures, "traditional" is ever-changing. Native Americans have incorporated items from modern times into much of their dancewear and pow wow dress. Synthetic elk teeth, replicas of bear claws, and even sunglasses are sometimes part of a dancer's wardrobe. (Courtesy of MSU Communications.)

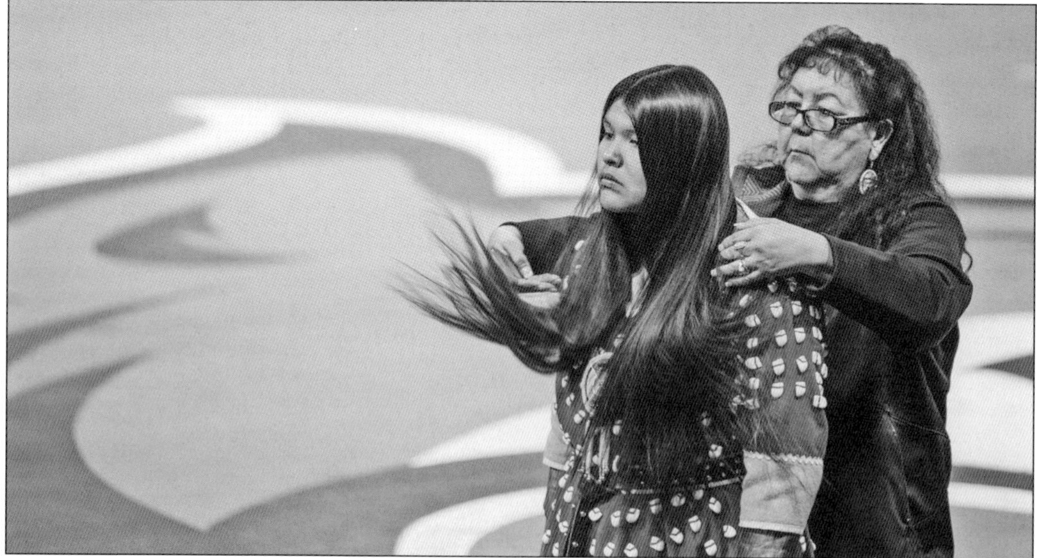

A young woman gets the final details on her hair and dress at the 2017 pow wow. The MSU Bobcat logo can be seen on the floor behind her. Her dress is studded with elk teeth. Only two teeth from an elk are used (their canine teeth), and each dress represents years of hunting and hard work; they are often passed down through generations of women in the family. (Courtesy of MSU Communications.)

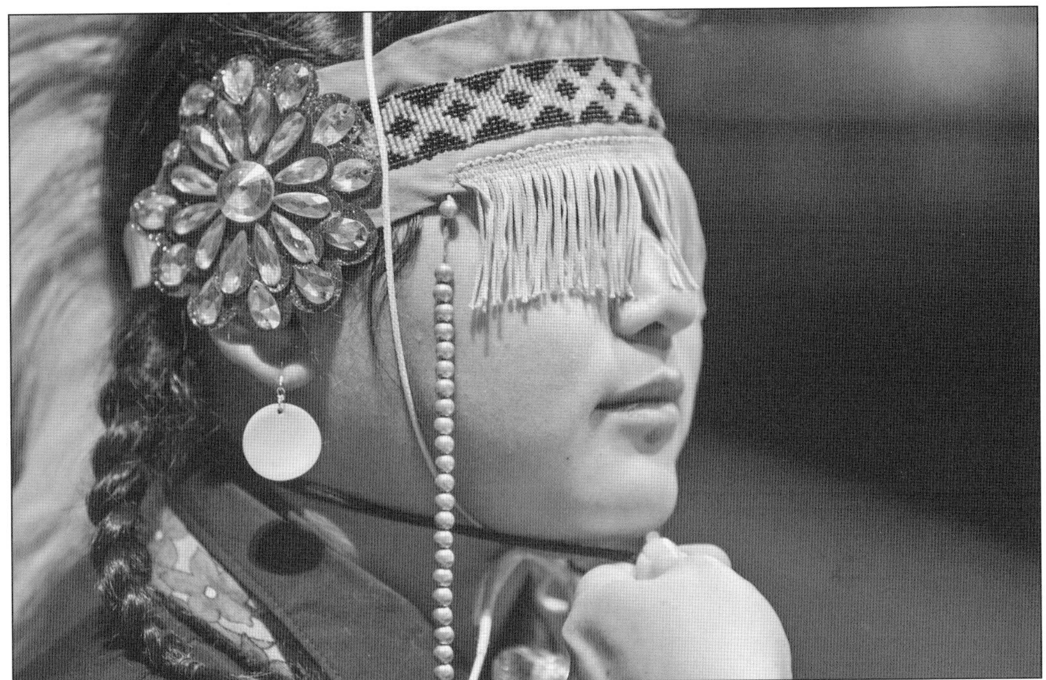

A young dancer wears a traditional headdress and braids at the 2017 pow wow. The pow wow is held each year at the Brick Breeden Fieldhouse, which offers 50,000 square feet of usable space and seating for over 8,000 people. In addition to official events, there are numerous vendors every year selling everything from clothing to beads. (Courtesy of MSU Communications.)

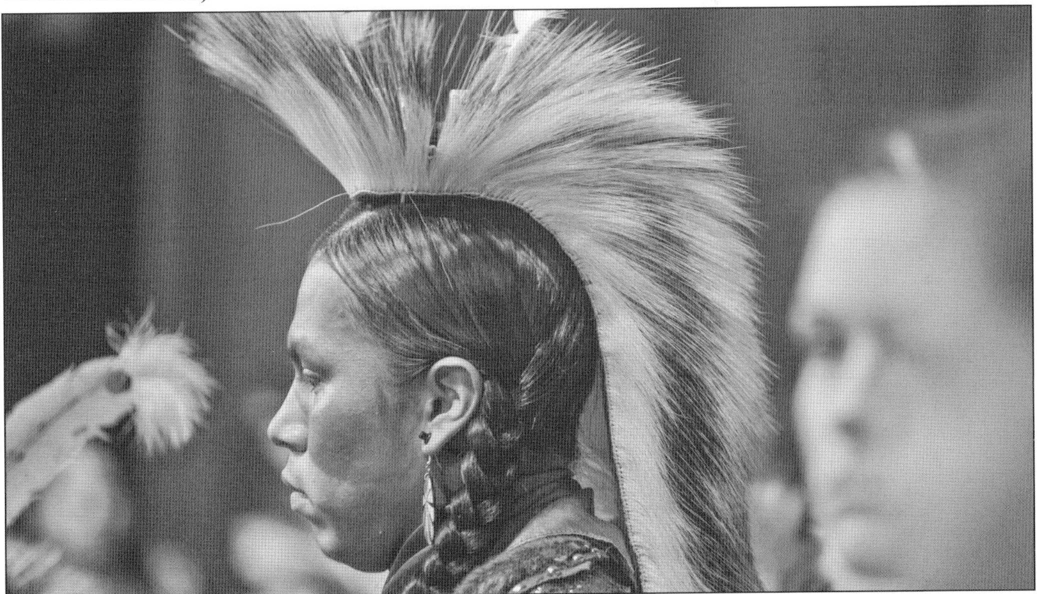

A young man wears a traditional roach headdress at the 2017 pow wow associated with the Mohawk, a tribe originally from the East Coast. The Mohawk were part of the Iroquois Confederacy, along with the Onondaga, Oneida, Cayuga, Seneca, and Tuscarora people. (Courtesy of MSU Communications.)

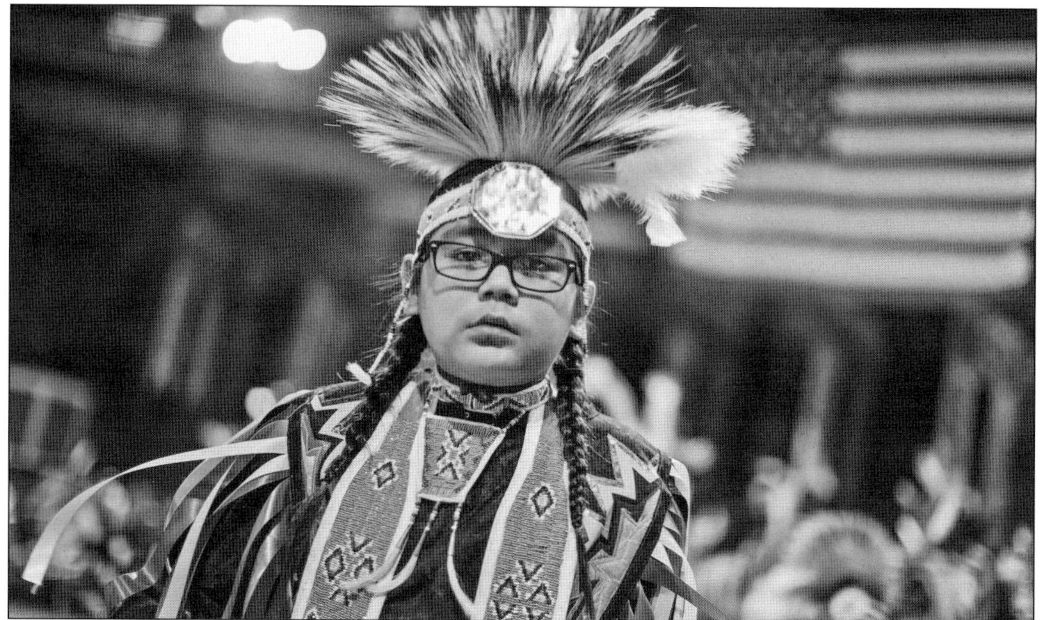

A young boy sports a headdress, braids, and a great deal of beadwork. Manufactured beads were some of the first items used for decorating in Native American tribes. Beads were some of the first items traded with the tribes when Europeans came to the New World. Porcupine quills, elk teeth, and polished stones are also often used in the same manner. (Courtesy of MSU Communications.)

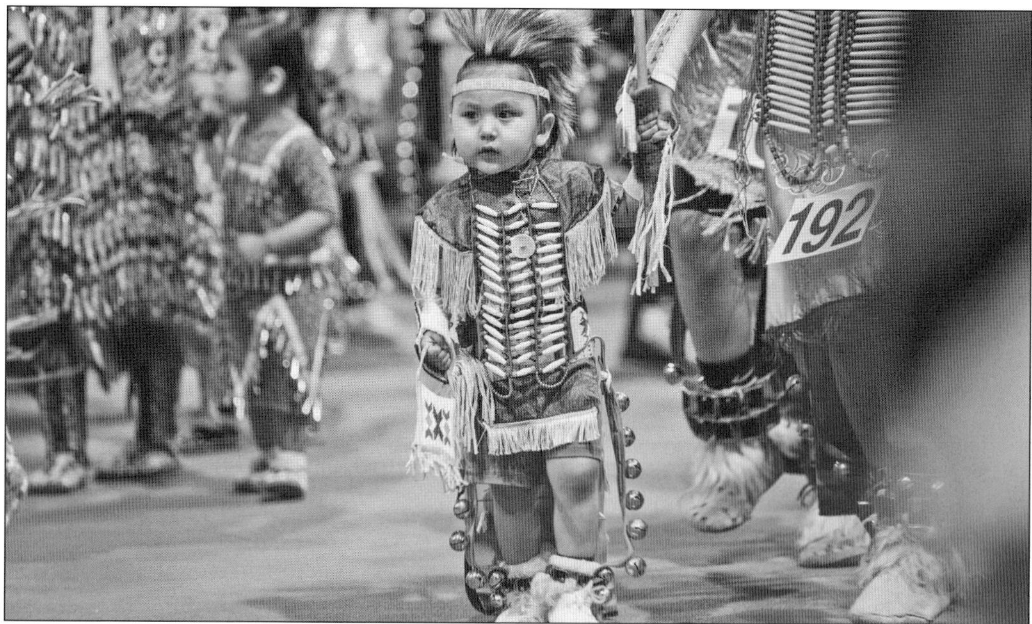

A young boy with a headdress and bone breast plate walks at the 2017 pow wow. There are awards for dancers in several categories, including juniors and teens. Royce Jarvey took first place for Junior Boys Fancy, Andre Lamb for Junior Boys Grass, and Alberto Spotted for Junior Boys Traditional in 2017. There are often cash prices associated with winning dance, drum, and singing competitions. (Courtesy of MSU Communications.)

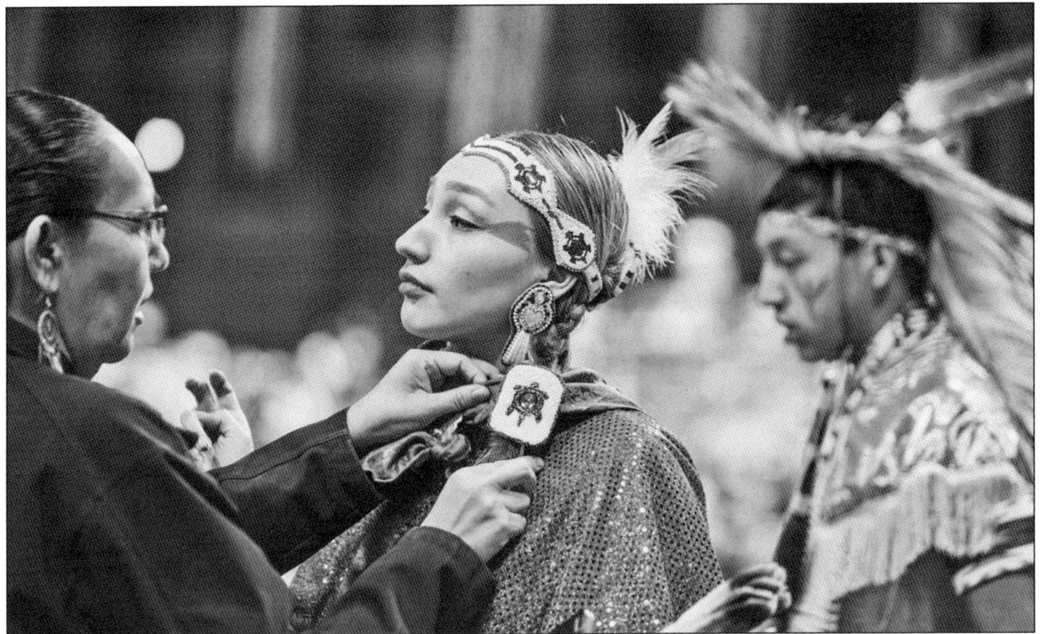

A young woman gets the final touches on her outfit at the 2017 pow wow. Note the turtles in her beadwork. The turtle is a sacred animal for many tribes; for some, it is a central figure in their creation stories. (Courtesy of MSU Communications.)

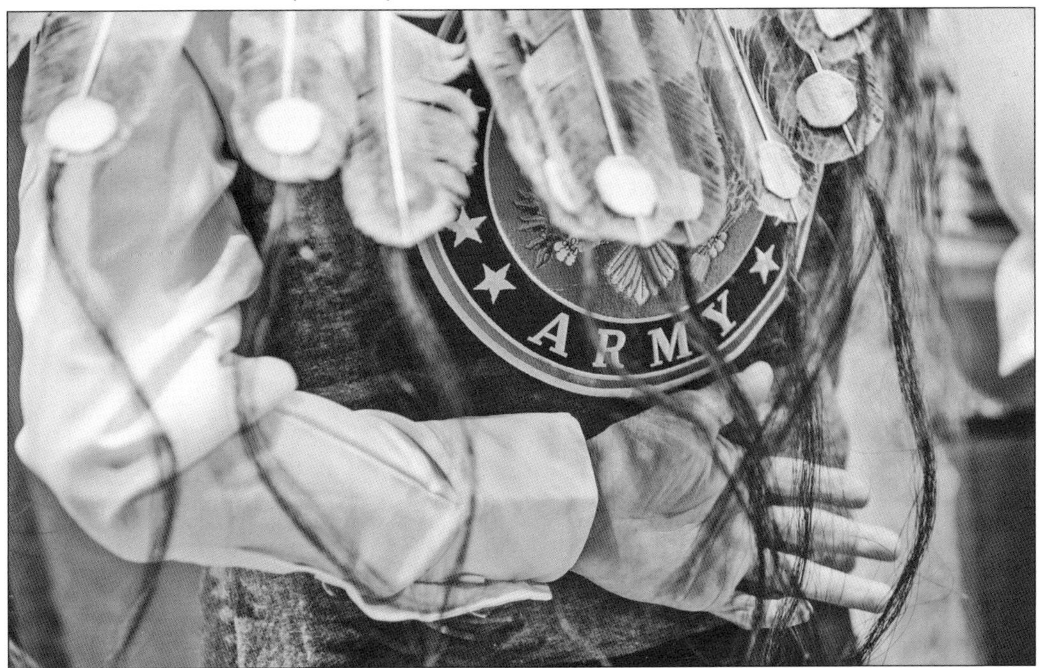

The loyalty, service, and sacrifice of Native Americans serving in the military is legendary. There are several stories of heroism from nearly every recorded US conflict. In World War II, Navajo native speakers, referred to as "Code Talkers," are credited with helping to win the war by serving on the front lines and communicating messages in their native tongue, a code the Japanese never broke. (Courtesy of MSU Communications.)

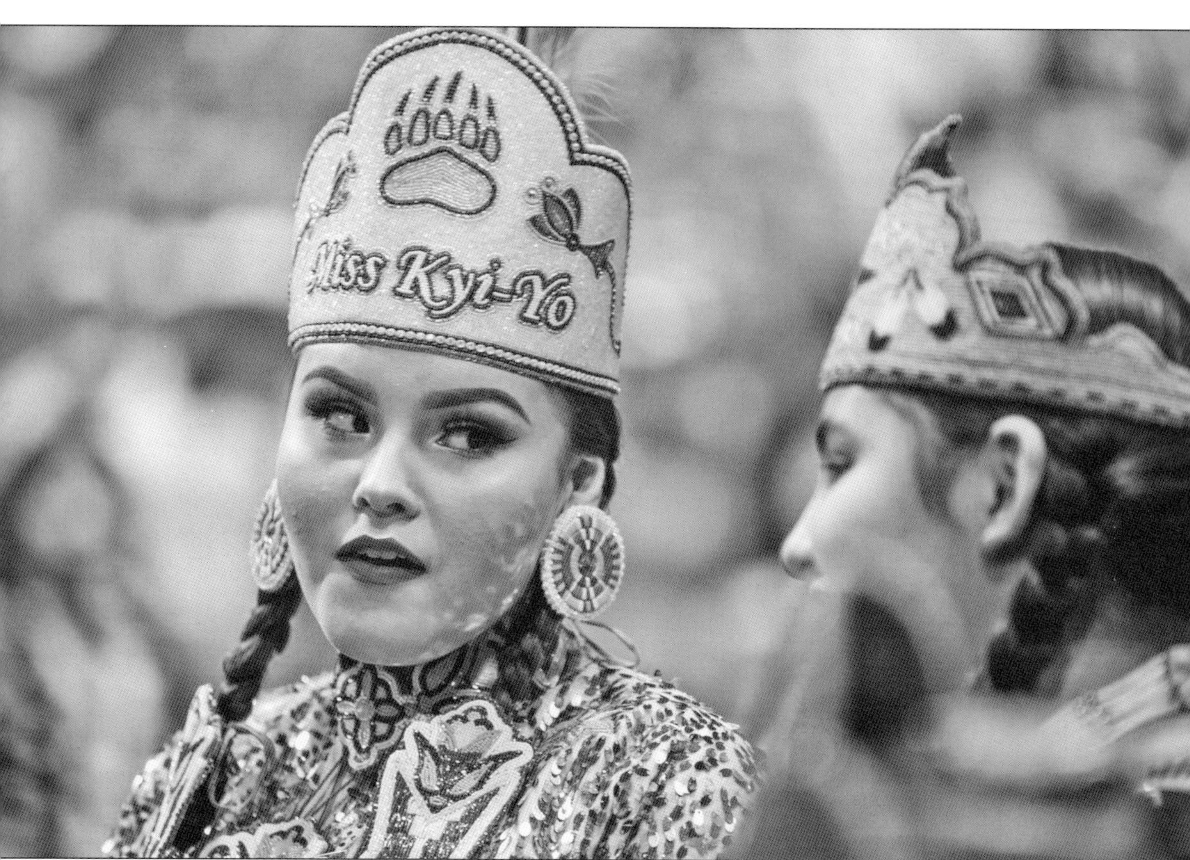

Wozek Chandler, Miss Kyi-Yo 2017, wears a headdress with a beaded image of a bear paw. The bear is a significant animal for many tribes and a central figure in many traditional stories. These stories preserve traditions and tribal narratives through insights into their beliefs. One of the more famous is of a giant bear who chased two Crow girls and, in his attempt to reach them, made claw marks in the rock that now forms the Devils Tower National Monument. The Crow girls were playing near the big rock and appeared to be a tasty meal. Upon seeing the giant bear, the girls scrambled on top of the rock where they were playing. The girls' rock grew thanks to the help of the creator, and the bear scratched the rock as he fell to the ground. (Courtesy of MSU Communications.)

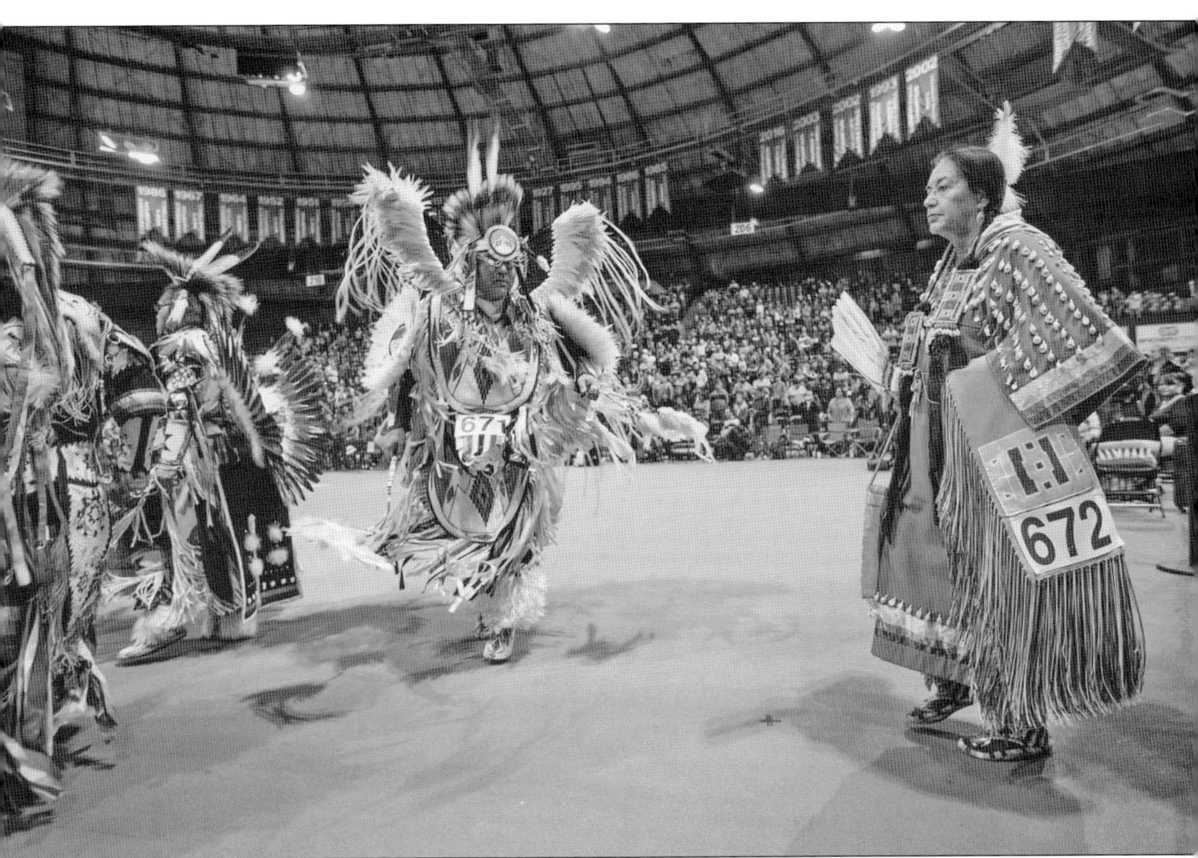

Male and female dancers are pictured at the 2017 pow wow. The Northern Cree were the host drum group, and the head dancers were Trisheena Kills Pretty Enemy (Crow) and Dion Killsback (Northern Cheyenne). The drum group provides music for dancing throughout the pow wow; while the number might vary, it normally consists of four members. The head dancers are the first to dance, encouraging others to join in. The head dancers guide the other dancers in the parade that opens the pow wow. In conjunction with the regular events, there was also the American Indian Council 5-Kilometer Pow Wow Fun Run in 2017, where participants were able to walk or run together. Another event is the annual MSU Pow Wow Basketball Tournament. Both the fun run and basketball tournament provide participants with the opportunity for enjoyment and friendly competition. (Courtesy of MSU Communications.)

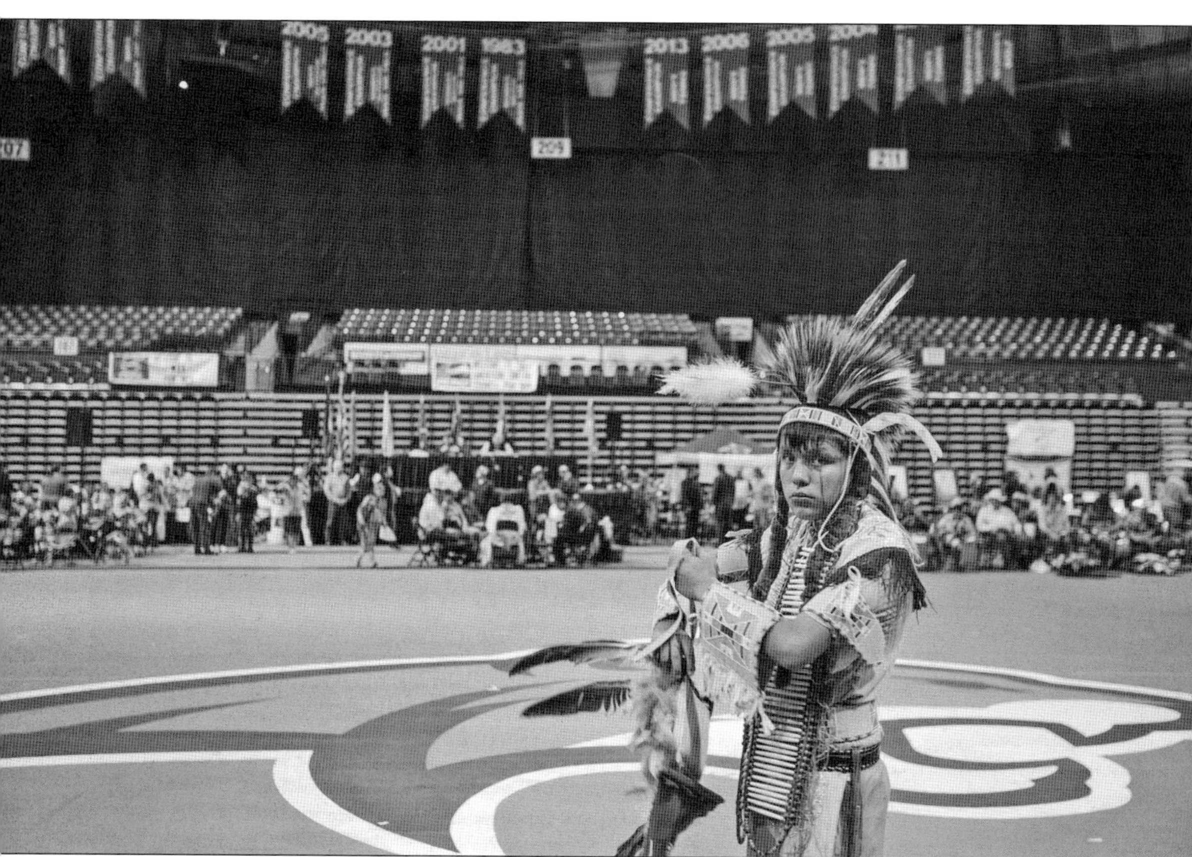

A young dancer is pictured at the 2017 pow wow. While the pow wow includes social dancing, called "intertribal dances," many dancers also compete in contest dances. Intertribal dances are open to anyone, Native or non-native, dressed in dance regalia or not. The American Indian Council works for months to prepare for the annual pow wow, raising thousands of dollars primarily through Indian taco sales at the Christmas Stroll, the International Food Bazaar, and other MSU and Bozeman community events. The fry bead used in an Indian taco is a flat dough bread that is deep fried and can be made with flour, sugar, salt, and lard. (Courtesy of MSU Communications.)

Six

Outdoor Recreation at Montana State University

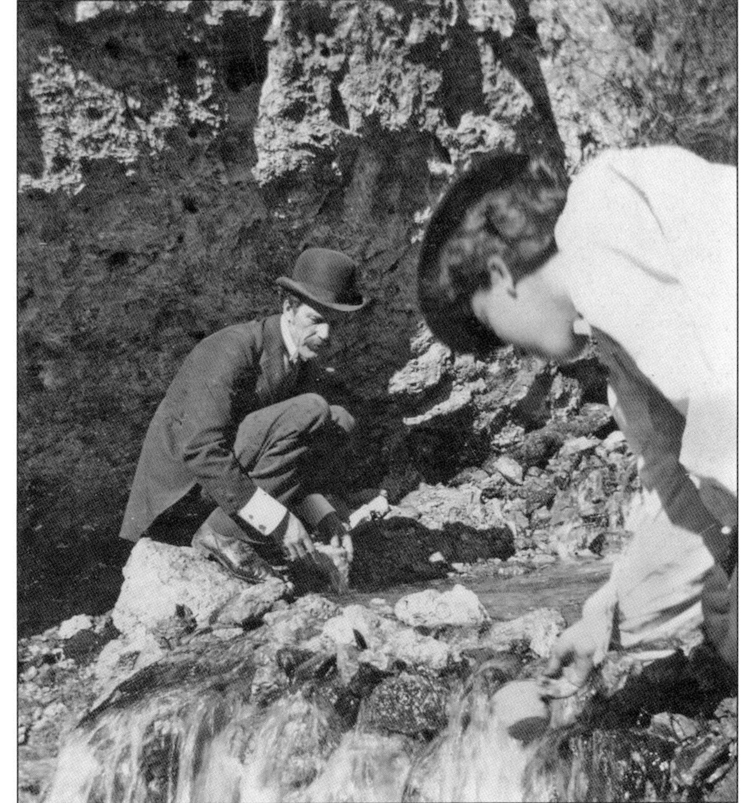

Faculty member James R. Reid is seen here crouching near a spring with a woman filling a cup with water at Rocky Canyon near Townsend, Montana, around 1897. Reid was a professor at Montana State University from 1894 to 1904. He also served as university president from 1894 to 1904. (Photograph by Bozeman Camera Club.)

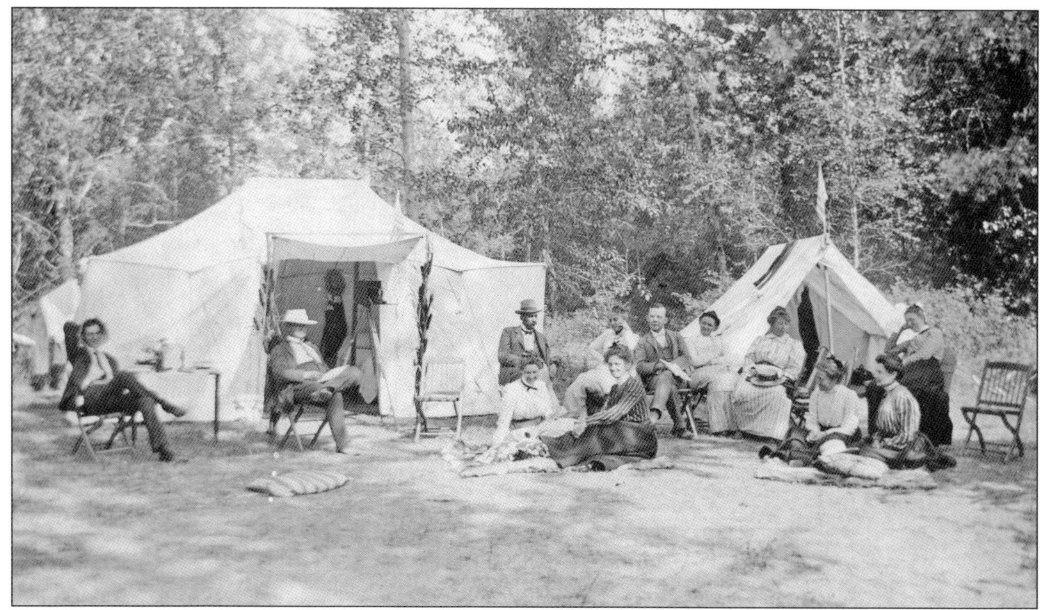

James M. Hamilton and other campers are pictured at the University Biology Camp near Flathead Lake. Hamilton was the third president of Montana State University, serving from 1904 to 1919. He was an author and historian who wrote the comprehensive history of Montana, *A History of Montana 1805–1900*. Hamilton Hall is named for his wife, Florence.

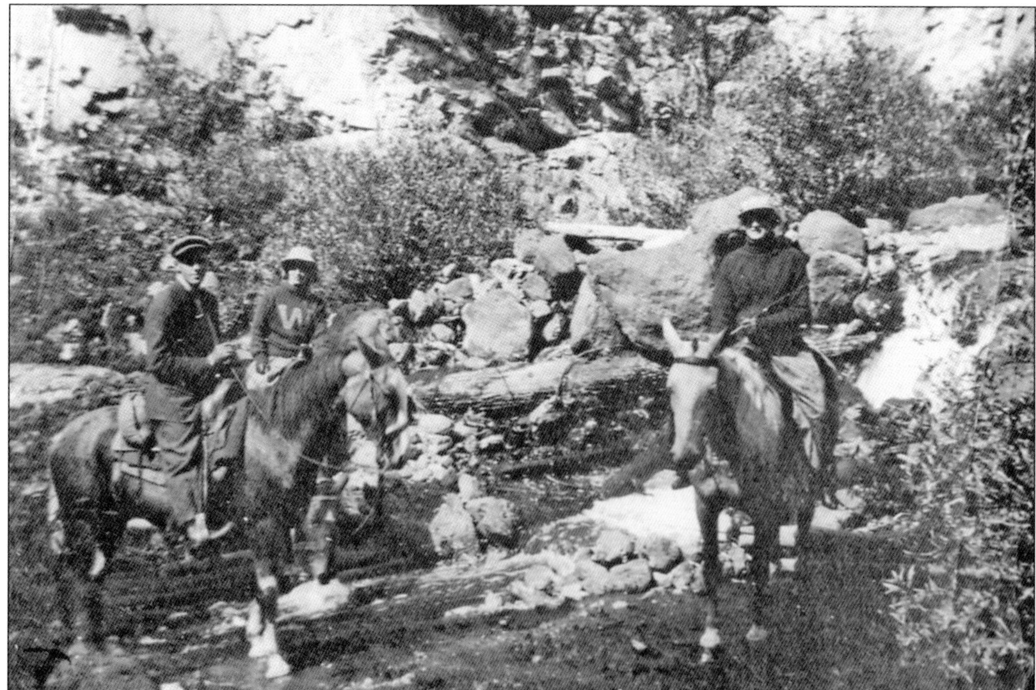

Bess, Rhoda, and a friend are on horseback with a stream flowing between them and bushes and a rock face in the background of the gorge near Mystic Lake. Horseback riding is a Montana tradition, and horses have been used by Native Americans, cowboys, farmers, and the students of MSU for recreation, work, and transportation for hundreds of years.

William M. Cobleigh eats at a picnic near the Gallatin River. The caption on the back of the photograph reads, "Mr. Cobleigh. Picnic grounds near Shedd's Bridge, West Gallatin." Cobleigh was an engineering professor, served as interim president of the university in 1942, and has Cobleigh Hall named in his honor.

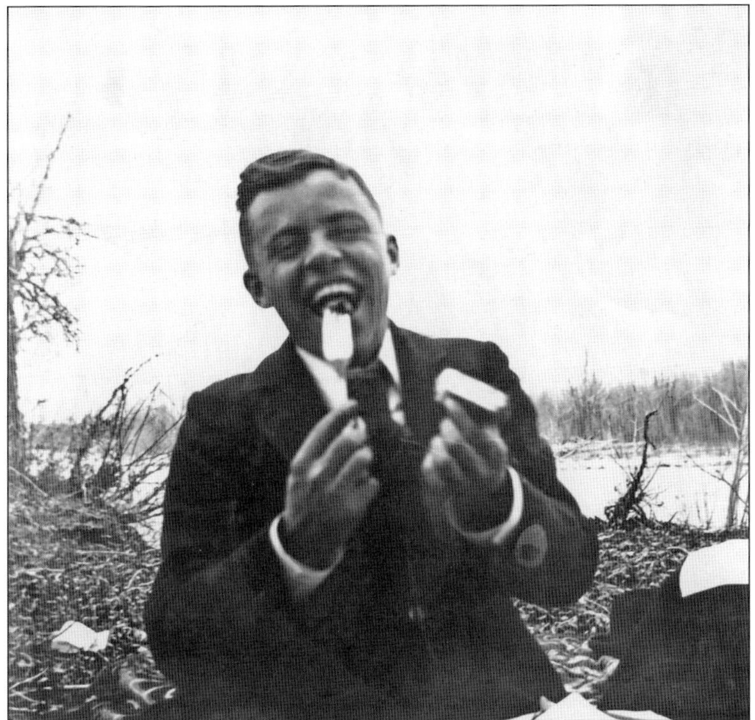

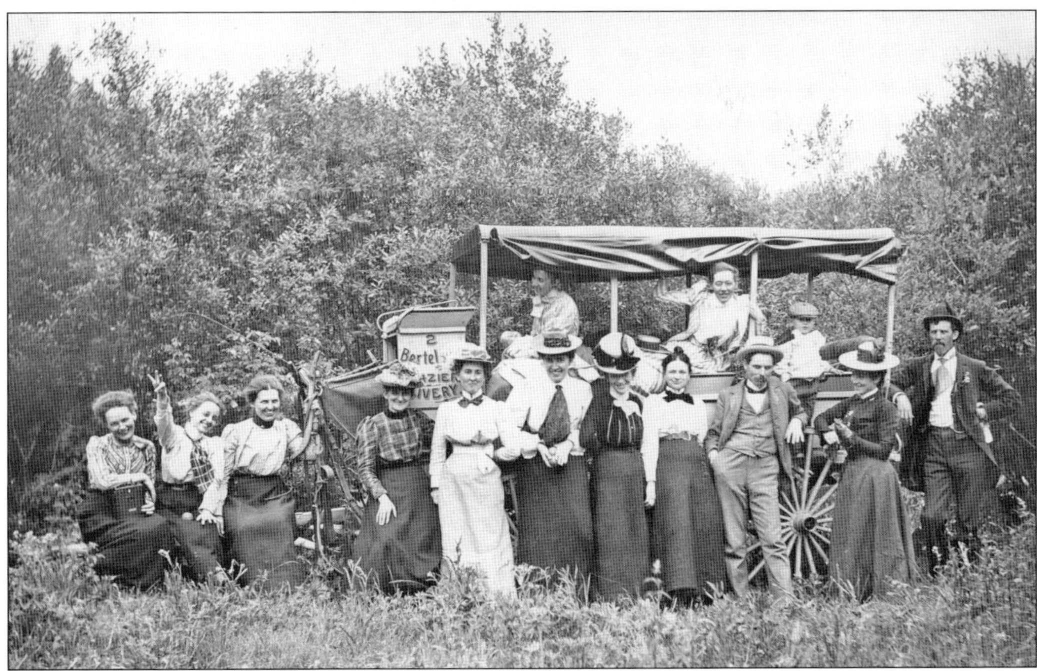

James R. Reid is pictured with several friends leaning against or sitting near a buggy. The caption on the photograph reads, "in wagon –, Mabel Hall (right), Paul Davidson (boy), –, Esther R. Cobleigh, Matty Gardner, Helen Brewer, Miss Cantwell, Lucy Ballinger Davidson, President James R. Reid, Frank Traphagan." Reid served as the second president of Montana State University from 1894 to 1904.

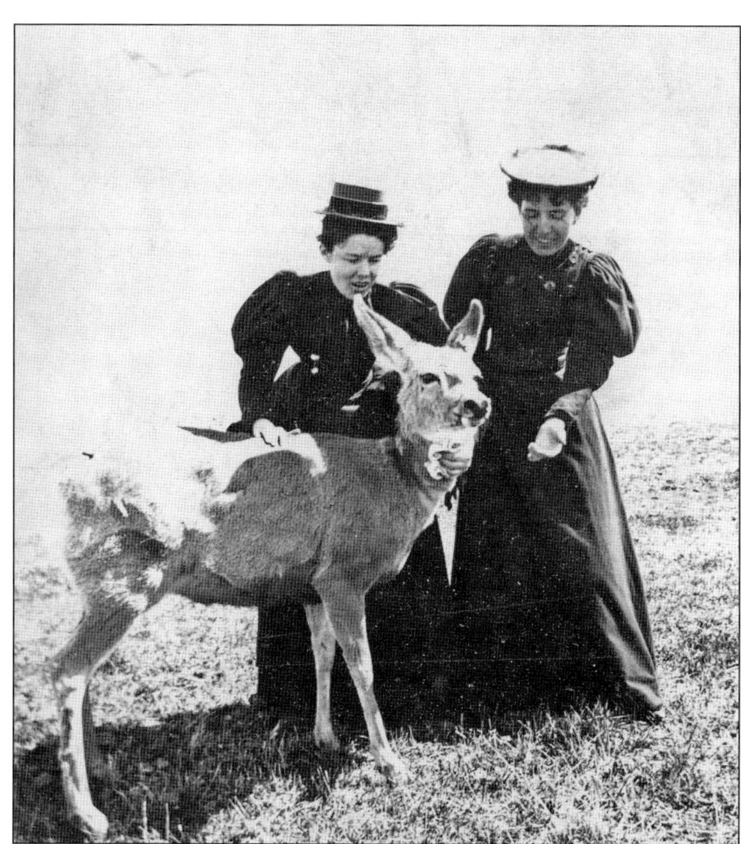

In this 1895 photograph, two women hold on to a deer. Abundant and diverse wildlife are one of the great natural resources of Montana. Black bears, moose, rattlesnakes, deer, foxes, coyotes, elks, antelopes, and a huge variety of birds can be seen around campus and on nearly every hike in the mountains and wild areas surrounding Bozeman.

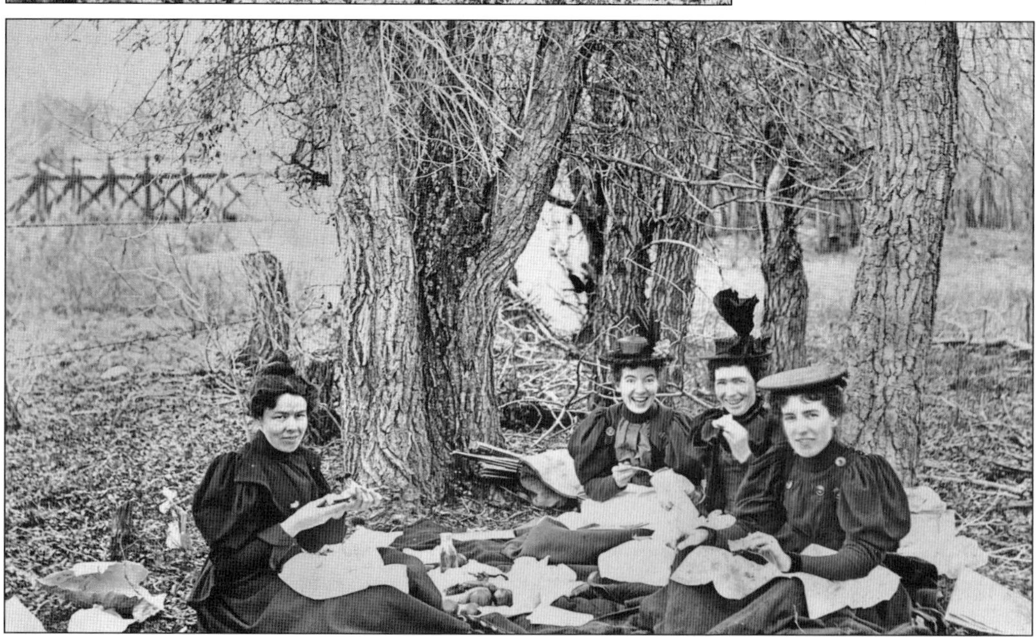

Four women enjoy a picnic near the West Gallatin River in approximately 1895. The Gallatin River joins the Jefferson and Madison Rivers near Three Forks to form the Missouri River. In the background is possibly Shedd's Bridge.

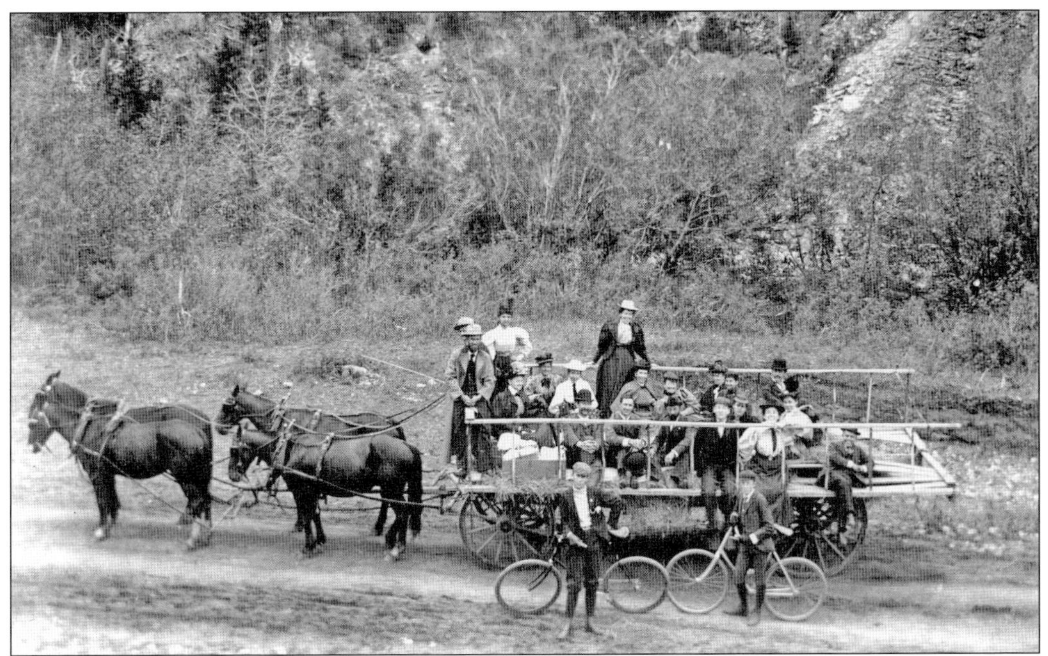

Outdoor activities were not just for students and staff; the university's faculty needed a chance to relax as well. This image shows attendees from an 1898 Montana State University faculty picnic. Individuals pictured are James R. Reid, William Cobleigh, William Brewer, Frank Traphagen, Mattie Gardner, and May Travis. (Photograph by Bozeman Camera Club.)

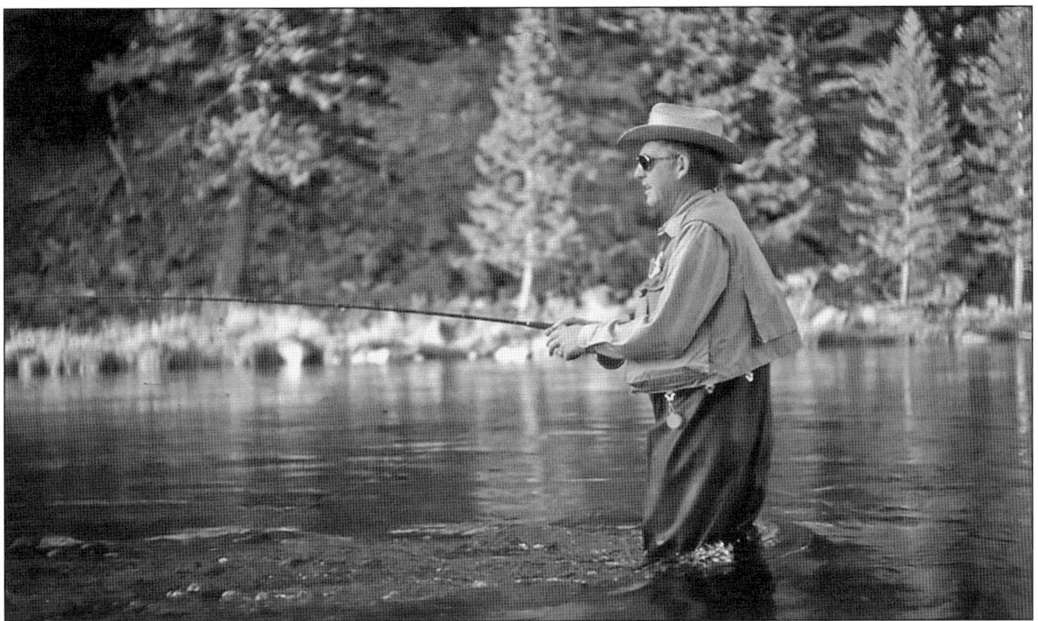

Alumnus of Montana State University and world-famous angler Bud Lilly makes a cast. Lilly went to MSU on the GI Bill after his service in the Navy during World War II. He was instrumental is starting the trout and salmonid special collection at MSU, which has grown into the world's largest collection of materials on the species. MSU is also the home of the Bud Lilly Archival Collections.

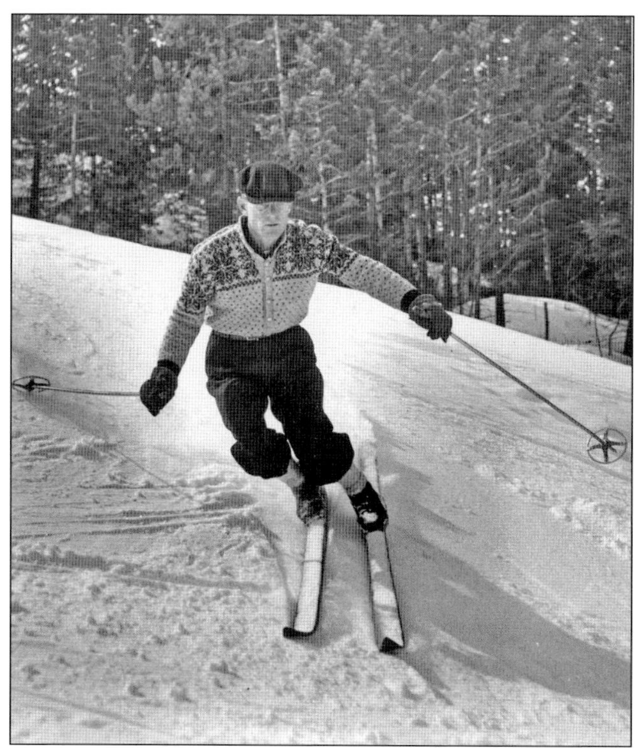

Robert S. Beck was a professor of physical education and health and coached the ski and golf teams. Beck is pictured taking a turn on the slope. Skiing is popular around Bozeman, and several destinations are nearby, including Bridger Bowl, Big Sky, and Moonlight Basin. There are also hundreds of miles of trails in the area for cross-country skiing. (Photograph by MSU Office of Information.)

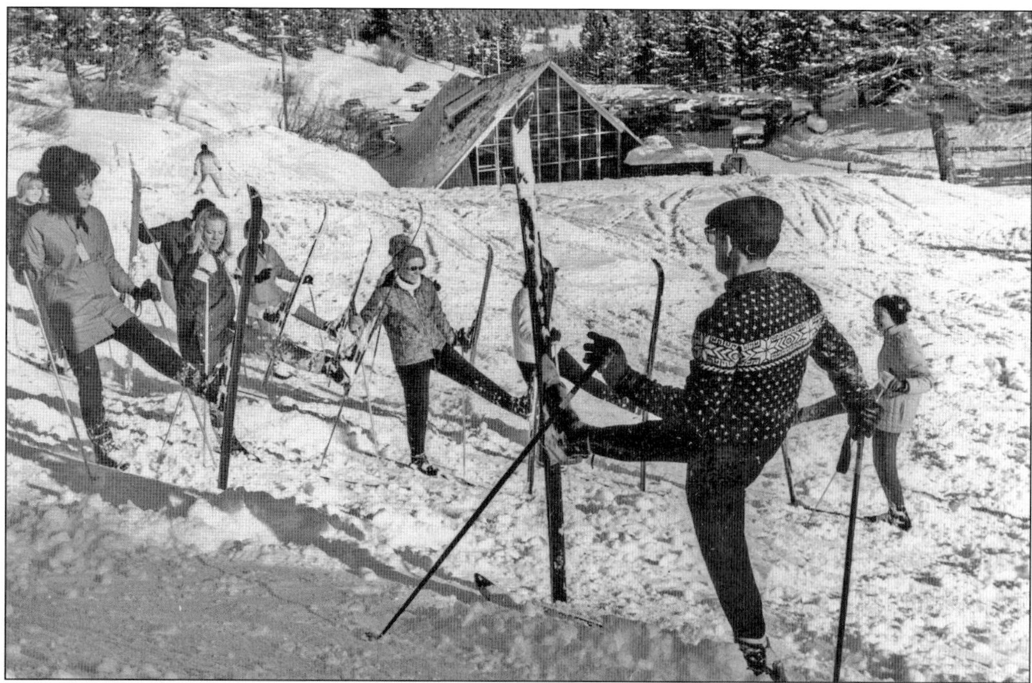

A group of students learn to ski. Montana State University has men's and women's ski teams and an Alpine Skiing Student Club that competes in intercollegiate ski competitions around the Western United States. MSU students get discounts on local ski passes, and the local Streamline bus even offers a route from campus to Bridger Bowl.

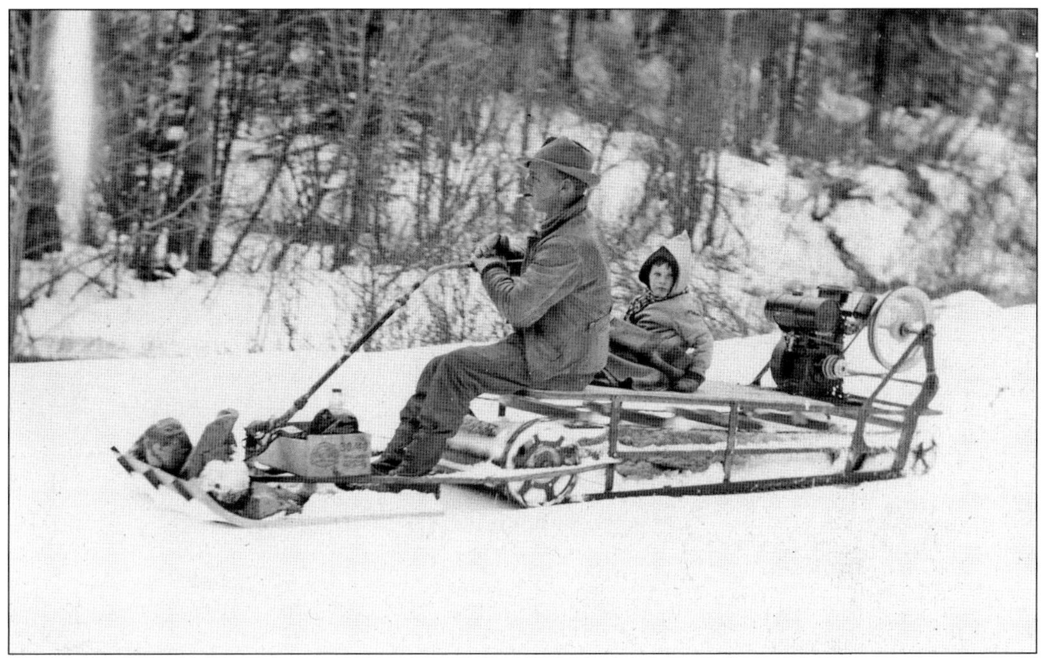

A man and child ride an early version of a snowmobile at Hyalite Canyon in the spring of 1945. Snowmobiling is a popular activity in Montana, and while largely recreational, it is a mode of winter travel used by some more perseverant residents to access mountain homes in the depths of winter.

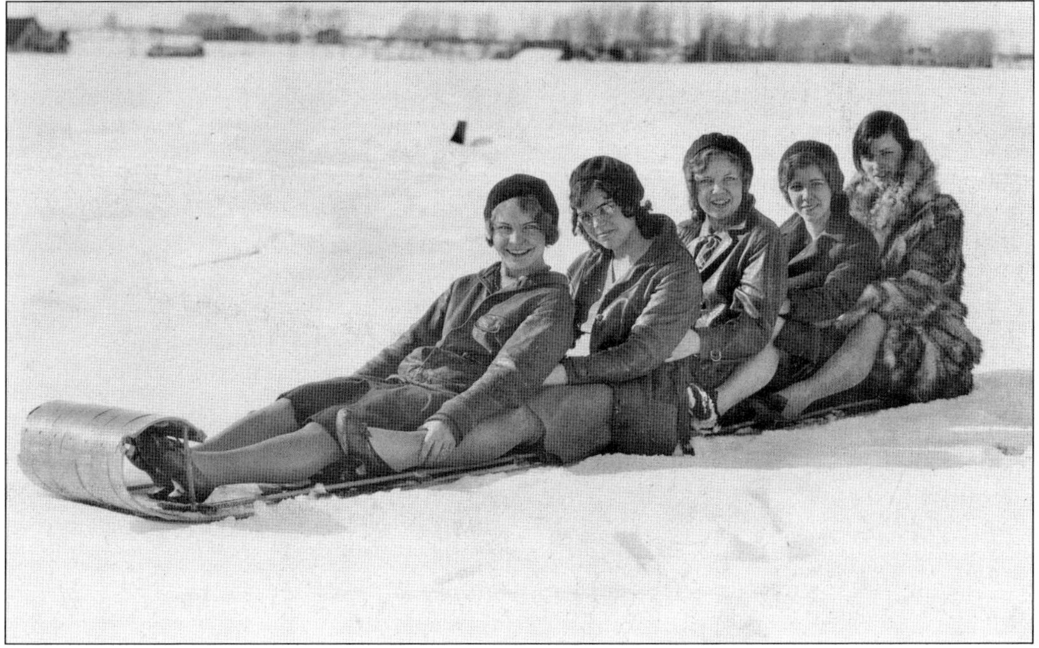

A group of young women ride a sled in the winter of 1931. Sledding opportunities surround campus and the Bozeman area. A popular local destination for sledding, as well as dog walking, hiking, and jogging, is Peets Hill on the east side of town. For the more adventurous, some local ski hills also offer opportunities for sledding.

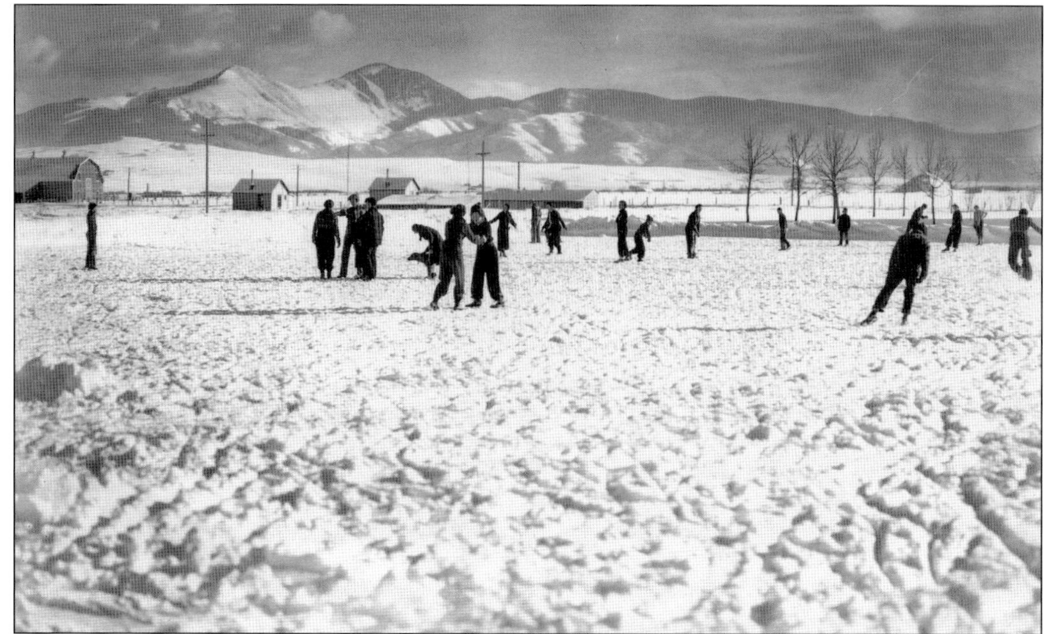

Students ice skate on a local pond. Winter sports are a mainstay of life in Montana. The season can be long and there is always a chance of a snowball fight or building a snowman in the middle of summer, as snow storms have been recorded during all 12 months of the year.

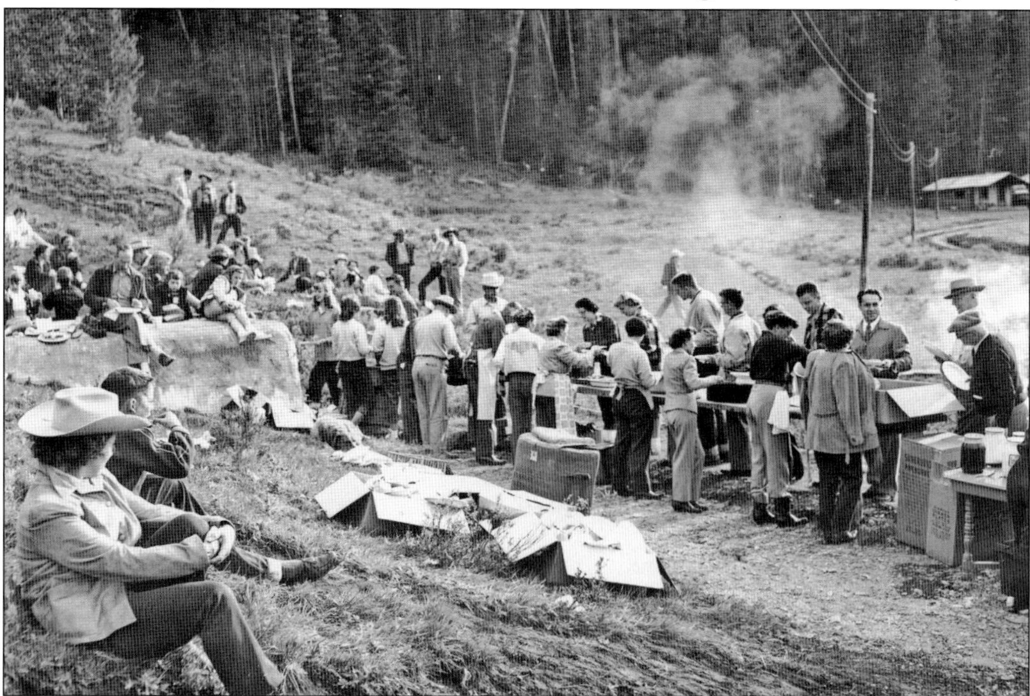

Men, women, and children attend a summer school picnic. They are enjoying a buffet-style lunch and relaxing in the sunshine. Note the number of individuals sporting cowboy hats. A cooler, possibly containing some ice cream for dessert from Kessler Dairy in Bozeman, can be seen near center behind those serving the meal.

Even successful poultry experts need a little downtime when they can explore the great outdoors and have a cup of coffee. Harriette E. Cushman was the poultry specialist for Montana State University from 1922 to 1955. She was one of the nation's few women specialists in agriculture and provided valuable knowledge and expertise on poultry raising to the extension service.

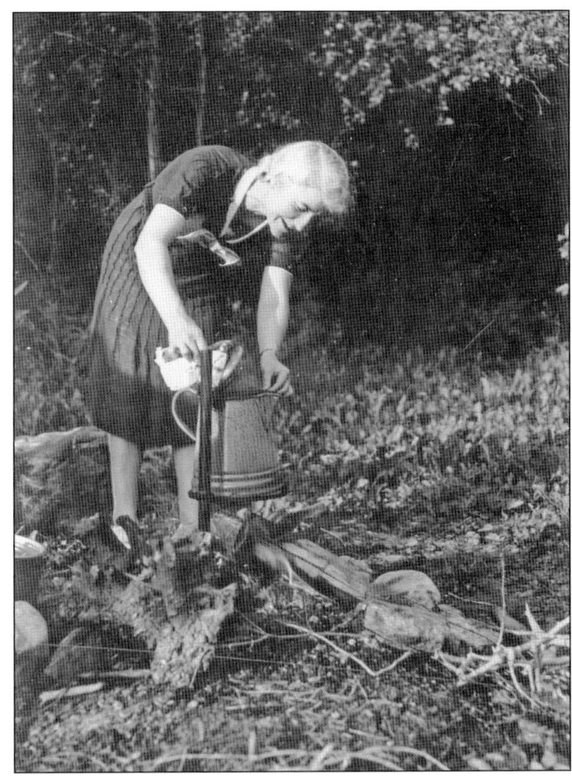

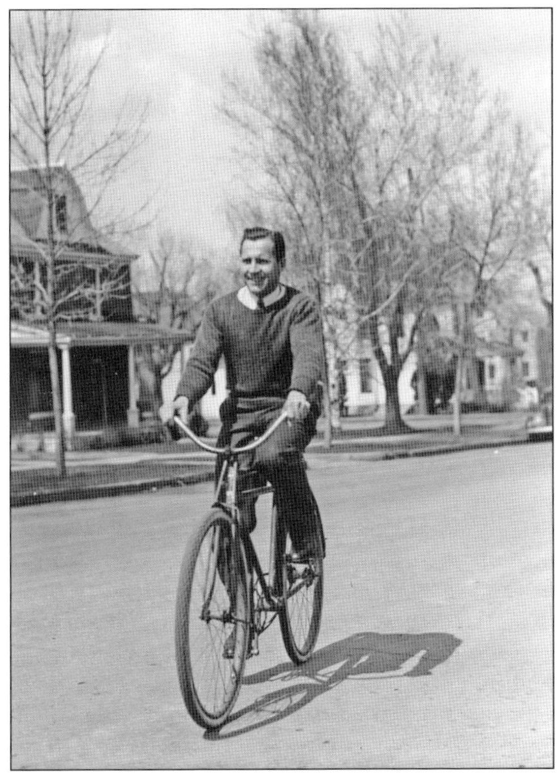

Roland R. Renne rides his bicycle in Bozeman. Renne was an agricultural economics professor and served as president of what was then Montana State College. He left the university to work for the federal government, where he served in many positions, including as assistant secretary of agriculture for international affairs. Renne Library is named in his honor.

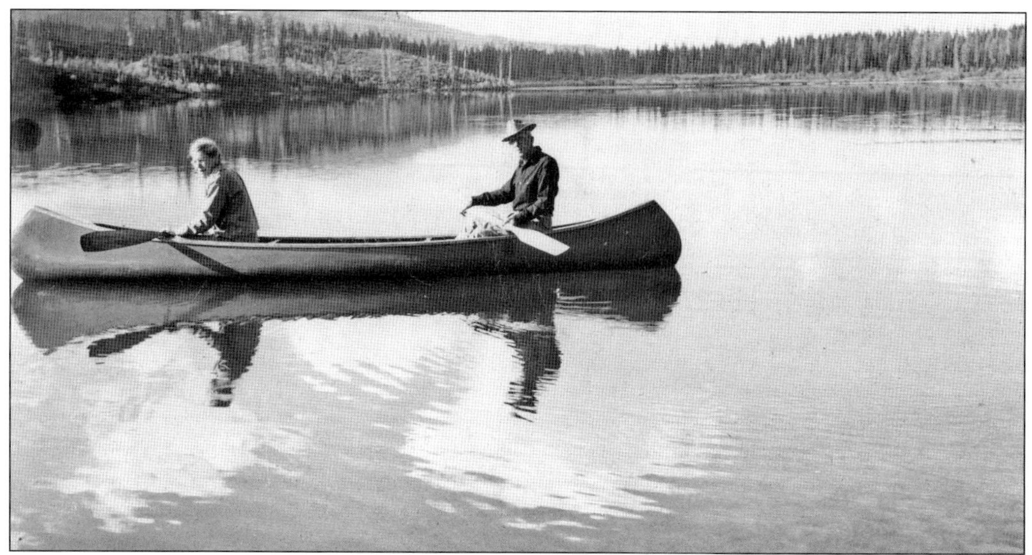

Gertrude Roskie is pictured in a canoe at Seeley Lake, Montana, in 1947. Canoeing, boating, swimming, and other water sports are popular summer activities for students and all Montana residents. Roskie Residence Hall was built in 1966 and is named for Gertrude Roskie. She was an instructor in home economics, head of the Home Economics Department, and later dean of the professional schools.

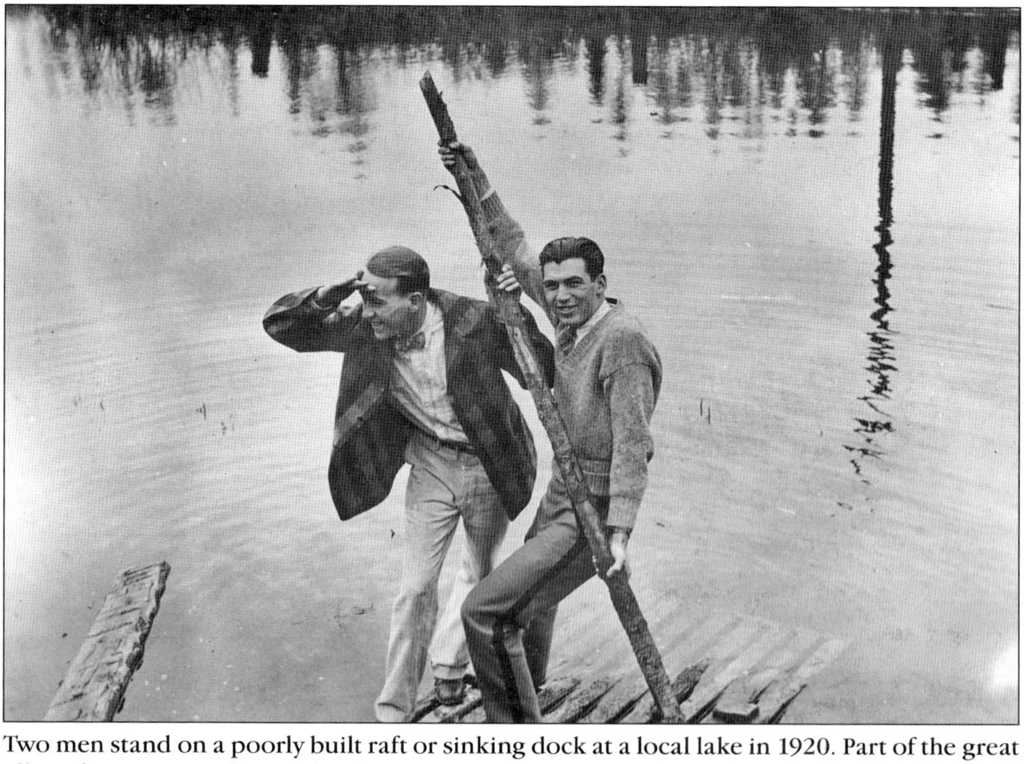

Two men stand on a poorly built raft or sinking dock at a local lake in 1920. Part of the great allure for many students who choose to study at MSU is its beautiful location high in the Rocky Mountains. Parks, state and national forests, and national parks like Yellowstone and Glacier are used and enjoyed by the student body.

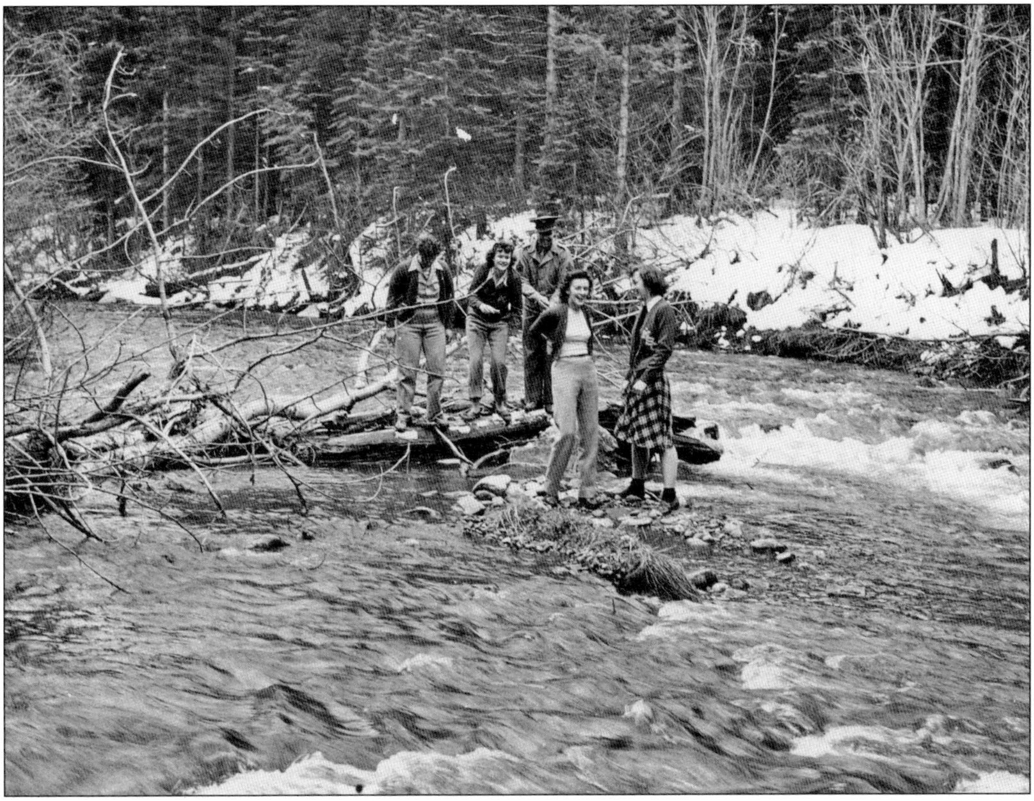

Five students enjoy a local river in 1940. Rafting, swimming, fishing, tubing, hiking, bird watching, canoeing, and kayaking are all popular local activities for students. This photograph was likely taken in the early spring or fall, based on the snow and the flow of the river.

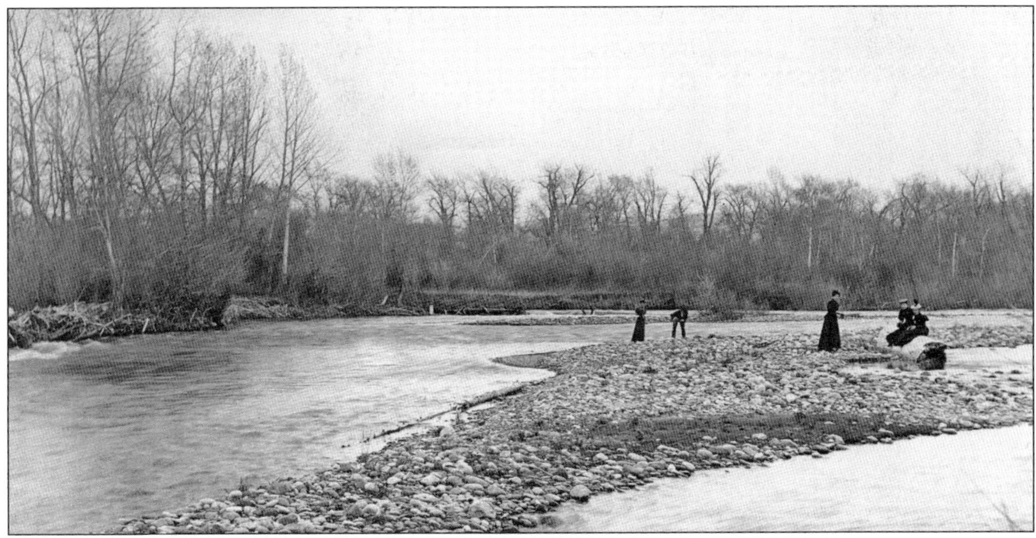

A group of friends hang out on a rocky bar in the middle of the Gallatin River in 1895. The river starts its journey in Yellowstone National Park and flows approximately 30 miles west of Bozeman to help form the Missouri River. The Gallatin was named in July 1805 by Meriwether Lewis for Albert Gallatin, the US treasury secretary from 1801 to 1814.

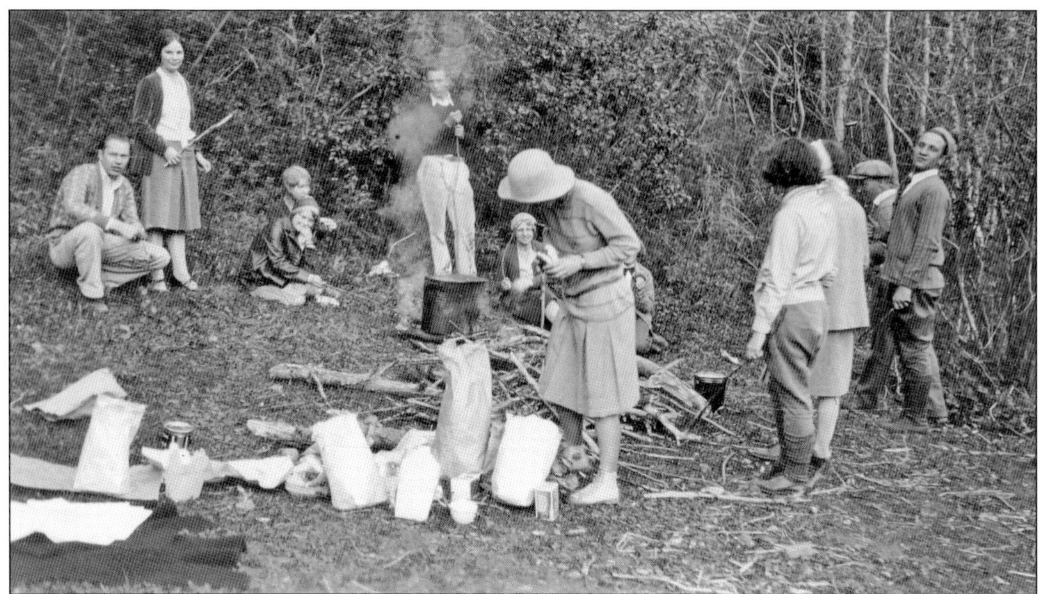

A group of Art Club students enjoy a meal around a campfire in June 1930. They are roasting hotdogs on sticks and making some sort of deliciousness in a large pot. Camping is a popular activity for MSU students. There are camp sites, national forests, state parks, and of course, Yellowstone National Park all within reach for a weekend camping trip.

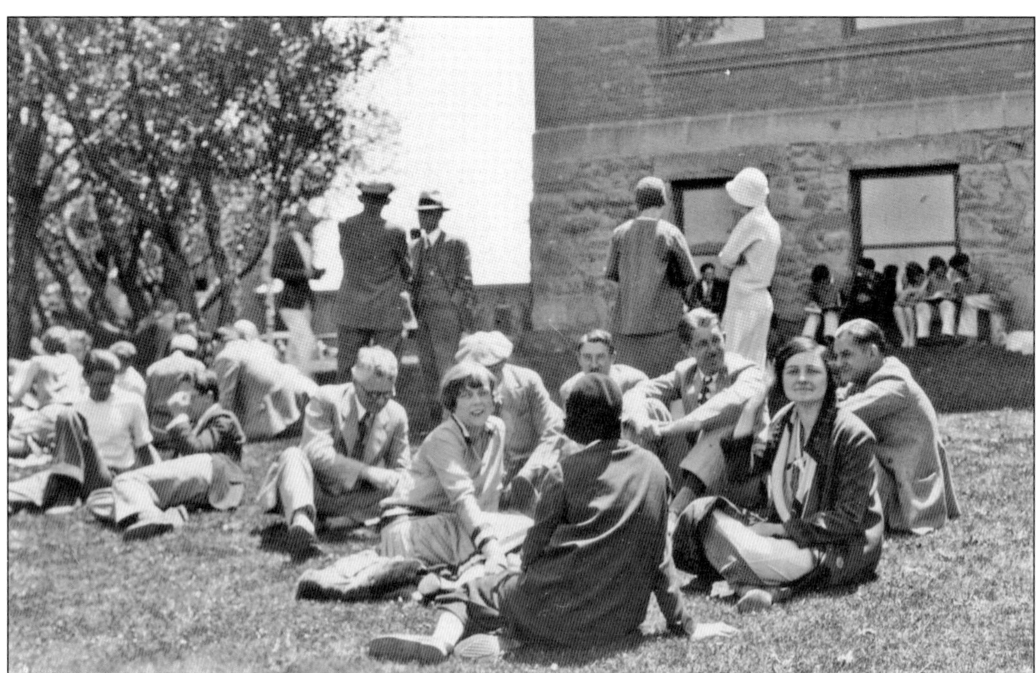

A group of students enjoy a picnic on the lawn just outside Montana Hall. Montana State University still hosts annual picnics, barbecues, and other events using the green space surrounding campus. On a nice fall or spring day, it is not uncommon for a professor to move class to a sunny spot outside.

Seven

Montana State University Student Life and Groups

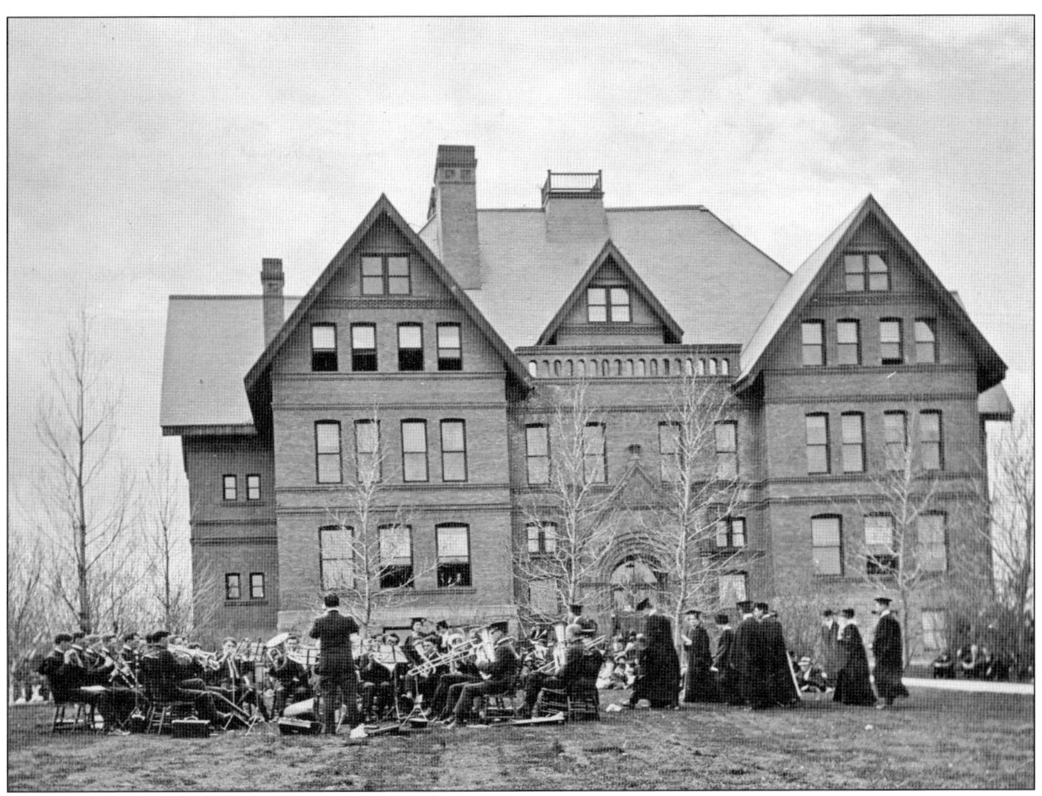

In the 1920s, Montana State University's band was led by Lou Howard, who worked tirelessly to improve the music program and ensure that his band played a variety of roles on campus from concerts and dances to athletic events. In this image, the band can be seen performing its semiannual concert on the lawn outside Montana Hall in 1920.

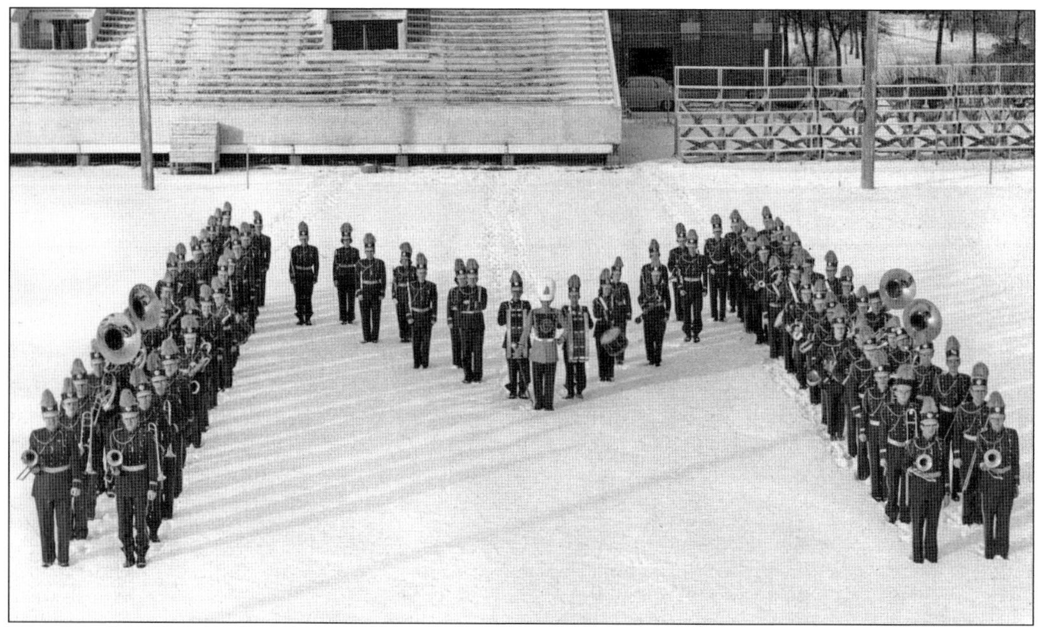

Colorful halftime shows add pep and vigor to Montana State University football game halftime shows. In this image, the MSU Bobcat marching band stands in an *M* formation on a snow-covered Gatton Field in 1968. Membership in the marching band provides students with the opportunity for hands-on application of classroom experience and participation in a rewarding extracurricular activity.

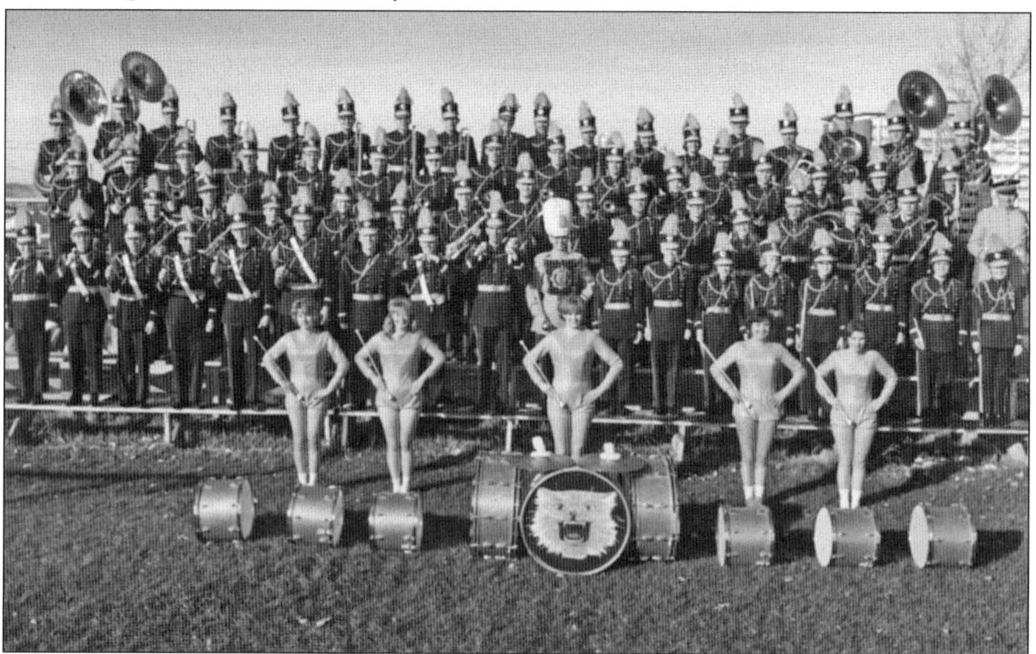

Practice makes perfect, and when MSU's marching band, led by Ed Sedivy, performed in the 1960s, they added flair to Bobcat football games and halftime entertainments, homecoming, and Armed Forces Day. In this 1966 image, the Montana State University Bobcat marching band poses on bleachers, with Hedges South visible in the background.

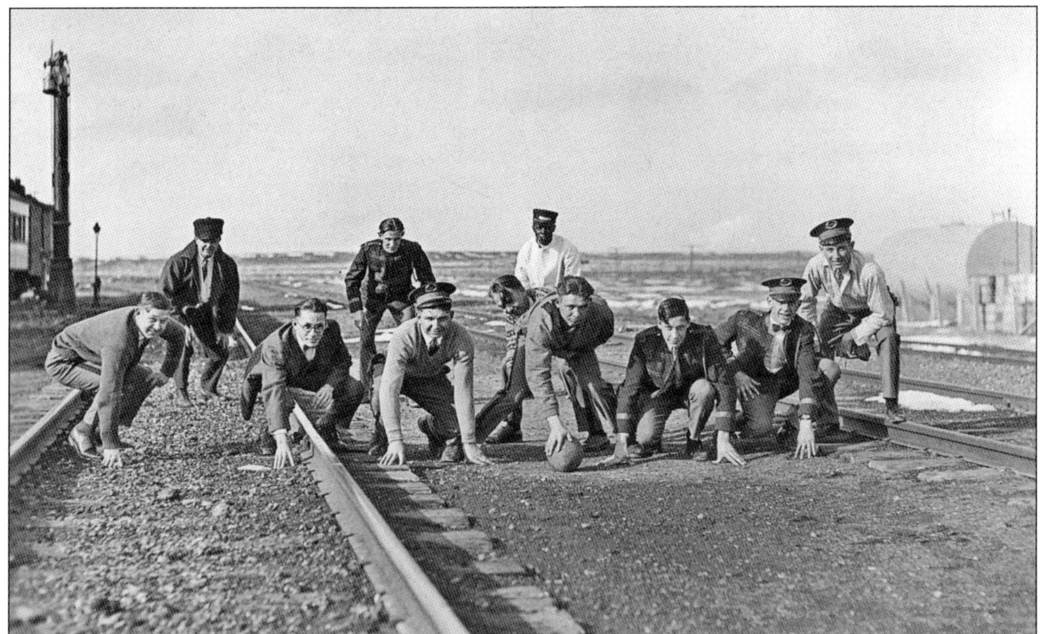

Taking time to relax during their annual tour, the members of the Bobcat band look ready to play a quick game of football in the 1920s. Each year, the band would tour Montana to perform concerts in various locales to generate awareness and encourage donations that helped maintain the program.

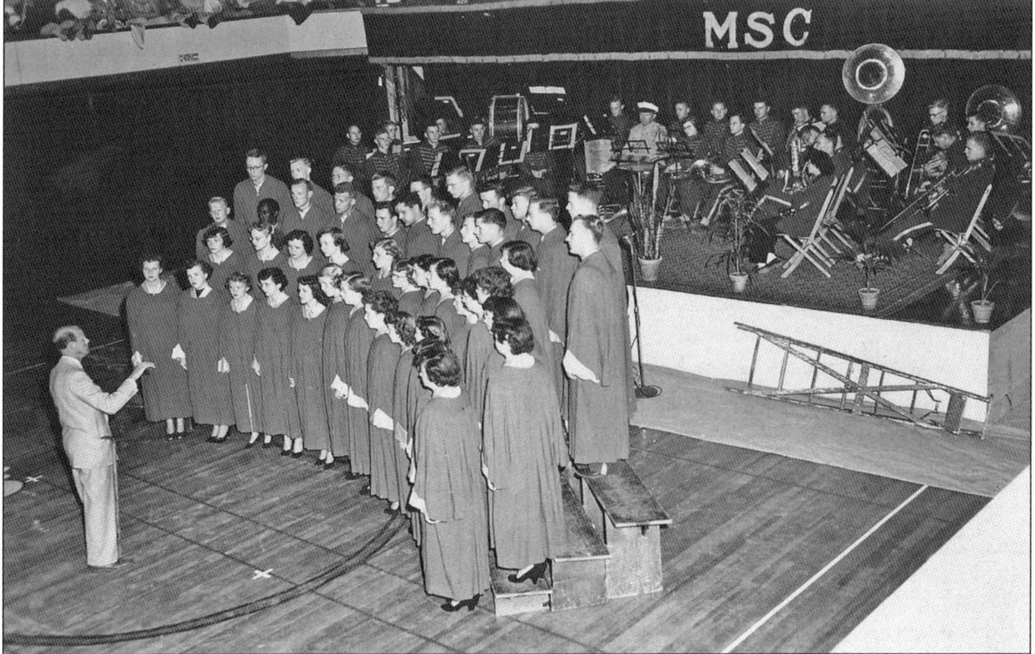

In the 1920s and 1930s, Romney Gymnasium offered avenues of opportunity for more than indoor sports. In this image from that time, several members of the Montana State College Chorus are intent on observing their conductor as he directs their actions from the floor, with the orchestra seated on the stage behind them.

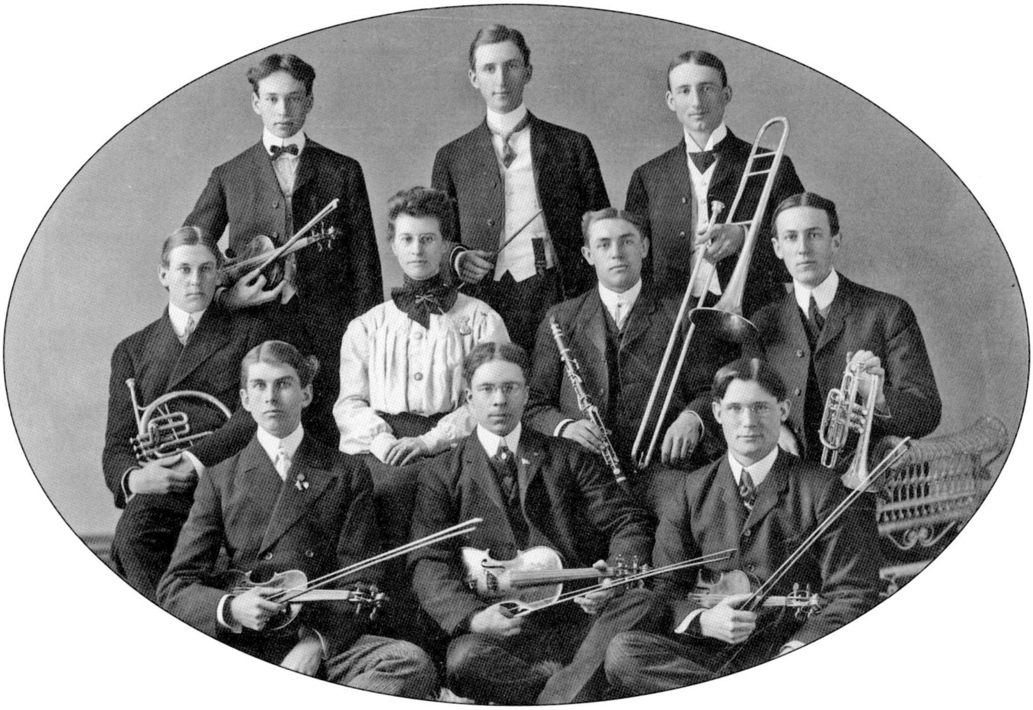

Organized in 1904, the then–Montana State College Orchestra was composed of seven men and one woman. From left to right are (first row) Charles M. Fisher, W.S. Bole, and unidentified; (second row) J. Wilbur Robinson, Macey Nelson, Clyde C. Penwell, and Charles C. Backes; (third row, standing) Lawrence Eukes, D. Earl Evans, and Stanley Yergey.

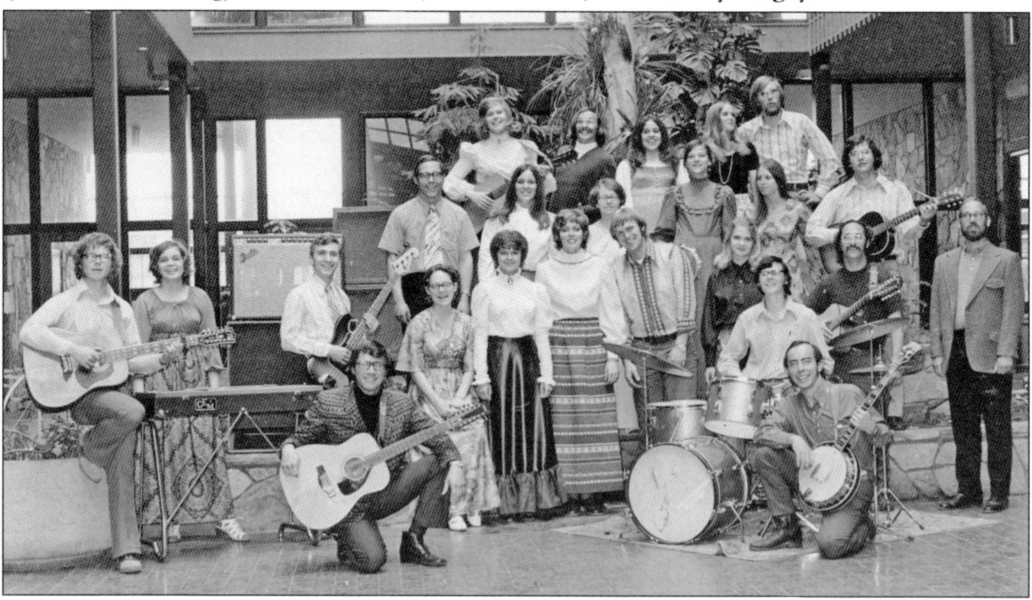

Montana State University's New Genesis singing group was sponsored by the Ecumenical Campus Ministries. In 1972, the group traveled across Montana and Idaho to introduce the folk-rock sound. Seen here are several members with their leader, Jack Jennings, kneeling with his guitar in front of the keyboard.

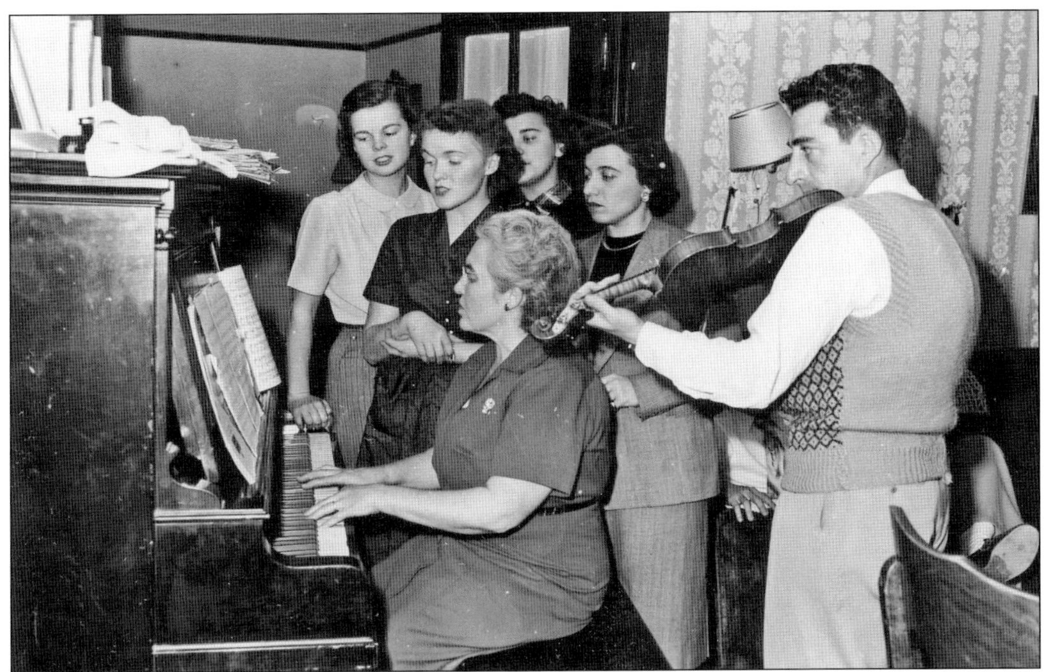

Opportunities in the 1950s abounded for hearing live music, ranging from concerts and recitals to informal entertainments and musical events. In this image, a group of female foreign students gather to sing accompanied by a young man playing the violin and a woman playing the piano.

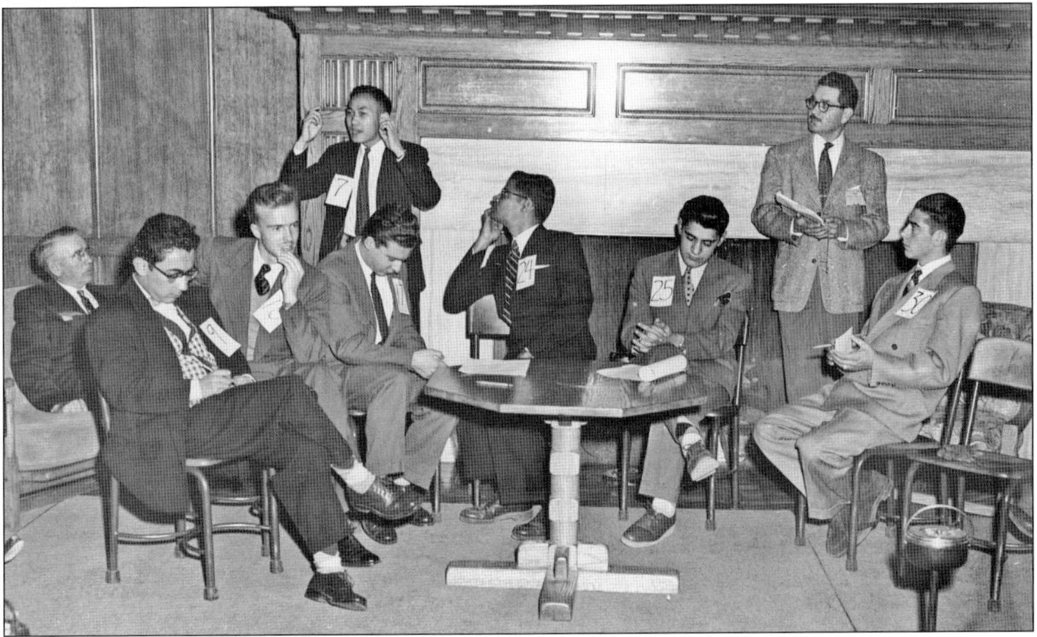

Encouraging students to enroll at Montana State University provides the opportunity for campus-wide enrichment through the diverse cultures and traditions of other nations. In 1952, a group of male international students are pictured in the Leigh Lounge at the Strand Union Building.

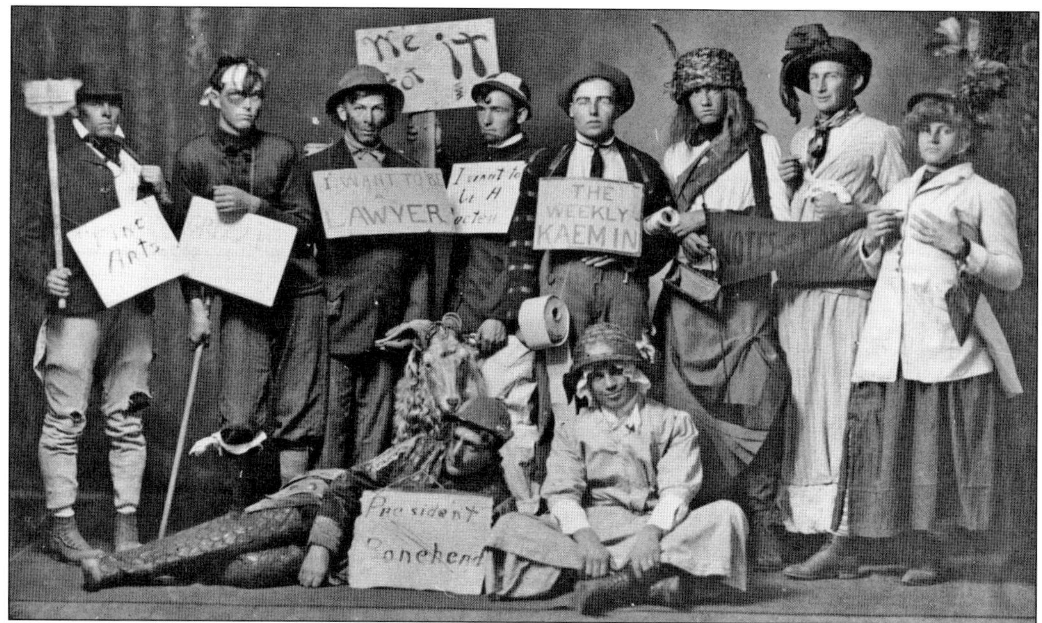

For the MSU football team, pranks were not limited to the field. Sometime between 1900 and 1916, these "Aggie" boys dressed up in costumes and posed with a goat before a game in Missoula. From left to right, team members are (first row) Floyd Crittenden and Hubert Rice; (second row) Fred Bullock, Ray Dunean, Don Langhor, Whit Manning, Arthur Fox, Bob Kelly, Russell Jackman, and Manfred Snow.

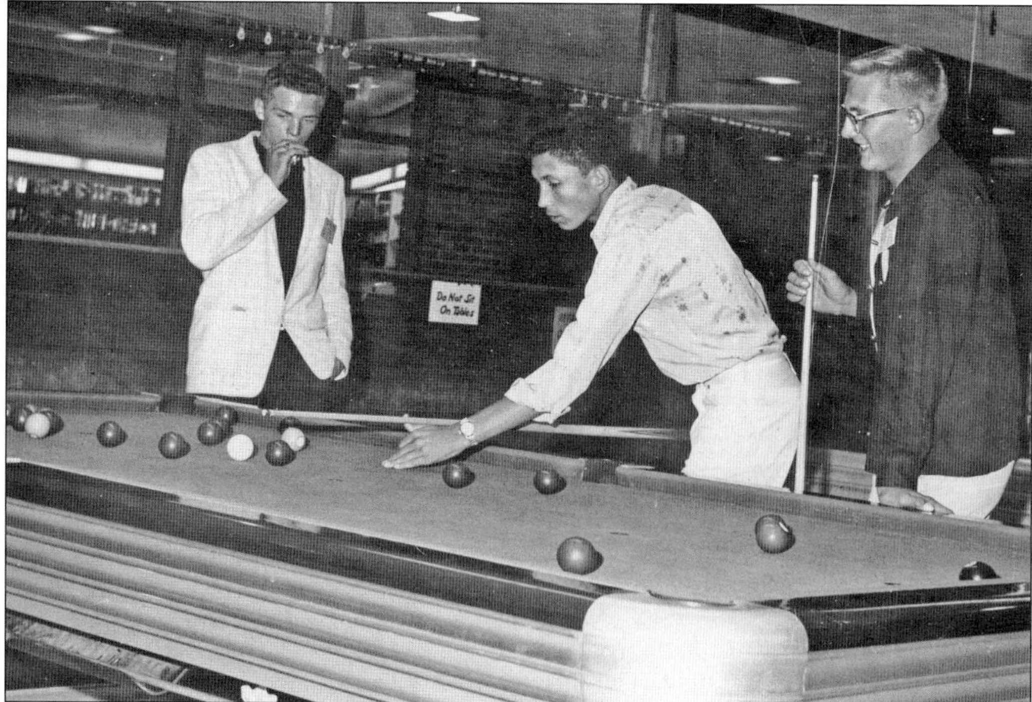

Taking time to enjoy good conversation and some downtime from 4-H activities, these three young men enjoy a game of pool in the 1960s.

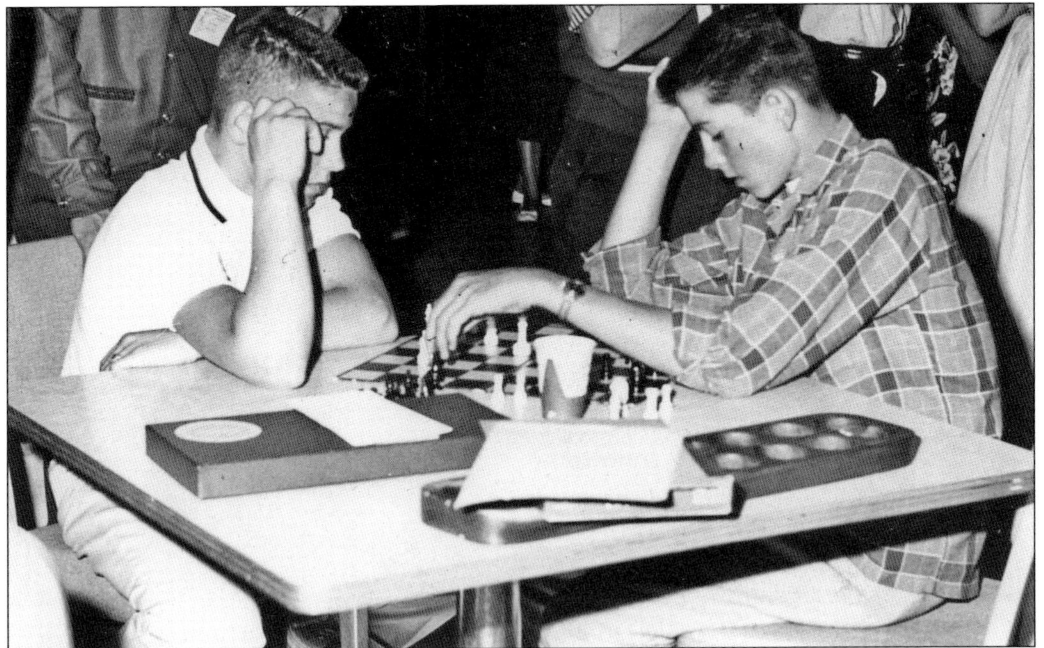

Players use skill and strategy to attack and capture opposing pieces during chess, and according to the April 3, 1979, *Exponent*, chess provides the player with the opportunity to learn more than winning. Contemplating one of a myriad of combinations, these two young men take time away from the different programs at a 4-H congress to play a game at the Book Lounge in 1961.

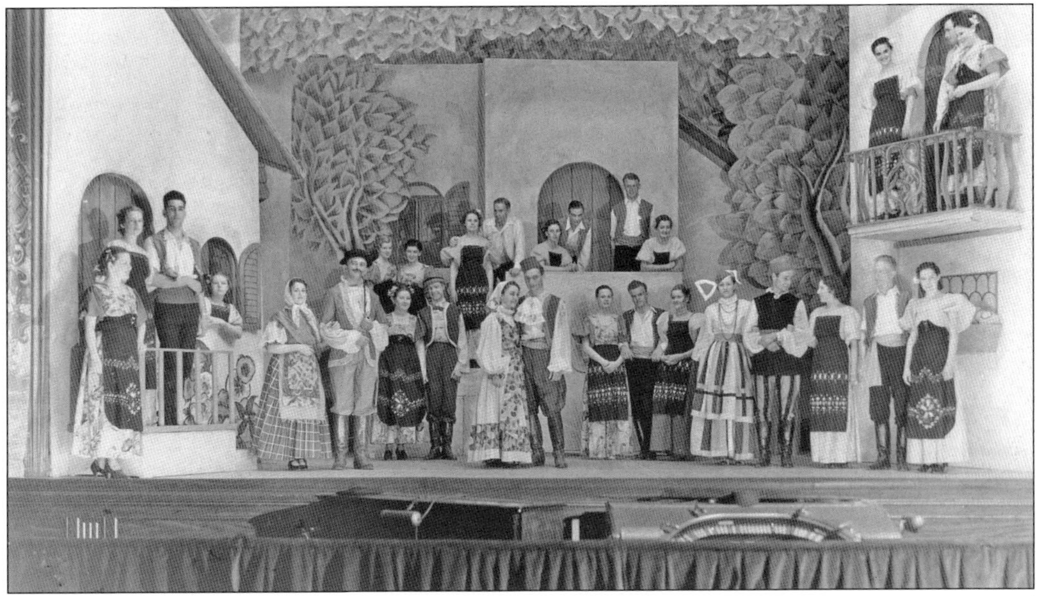

According to the *Montanan*, the Dramatics' performances of three plays during the 1935–1936 academic year were "outstanding." This image portrays the cast of *The Bartered Bride*, which was the last play of the season in 1936. Cast members included Lester Willson, Brownie Greene, Robert Hyink, Jean Durland, James Finn, Lillie Mae Hellen, Charles Heidel, Jack Boetcher, Ed Exum, and George Sime.

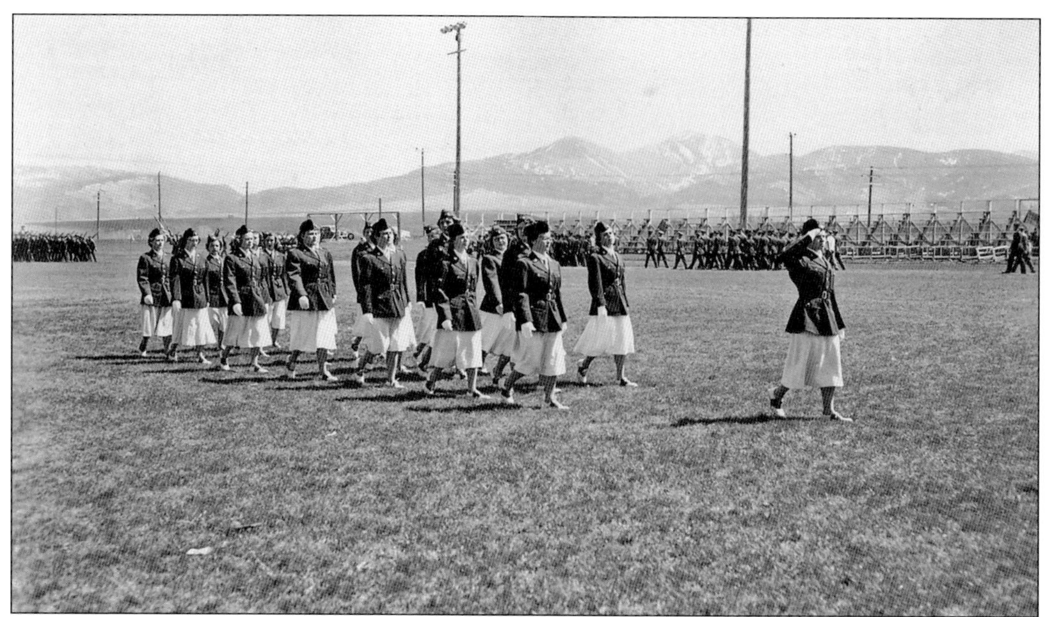

Military science and tactics in World War II were not just for young men; the armed forces also offered women the chance to serve their country. In this 1944 image, several young Women's Army Auxiliary Corps cadets march and drill in an open field with the male ROTC cadets in the background.

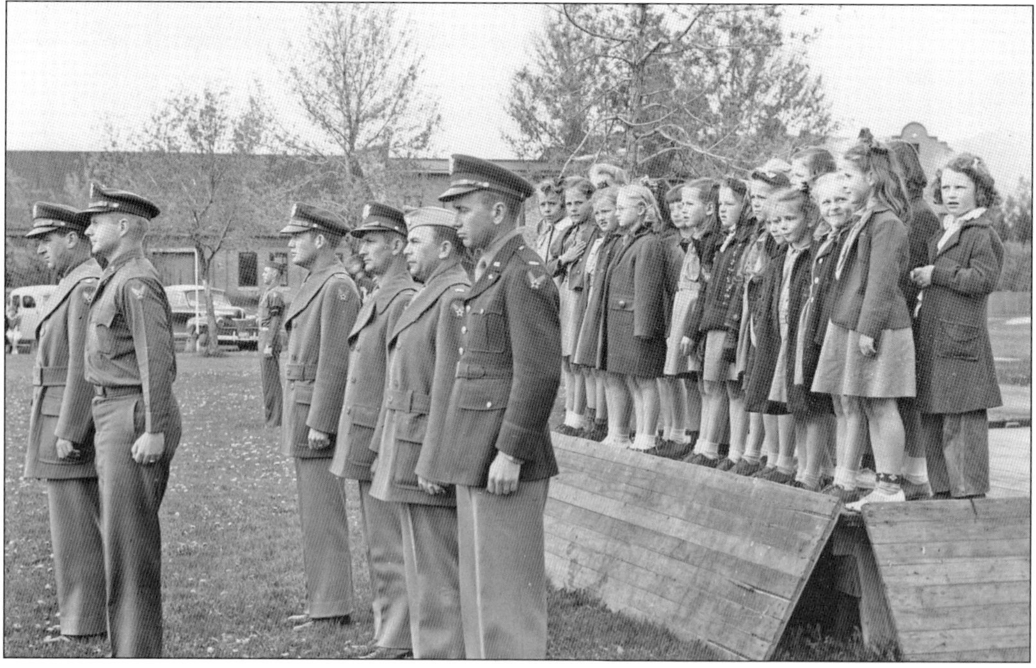

Support comes in all shapes and sizes. Here, several children stand behind a group of ROTC cadets in 1944. Individuals successfully completing courses in military science for four years could be commissioned as second lieutenants of infantry in the Organized Reserve Corps on the support and recommendation of the university president and the professor of military science.

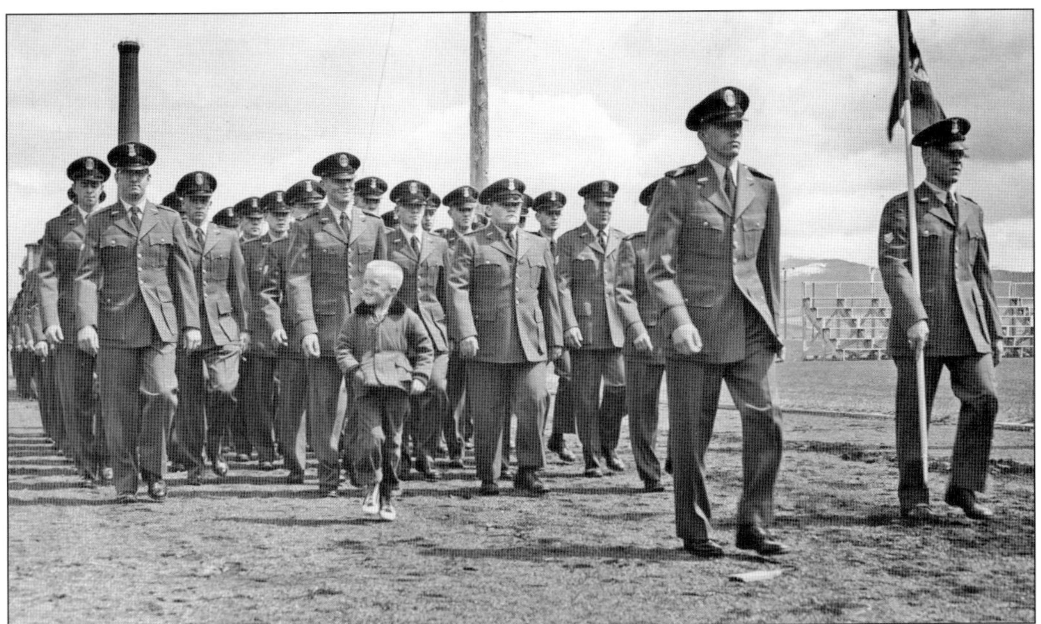

Emulation is one of the sincerest forms of flattery. In this 1944 image, a young boy marches with the ROTC cadets. Montana State University was designated by the War Department as a higher-education institution with the provision for maintenance of ROTC. The courses in military science and tactics included two years in military drill and instruction.

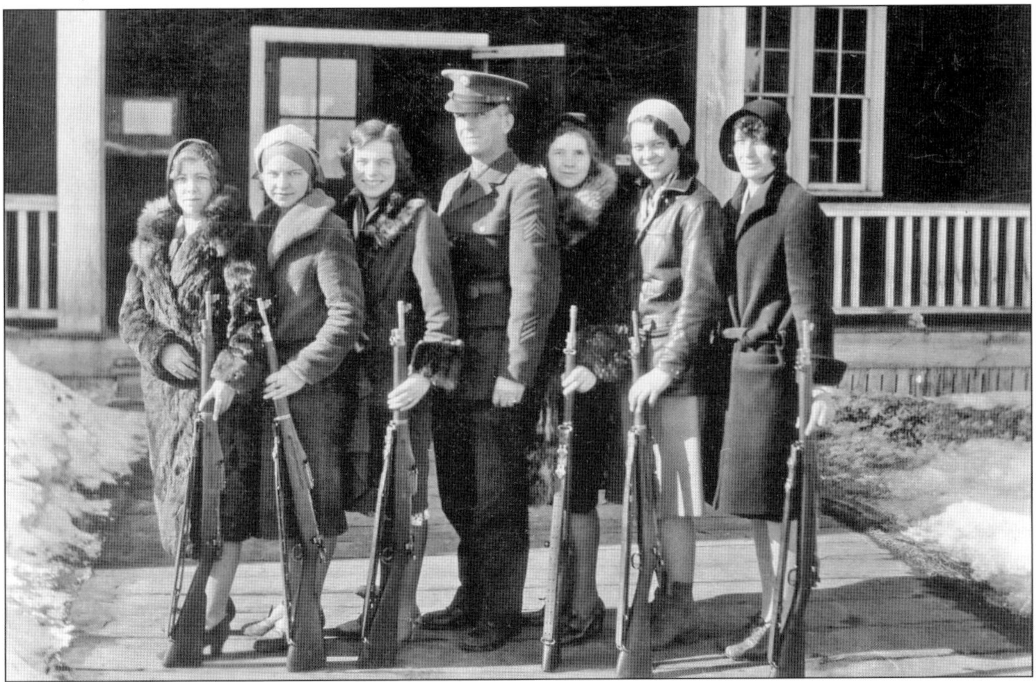

Competitive shooting provides tests of accuracy and speed with firearms against targets. In the 1930s, Montana State College boasted not only a men's rifle team but a women's team as well. Members of this 1931 team include Margaret Aakjer, Helen Albrecht, May E. Boyd, Mildred Erb, and Leone Lynn.

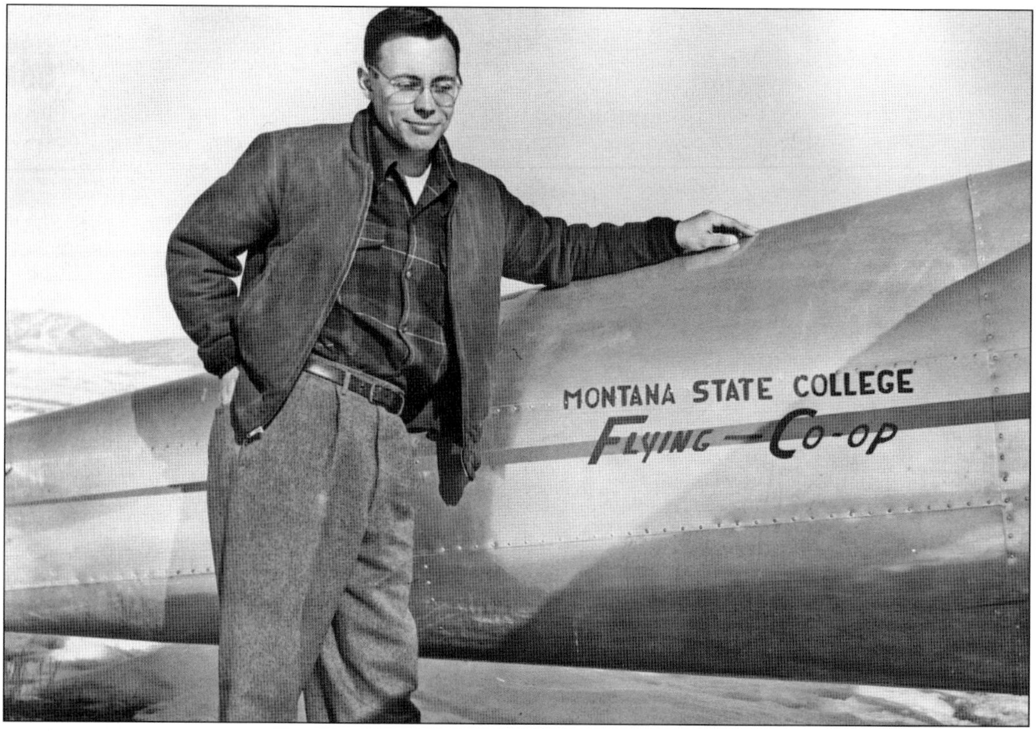

In the early 1960s, the Flying Bobcats were chartered to provide Montana State College students with the opportunity to learn to fly at low rates. The group belonged to the National Intercollegiate Flying Association and met to compete with other amateur-sponsored flying groups. In this c. 1960–1964 image, a man stands next to the MSC Flying Co-Op plane.

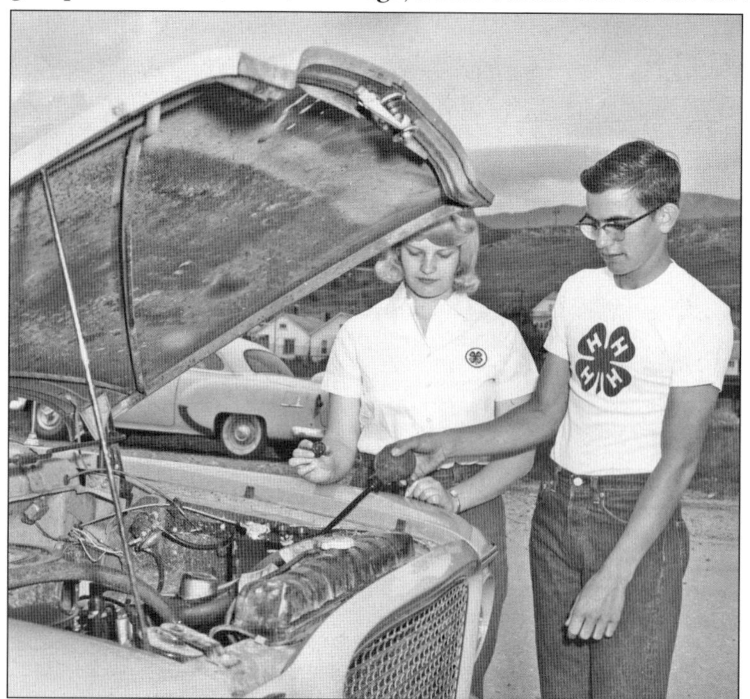

The 4-H youth education program of the Montana Cooperative Extension Service provides useful skill sets to youth. In this 1960s image, Judy Rintala and Jerome Besel from Silesia, Montana, learn how to check a car battery as well as how to add water to it.

Patty Crow, from Roberts, Montana, removes a loaf she baked as part of her 4-H breadmaking project in the 1960s. Crow's project demonstrates the 4-H mission in acquiring life skills through food production, health, and nutrition. (Photograph by Allison Lighthall Photographers.)

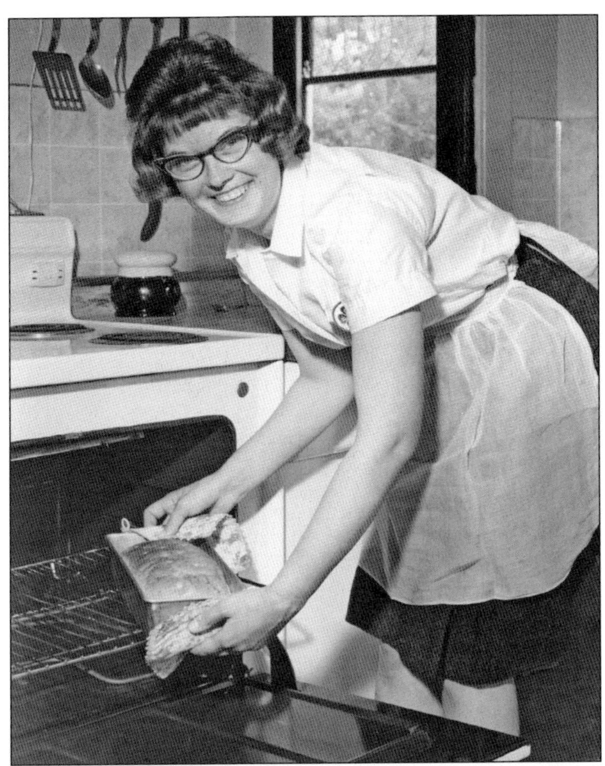

Phi Gamma had a busy year in 1919, with activities that varied from feeding "Prexy" (James M. Hamilton), hosting a dance, and hosting an auction. Members included in this image are Helen Lund, Marjory Quaw, Marie Bunnell, Ruth Noble, Dorothy Mills, Frances Kyle, Florence Noble, Dorothy Powell, Evelyn Watnerman, Josephine Kuntze, Stella Solberg, Lucile Monforton, Marie Waterman, Pauline Powell, Florence Switzer, Florence Wesch, and Edith Stanley.

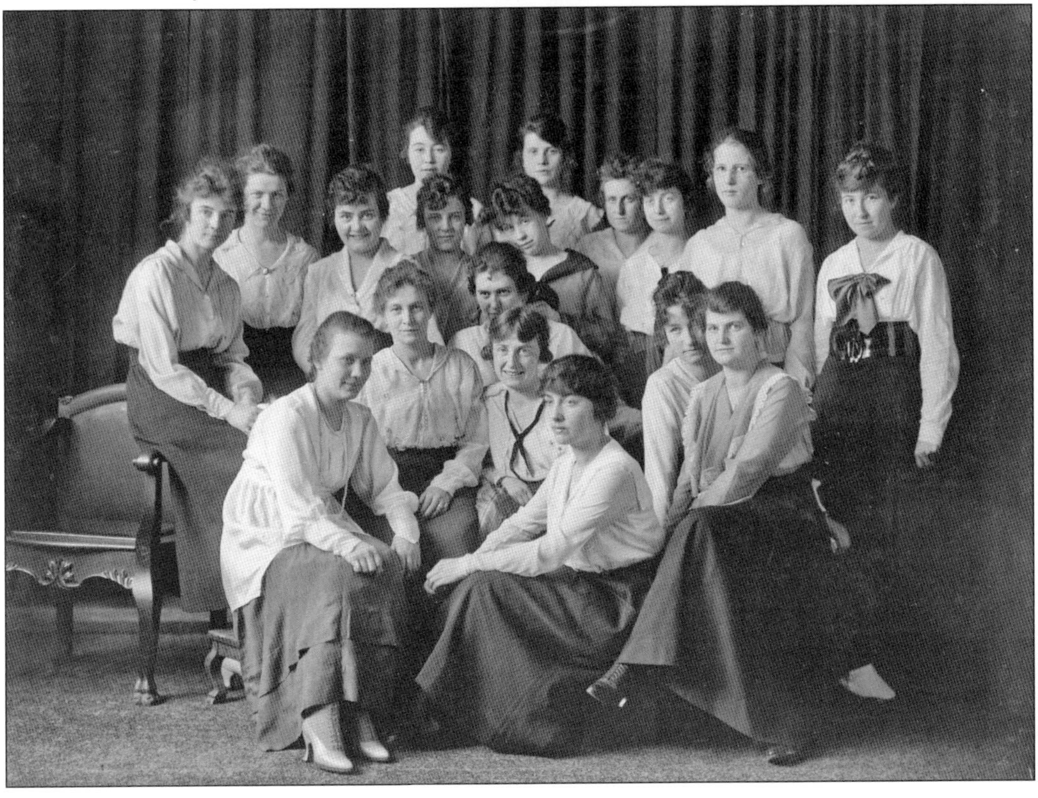

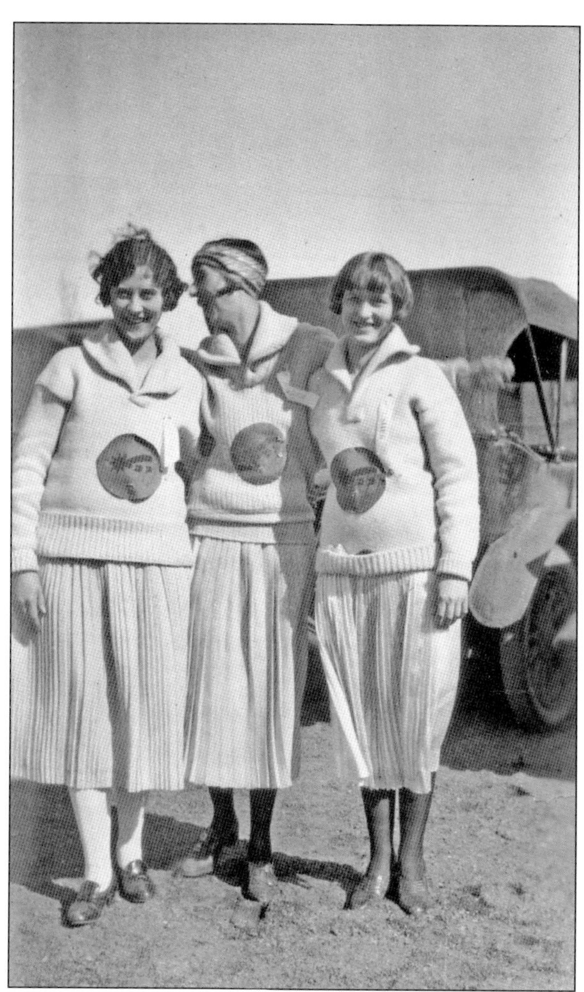

Montana State University's local Theta Xi sorority was successfully inducted as the Sigma Beta chapter of Chi Omega in 1920. The chapter started with 17 members and at that time was the only chapter in Montana. In this image are Martha Stevens, Vera Bartz, and Alberta Mitchell, three of the 1924–1925 Chi Omega members at MSU.

The 1921 members stand on the porch of Sigma Chi's fraternity house. Some of the members of the fraternity are Willard H. Tobey, Sigvald L. Berg, Lorren O. Bradford, August M. Schneider, Frank Harris, Edward Cates, Fred Stump, Hubert M. Rice, Harold Dickerson, and Havard Mann.

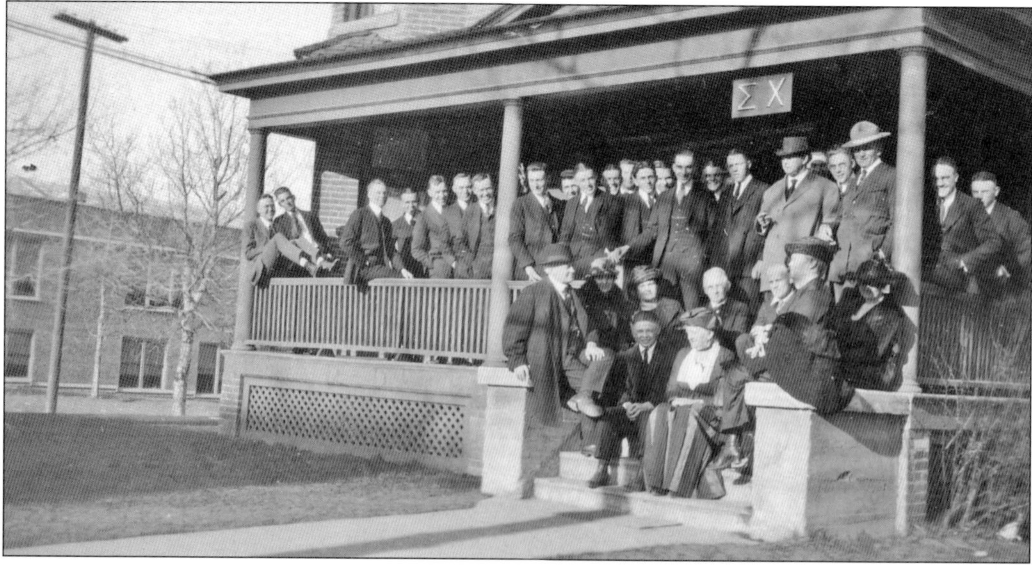

Sigma Chi was established in 1917 at Montana State University, bringing national fraternities to the university and providing an avenue through which young men could share common goals and find friendship. Sigma Chi members Leonard R. "Torchy" Swan and Lorren Bradford stand with an unidentified member on the porch of the house in 1921.

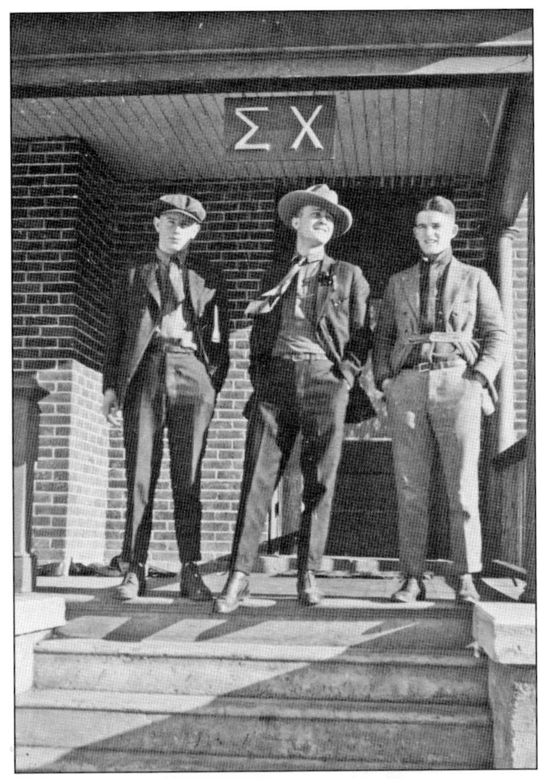

Montana State University's chapter of Sigma Alpha Epsilon was established in 1919. In this 1940 image, members stand in front of the SAE house. Some of the members include Frank Strong, Bill Roberts, Kirby Whitman, Joe Divine, Paul Waddell, Jerry Nagle, Ray Lakey, Bob Simkins, Al Johnson, Jean Berg, Steve Montil, Joe May, and Fred Williams.

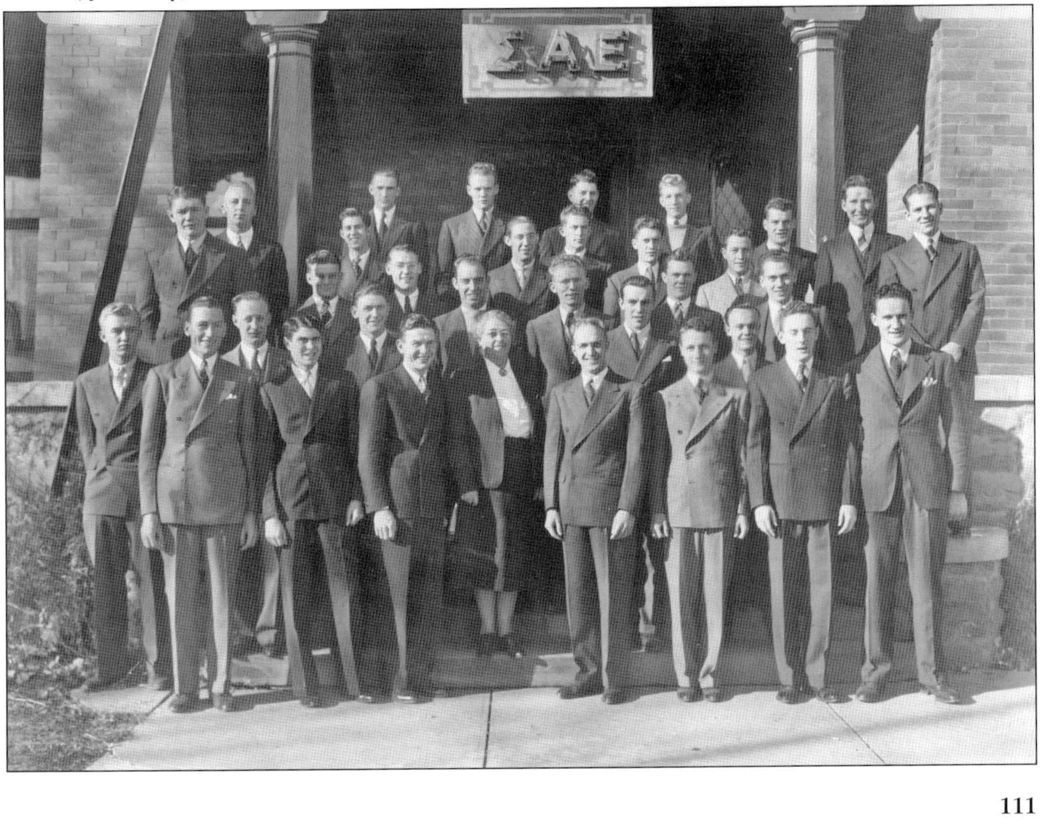

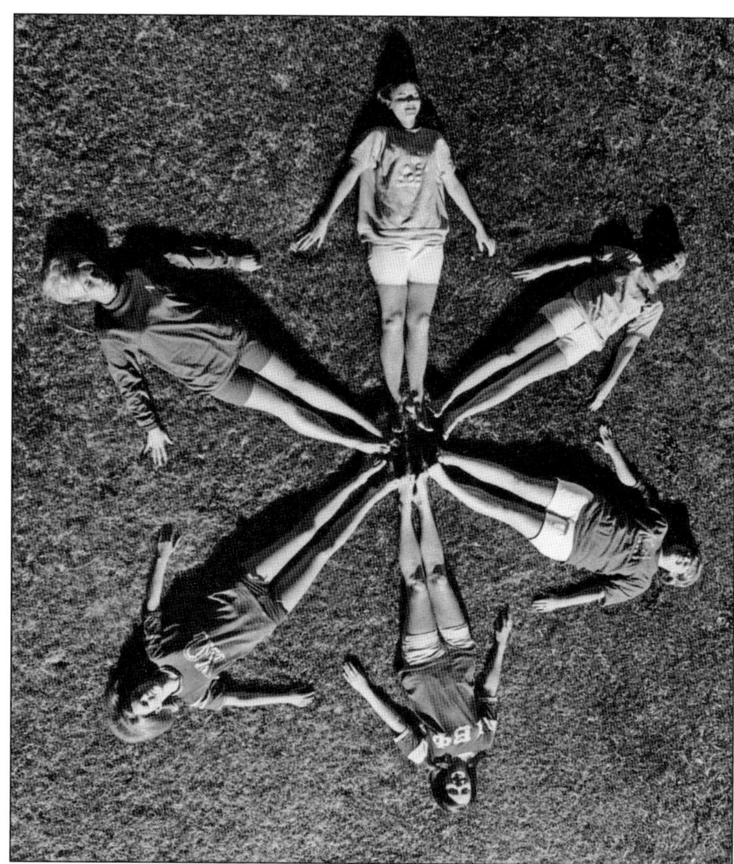

Taking time to relax in the grass with their fellow Greek sisters, these six women represent the different sororities at Montana State University in the 1960s. The women were the presidents of Alpha Gamma Delta, Alpha Omicron Pi, Chi Omega, Delta Gamma, Kappa Delta, and Phi Beta Phi.

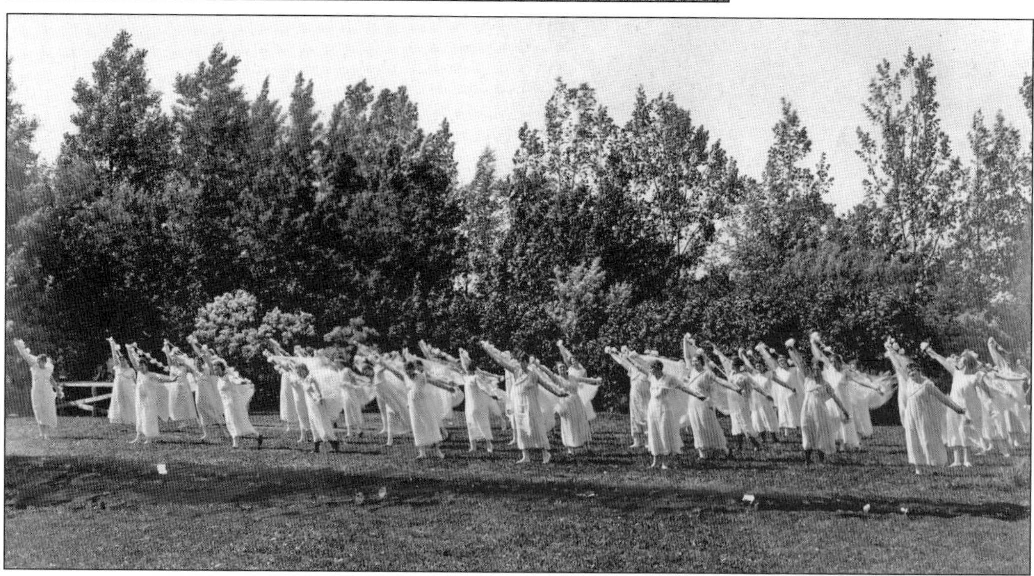

The Women's Day celebration in 1919 allowed Montana State University women to gather together on campus to view or participate in activities that illustrated the proficiencies learned through home science courses. It also allowed them to demonstrate their value outside of the home as accountable workers and citizens who provided useful skills to the community.

Eight

MONTANA COOPERATIVE EXTENSION SERVICE AND AGRICULTURE

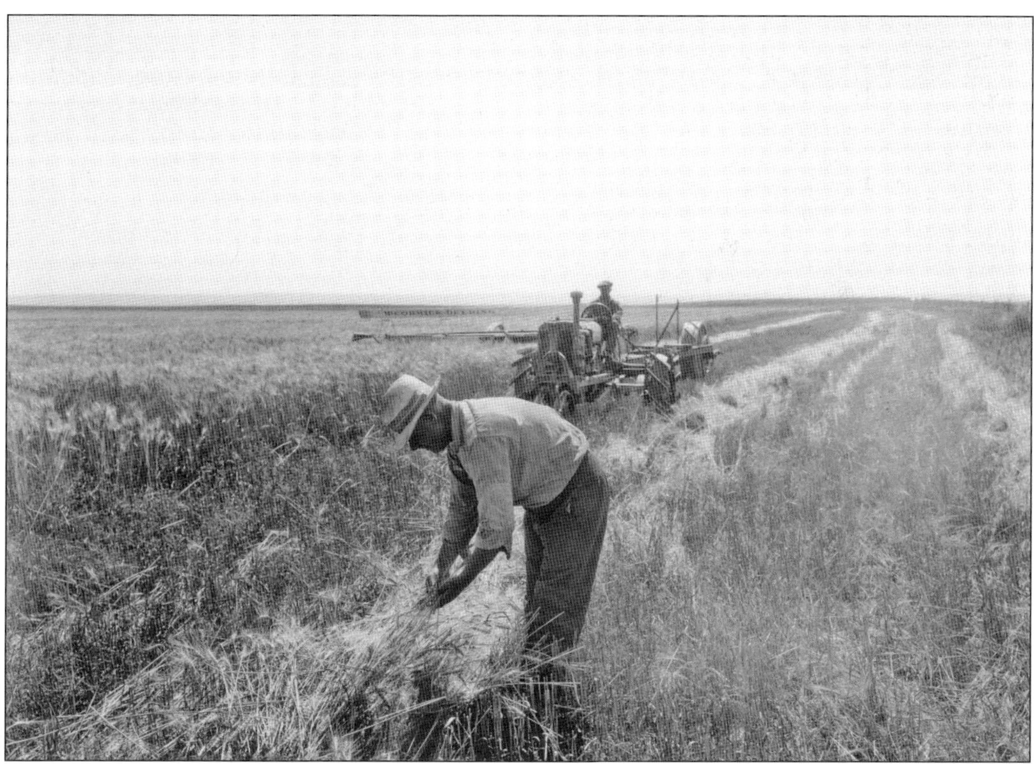

Agriculture is an integral feature of Montana State University. MSU was established hand-in-hand with the Montana Agricultural Experiment Station. Together, they work to demonstrate the importance of agriculture to the students and the greater community. The university works to educate students, who become valued members of the agricultural community, while the Montana Agricultural Experiment Station conducts research and experiments into plants, their diseases, crop rotation, and soil analysis.

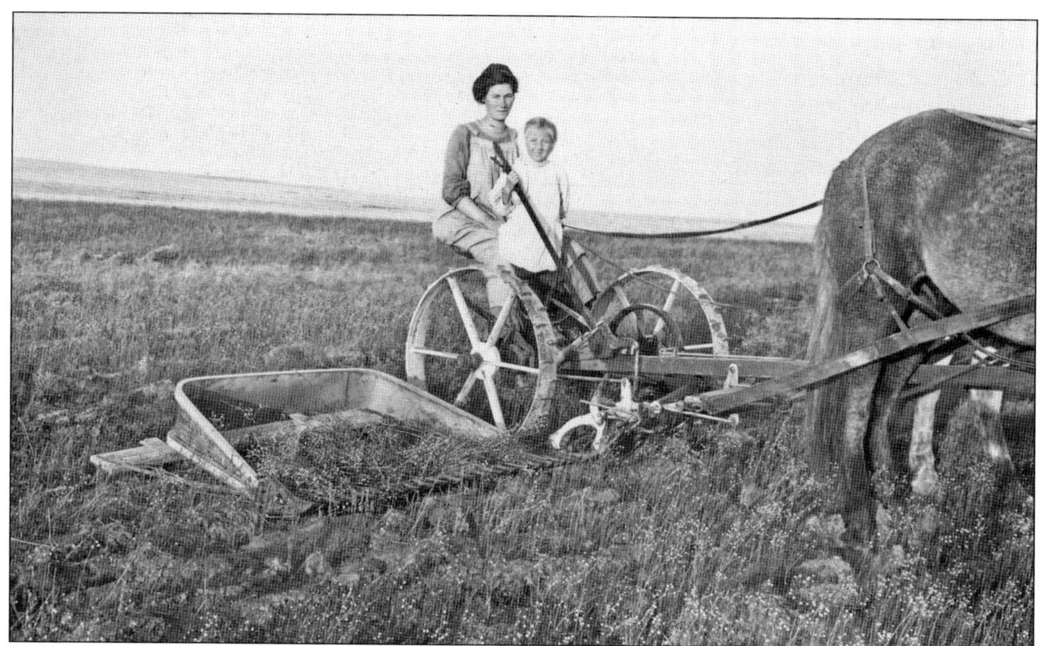

Flax is cultivated by Montana farmers for its seed and textile fiber, which is made from the plant's stalks. A woman sits behind a pair of horses with a child in her lap, attempting to operate a lever for a buncher on the mower next to them in 1912.

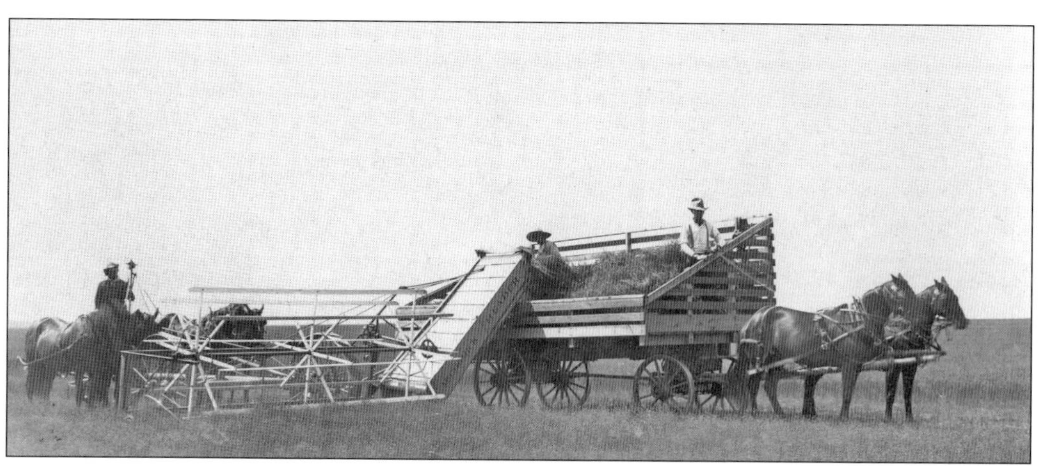

Interest in flax growing in 1911 encouraged the extension service to hire Milburn L. Wilson as an extension specialist to provide demonstrations and education on the flax culture to Montana Farmers' Institutes. As part of Wilson's flax series, men and horses are heading flax on the Bovee Ranch near Fallon, Montana, in August 1912.

Meeting a need for assistance to individuals and communities, Montana Agricultural Experiment Stations provided short courses of a practical nature; fulfilling this need in eastern Montana was the branch station established in Sidney in 1947. Here, a group of men examine small sunflower plants at the Eastern Branch Experiment Station in the 1950s.

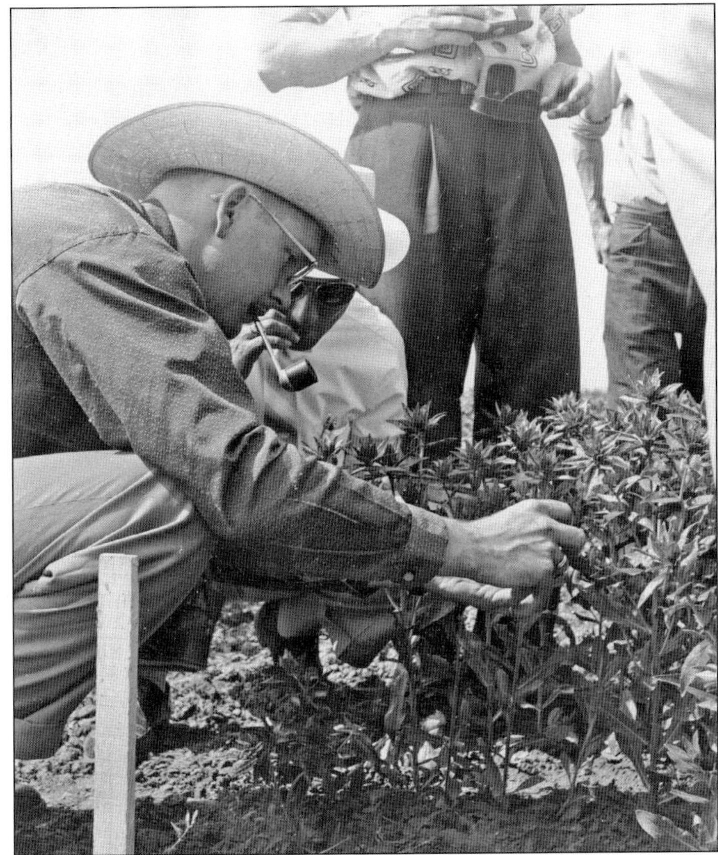

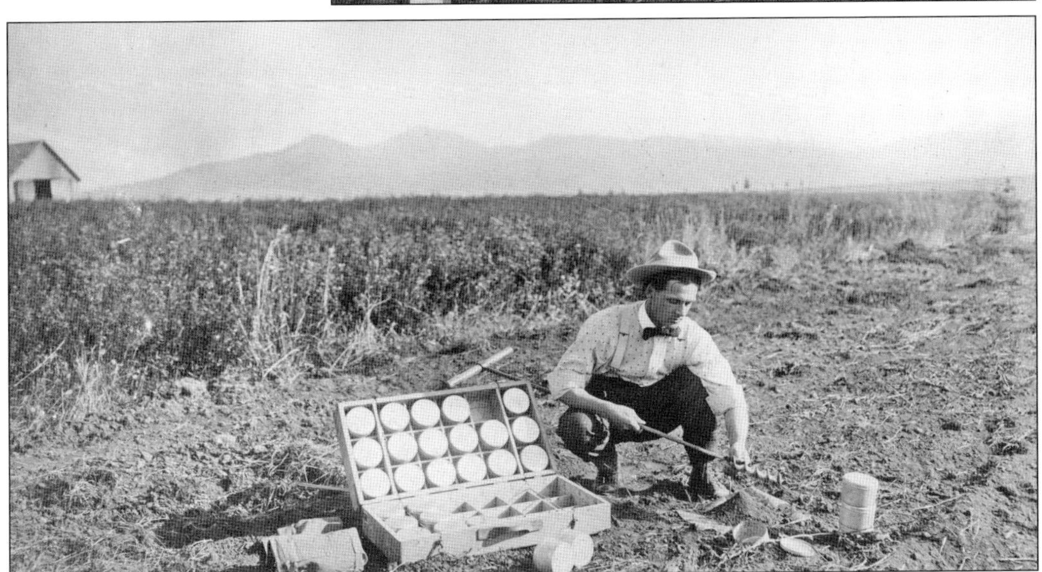

An experiment station employee retrieves soil samples with an auger; as he finishes retrieving his samples, he places them in containers to be transported in a sample box. Researchers utilize soil sampling to determine the nutrient content, composition, and other characteristics of the soil at Montana Agricultural Experiment Stations.

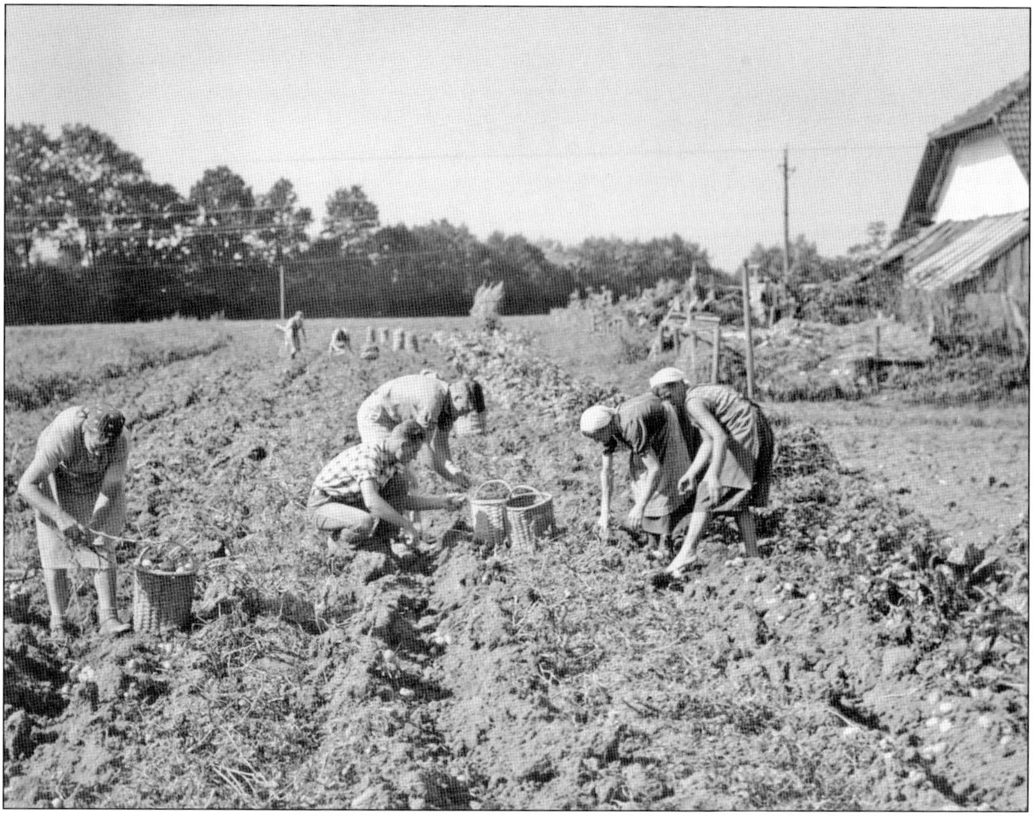

In 1948, Montana joined the International Farm Youth Exchange (IFYE), established in 1947. The program provided students with the opportunity to take an educational journey to a foreign land and learn about its people, language, and traditions. In this image, a group of IFYE students work in a field picking potatoes in 1959.

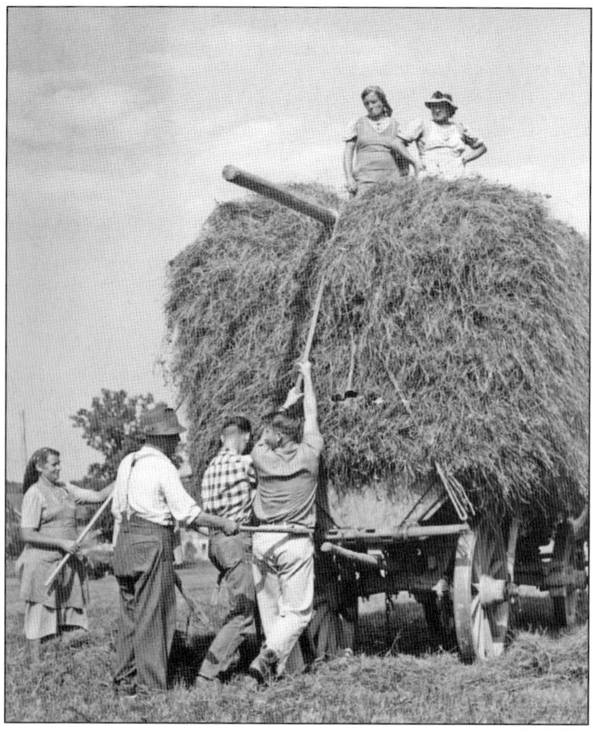

The culture exchange provided by the IFYE offered Montana youth the opportunity to share their once-in-a-lifetime experiences with individuals from their schools and communities as they returned home from their host country. Here, two IFYE students help a farmer and his hands load hay in a wagon in 1959.

Properly caring for sheep is not just an adult pastime. These two young children pose while feeding a bottle of milk to a lamb in June 1922. The consideration shown by the boy and girl demonstrates the care and management invested in the Thomas J. MacFarlane farm flock at Lothair, Montana. (Photograph by M.L. Wilson.)

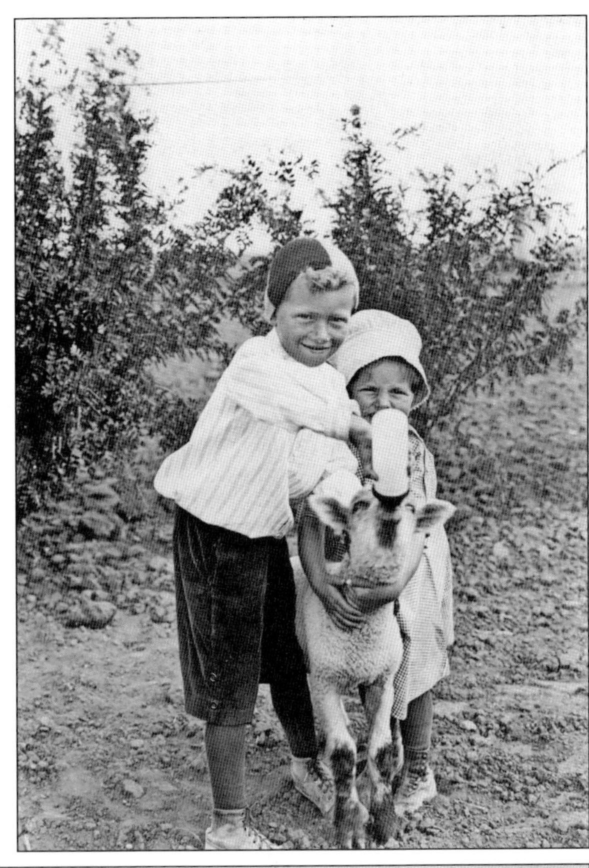

The extension service short courses lasted up to a week and were devoted to a specific subject. Success for the short courses varied; a subject that worked in one area did not necessarily work in another. Here, a group of students gather outside the horse barn with eight horses hitched to a sleigh for a farmers' short course in January 1911.

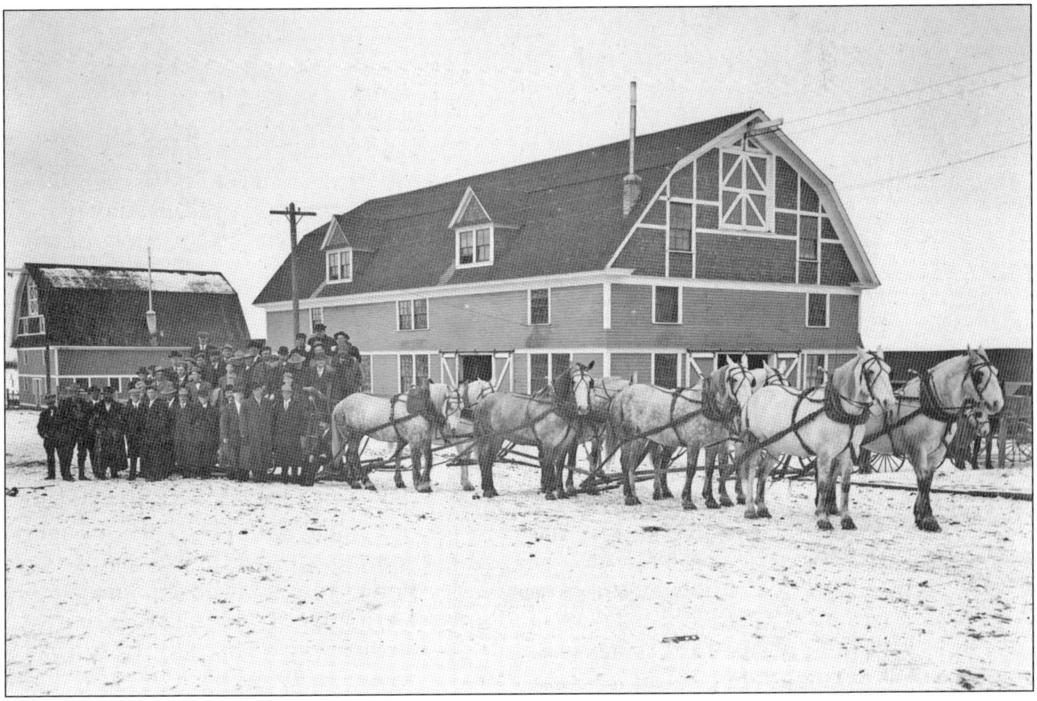

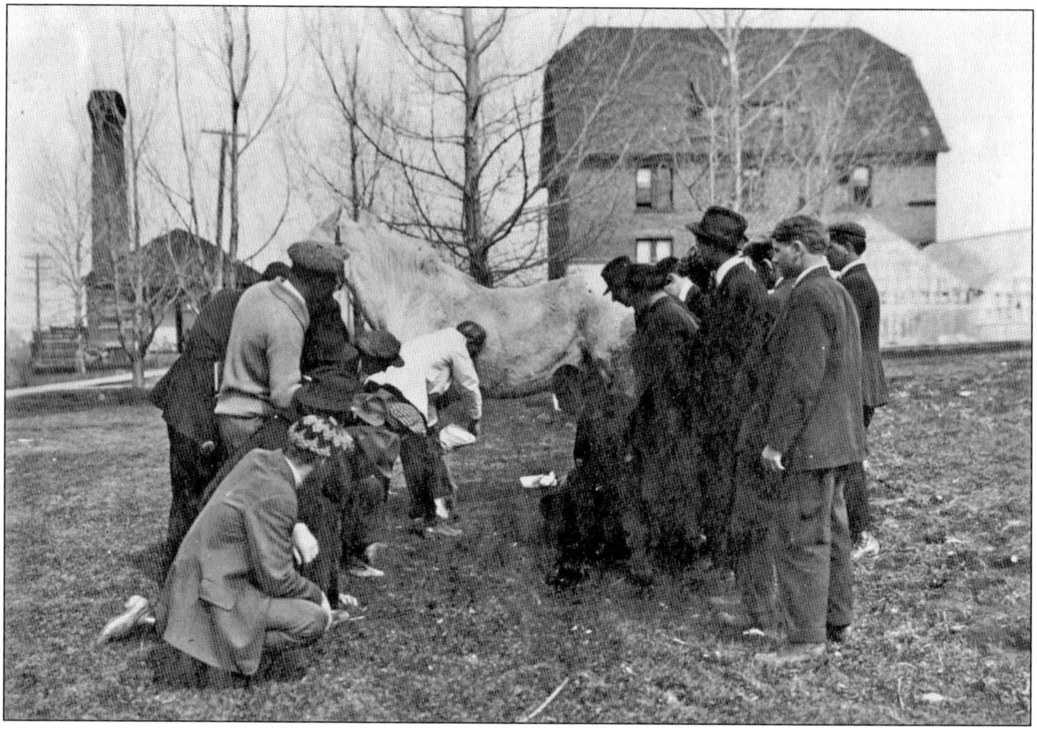

Located in front of the horse barn at then Montana State College, the demonstration in this image provided students with instruction in veterinary science and the care and management of livestock. A group of students gather around a veterinary instructor as he works on a horse's hoof in the 1910s.

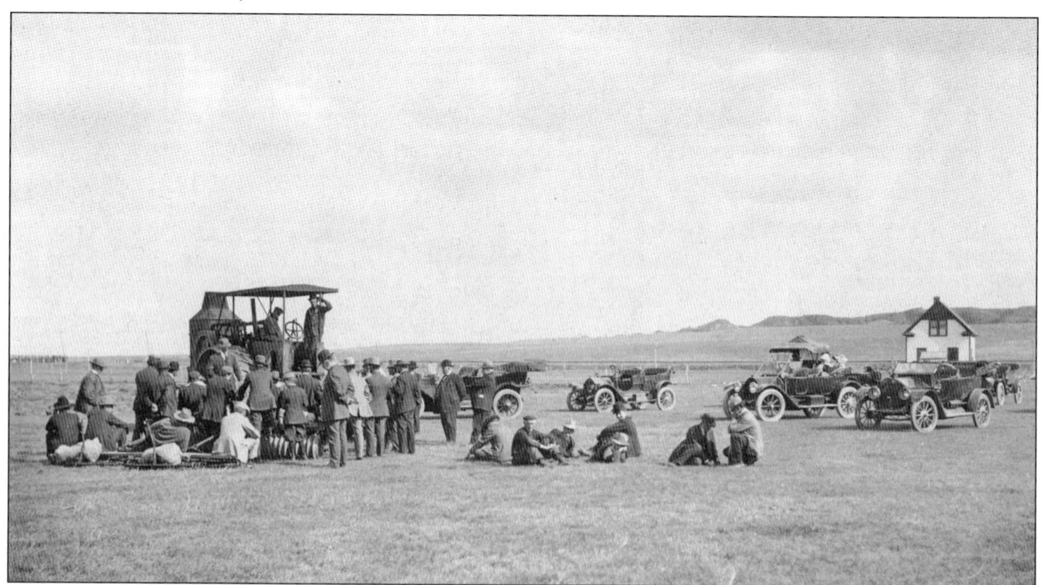

The American Flax Association promoted flax growing in Montana in 1912 through contributions to Milburn L. Wilson's salary at the experiment station. Wilson provided a variety of lectures and demonstrations to the citizens of Montana. Here, people gather to listen to part of Wilson's flax series in 1912 at Glendive, Montana.

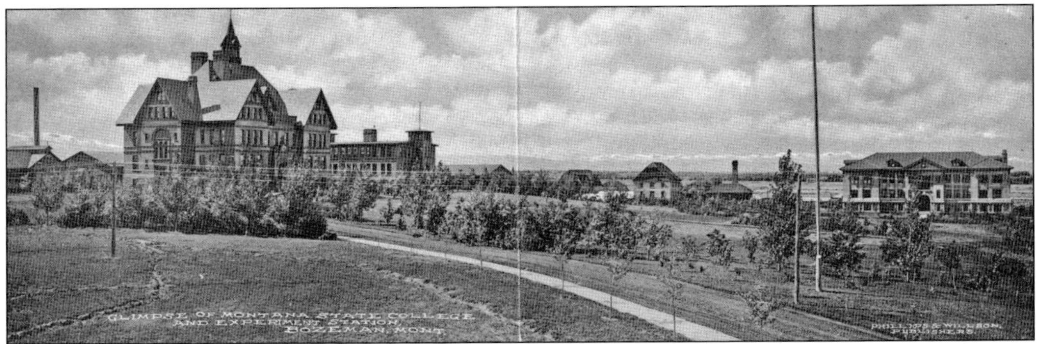

The Cooperative Extension Service at Montana State University grew from the founder's vision that there was a need for education beyond the traditional fields of study. The extension service provided research and dissemination essential to making Montana agriculture a successful and stable enterprise. It provided education to rural Montanans about livestock breeding, soil conservation, rodent control, and other subjects.

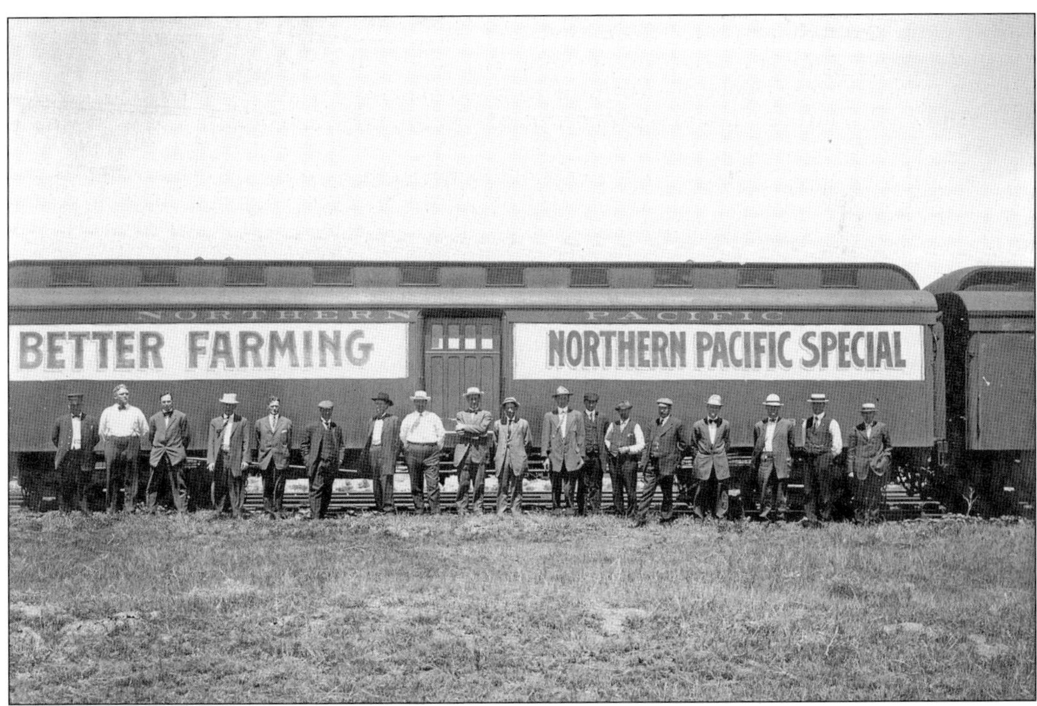

Interest in increasing the numbers of farmer-homesteaders sparked the development of specialized trains by Western railroads. Seen here is the 1910 Northern Pacific Better Farming special train in Wibaux, Montana. This train, with a 15-member staff, was billed as a "Farmers Institute on Wheels." The train made 44 stops on a 12-day run and attracted over 7,000 visitors.

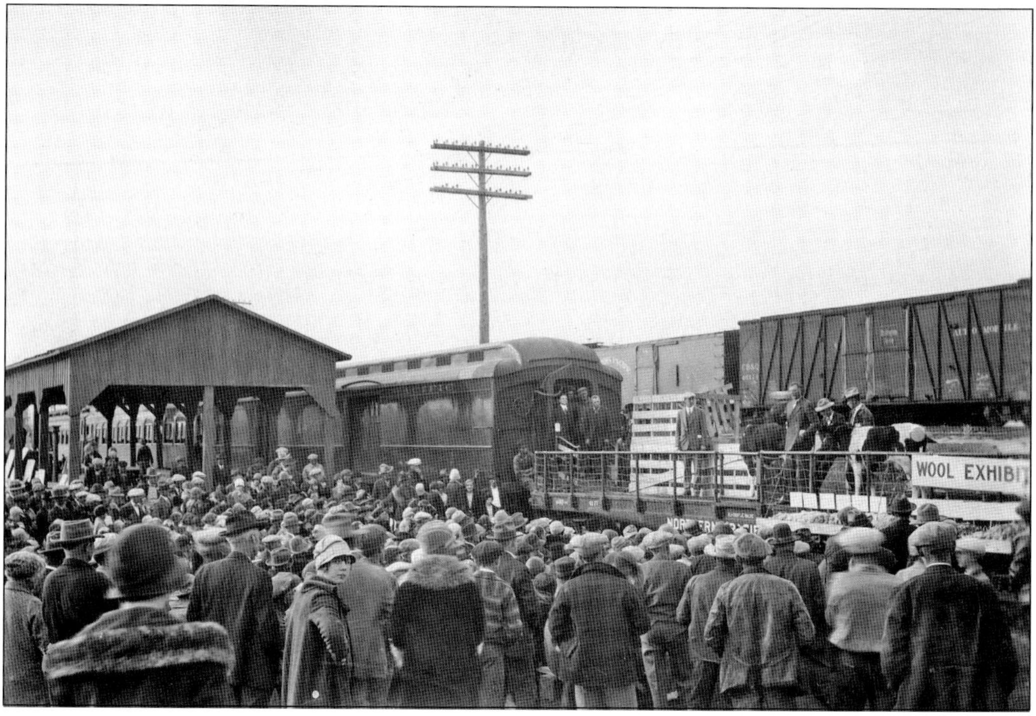

A man addresses a crowd from a flatcar of the Better Livestock special train as he conducts a presentation on cattle between 1908 and 1915. The Montana Cooperative Extension Service partnered with the Northern Pacific Railway, the Great Northern Railroad, and the Milwaukee Railroad to reach out to local communities in an effort to educate Montana citizens on new agricultural and livestock methods.

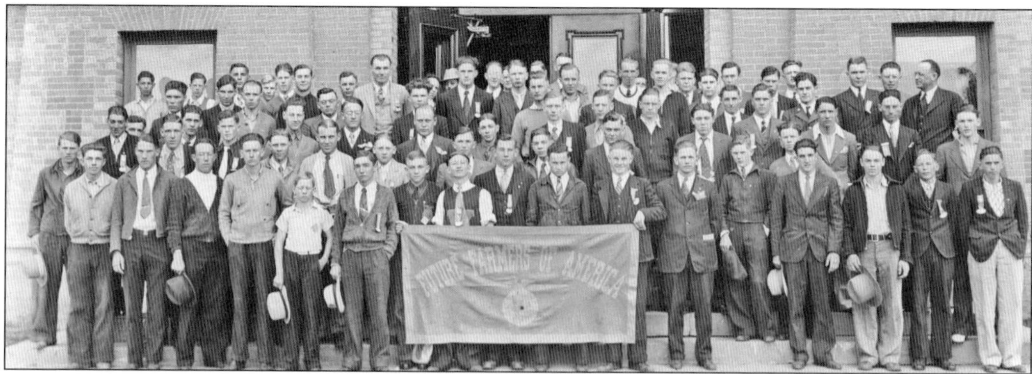

This large group of men and boys represented the Future Farmers of America at a convention at Montana State College in 1936. Beginning in 1917, federal funds provided through the Smith-Hughes National Vocational Education Act allowed Montana high schools to promote and support agricultural education. (Photograph by F. Bertil Linfield.)

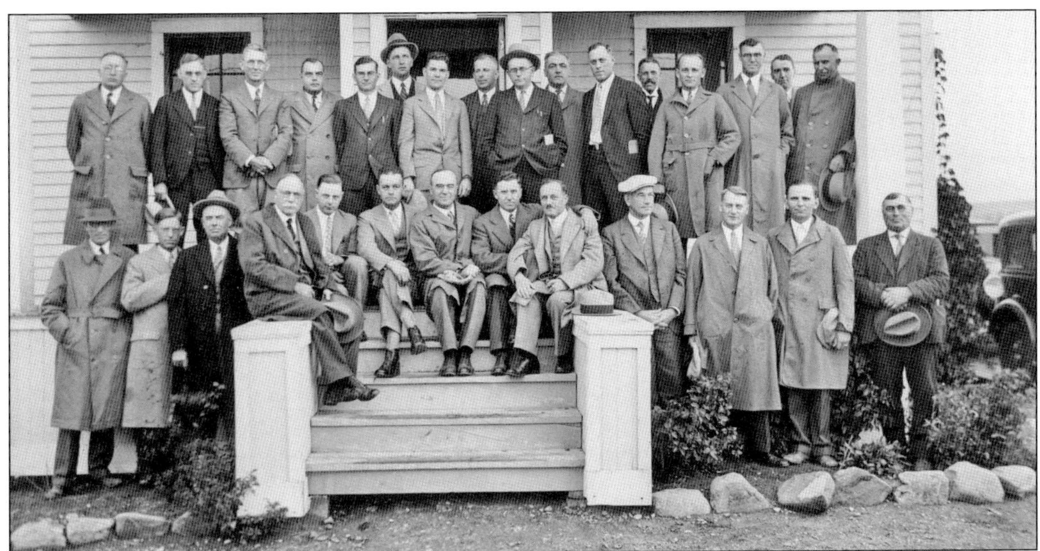

Montana's extension service employed a variety of individuals who provided specialized knowledge and support to the citizens of Montana. Extension station staff offered a variety of services, including conducting farming experiments, hosting farmers' institutes and farmers' picnics, and providing demonstrations and short courses. Several station staff members, including Milburn L. Wilson (first row, left of steps) and Frederick B. Linfield (seated to Wilson's left) are pictured sometime between 1930 and 1937.

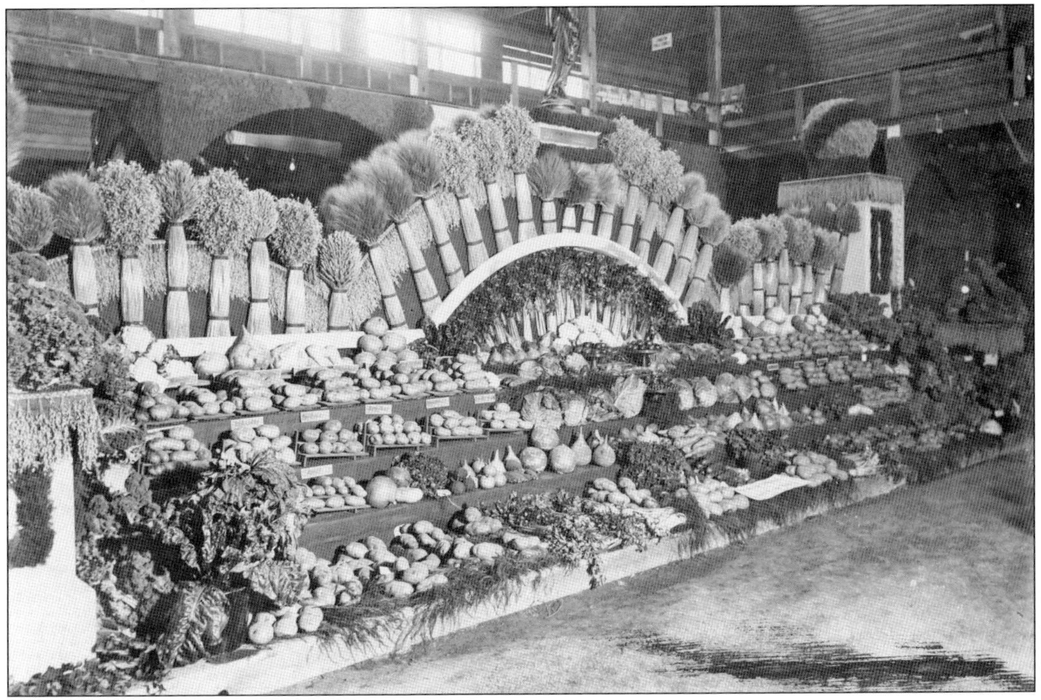

The Montana legislature established the Montana State Fair in 1903 to be held annually in Helena to provide information and encourage growth in topics such as agriculture, stock grazing, horticulture, and mechanical and industrial pursuits. This image highlights a country booth exhibit of grains and vegetables as natural products of Montana's soil in the 1910s.

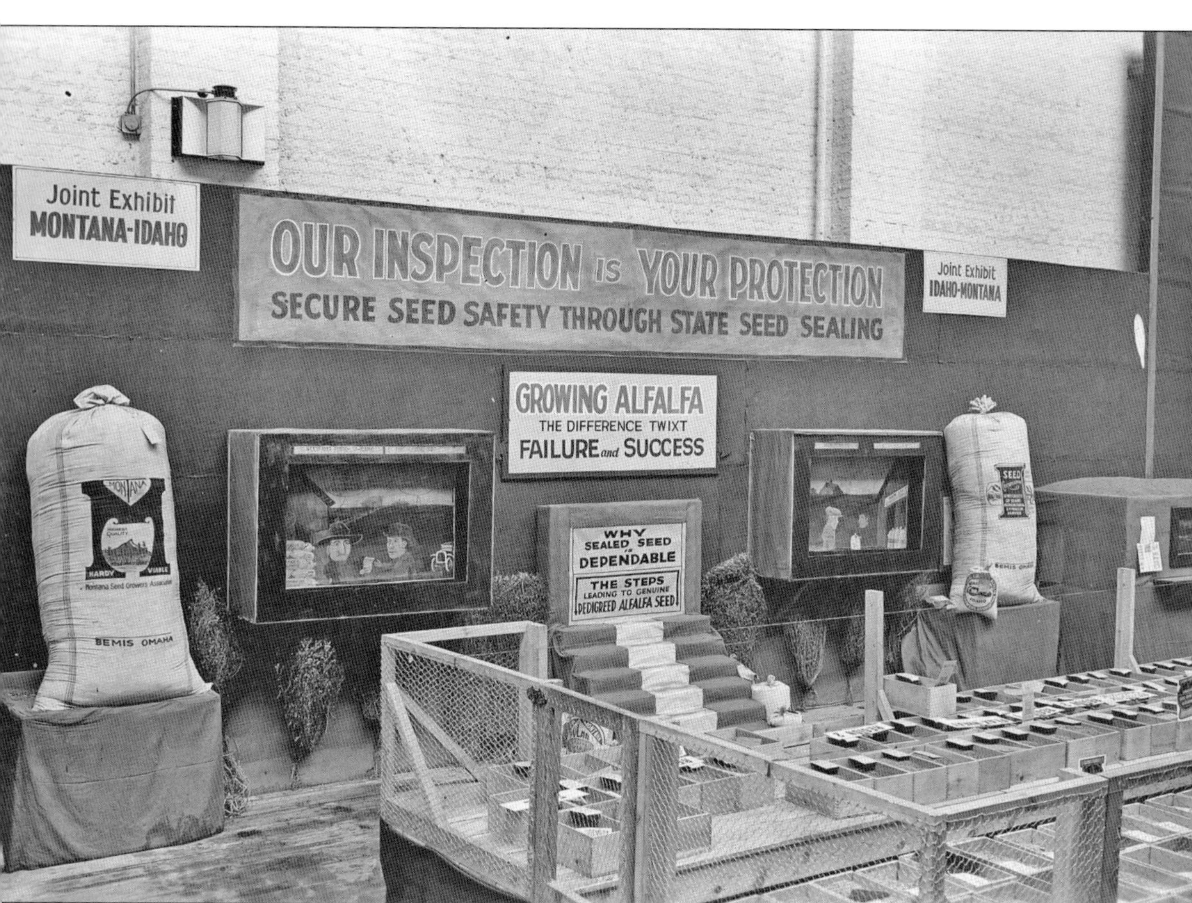

Working to provide Montana's farmers with options and information on quality seeds for the crops they plant, the extension service partnered with the Montana Seed Growers Association (MSGA) and Idaho Seed Growers Association in the 1940s in a joint exhibit. Exhibits were considered significant and appeared at many county fairs. The organizations work to ensure that Montana and Idaho seeds and crops are preserved as healthy and pure, which results in superior crops that keep pace with growers' demands. The certification process is designed to encourage high-quality seeds through extensive testing and inspection. The MSGA currently consists of approximately 500 members across Montana. This exhibit promoted the pros and cons of sealed alfalfa seed. (Photograph by J.C. Allen.)

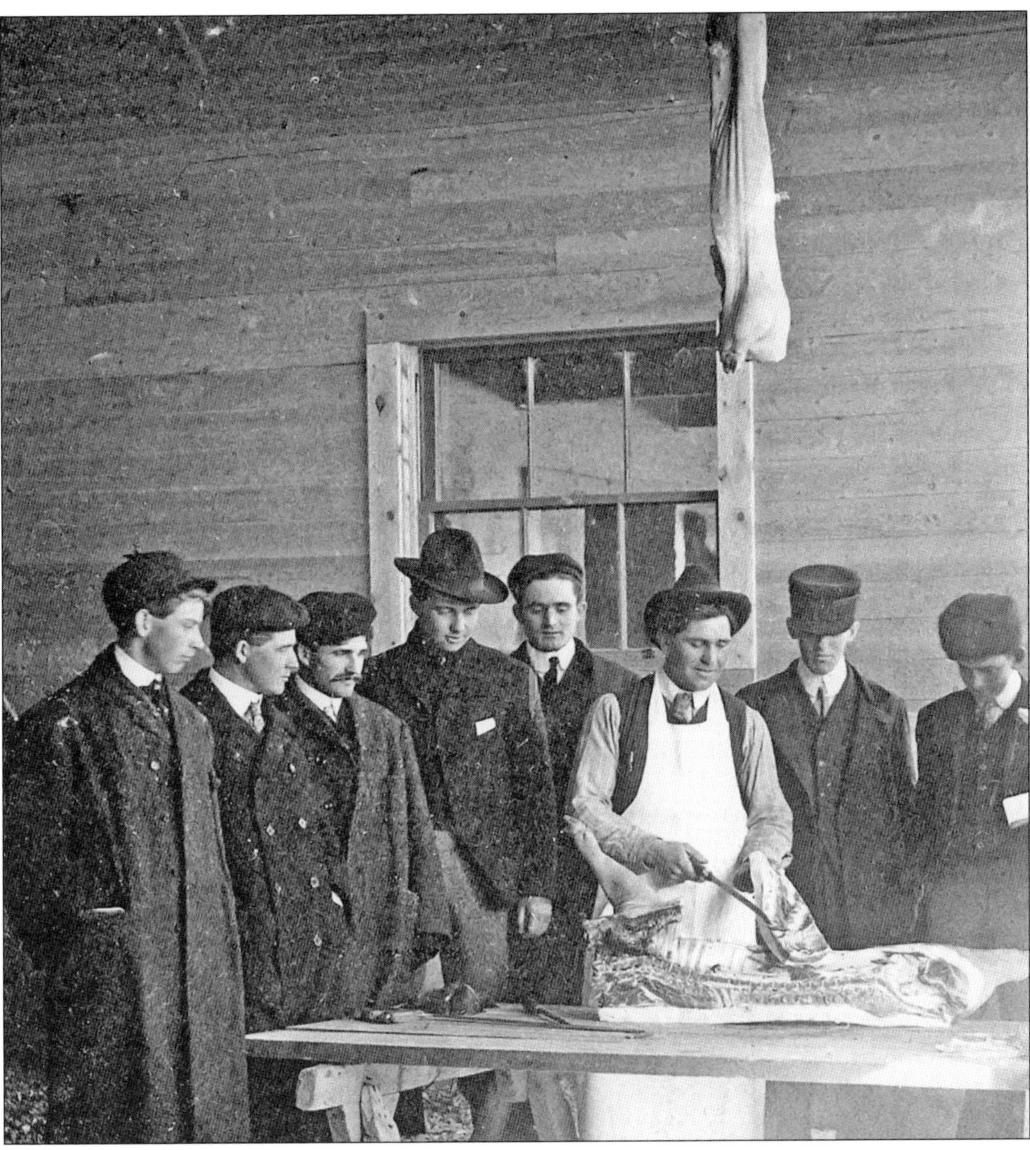

As part of a food demonstration to educate Montana citizens, W.O. Bohart provides instruction in how to cut meat in 1906. The extension service provided early farmers' institutes to meet community interest in the Montana Agricultural Experiment Station. The institutes provided lectures and demonstrations to local communities, farmers, and rural populations to promote specialized knowledge researched and developed by the extension service. Later food demonstrations encouraged larger production and efficient utilization and conservation of food. Other topics discussed at the institutes included meat adulteration, stock and stock feeding, and poultry. All topics were delivered on behalf of Montana State University by county extension agents. Currently, Montana county extension agents serve over 60 offices and communities statewide as they respond to the needs of families, farmers, businesses, and industry to enrich education and strengthen growth. (Photograph by William F. Brewer.)

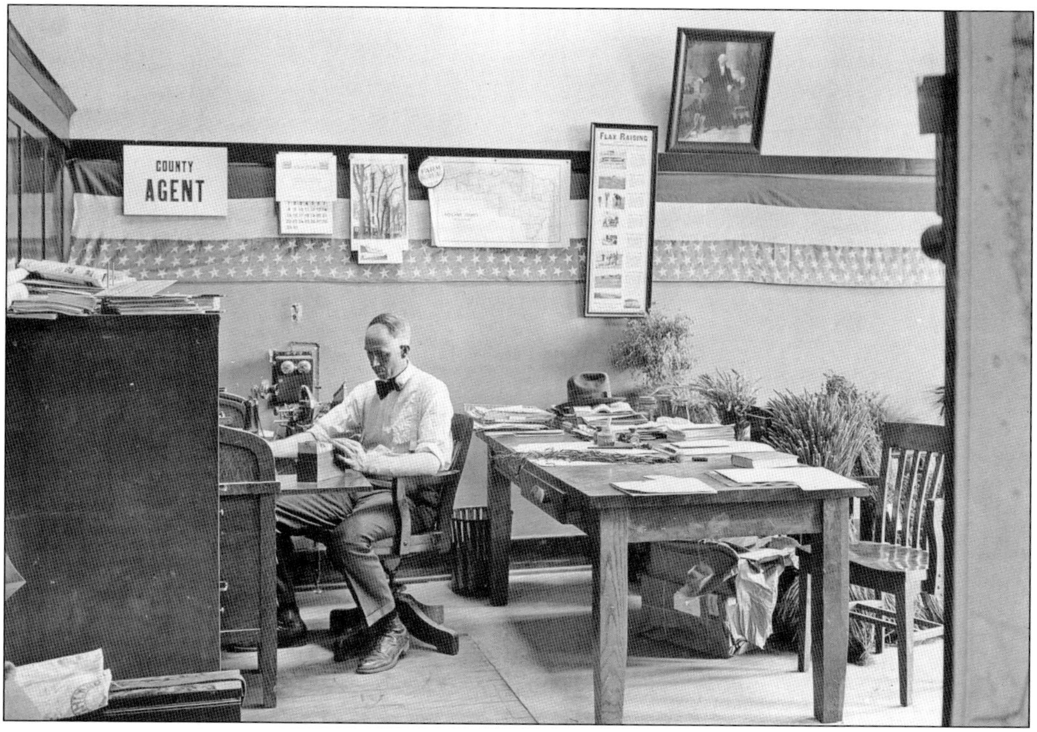

This extension service agent in 1921 in Richmond County, possibly Harold F. DePue, looks through an index at his desk. Behind him sit an assortment of samples ranging from flax to thistles that are waiting for his attention. DePue served as one of the Richland County agents from 1920 to 1930.

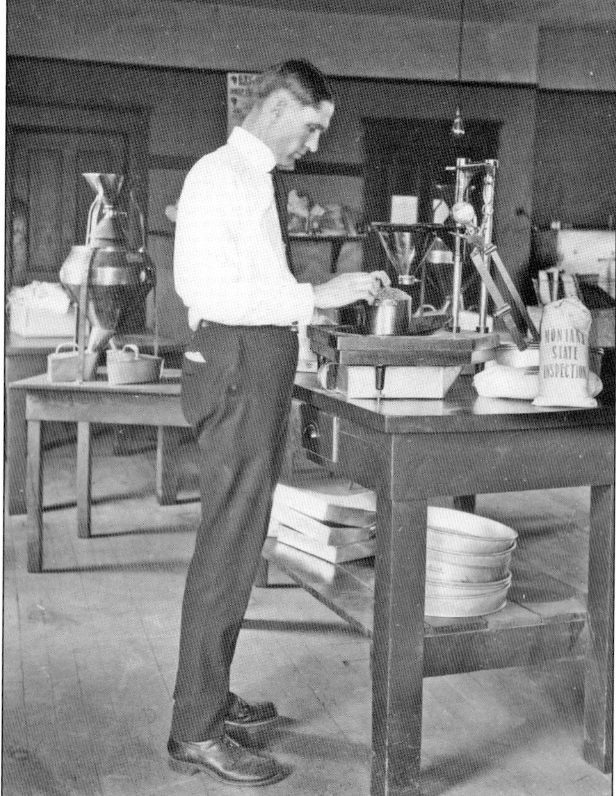

Extension station staff conducted experiments that helped determine bushel weight in pounds to help farmers talk intelligently to their buyers about the grading factor when discussing crop payments for grain. In this image, a man stands at a table testing the weight of grain per bushel in the 1920s.

Bibliography

Accession 00021, Montana State University Extension Service Records, 1912–1970. Merrill G. Burlingame Special Collections, Montana State University Library, Bozeman, MT.

Accession 00029, Montana State University Library Records, 1893–2004. Merrill G. Burlingame Special Collections, Montana State University Library, Bozeman, MT.

Accession 03001, Montana State University Faculty Biographies, c. 1900–1990. Merrill G. Burlingame Special Collections, Montana State University Library, Bozeman, MT.

Accession 12001, University Pictures Collection, 1983–1975. Merrill G. Burlingame Special Collections, Montana State University Library, Bozeman, MT.

Burlingame, Merrill G. *A History: Montana State University, Bozeman, Montana*. Bozeman, MT: Office of Information, 1968.

———. *The Montana Cooperative Extensive Service: A History, 1893–1974*. Bozeman, MT: Montana State University, 1984.

"Devils Tower—First Stories." National Park Service www.nps.gov/deto/learn/historyculture/first-stories.htm (last modified March 7, 2017).

The *Exponent* (MSU newspaper), 1895–present.

Lukas, John D. "Everybody's All-Americans." *Mountains and Minds* 6, no. 2 (Fall 2012): 52–57.

The Montanan. Bozeman, MT: Montana State College of Mechanic Arts, 1909–1991.

Rydell, Robert W., Jeffery J. Safford, and Pierce C. Mullen. *In the People's Interest: A Centennial History of Montana State University*. Bozeman, MT: Montana State University Foundation, 1992.

Shovic, Henry F. *Management Characteristics of Interdisciplinary Research: A Case Study of the Gallatin Canyon Study*. Bozeman, MT: Montana State University, 1973.

Undergraduate Bulletin. Bozeman, MT: Montana State University, 1883–1994.

Wessell, Thomas and Marilyn Wessel. *4-H, An American Idea 1900–1980: A History of 4-H*. Chevy Chase, MD: National 4-H Council, 1982.

Wilson, M.L. *Big Teams in Montana*. No. 70. Bozeman, MT: Montana State College Extension Service, April 1925.